AGONIZING QUESTIONS ABOUT SHATTERING SERIAL SEX MURDERS

Who was the "flat-nosed man" in a black truck who picked up prostitutes and brutally raped them— and was he the killer?

Who was the driver of the mysterious white pickup truck seen near so many of the victims' remains?

What did forensic examination show about what was done to the female corpses before, during and after their deaths?

What is former District Attorney Ronald Pina's explanation of his investigation of the Highway Murders—an investigation that not only failed to produce a conviction, but led to the tragic death of one of its targets?

Which police officials fumbled the ball—and which ones were hog-tied by departmental rivalries and bureaucratic bickering?

Why did a grand jury return one of the most startling murder indictments in the annals of the law?

Drawing on many hours of original interviews with police, prosecutors, victims' families, the suspects, journalists, and extensive documentary information never before published, this riveting account revisits the events surrounding one of the worst serial murder cases in the United States—an unsolved mystery that still casts a pall of terror.

KILLING SEASON

The Unsolved Case of New England's Deadliest Serial Killer

CARLTON SMITH

AN ONYX BOOK

ONYX
Published by the Penguin Group
Penguin Books USA Inc., 375 Hudson Street,
New York, New York 10014, U.S.A.
Penguin Books Ltd, 27 Wrights Lane,
London W8 5TZ, England
Penguin Books Australia Ltd, Ringwood,
Victoria, Australia
Penguin Books Canada Ltd, 10 Alcorn Avenue,
Toronto, Ontario, Canada M4V 3B2
Penguin Books (N.Z.) Ltd, 182–190 Wairau Road,
Auckland 10, New Zealand

Penguin Books Ltd, Registered Offices:
Harmondsworth, Middlesex, England

First published by Onyx, an imprint of Dutton Signet,
a division of Penguin Books USA Inc.

First Printing, September, 1994
10 9 8 7 6 5 4 3 2 1

For Judy, Jill, and Jolene

"Because the outcry against Sodom and Gomorrah is great and their sin is very grave, I will go down to see whether they have done altogether according to the outcry which has come to me, and if not, I will know."

—Genesis 18:21

"Such dreary streets! blocks of blackness, not houses, on either hand, and here and there a candle, like a candle moving in a tomb. At this hour of the night, of the last day of the week, that quarter of the town proved all but deserted. But presently I came to a smoky light from a low, wide building, the door of which stood invitingly open. It had a careless look, as if it were meant for uses of the public; so, entering, the first thing I did was to stumble over an ash-box on the porch. Ha! thought I, ha, as the flying particles almost choked me, are these the ashes of the destroyed city, Gomorrah?"

—HERMAN MELVILLE, *Moby Dick*, 1851

Contents

Major Characters

The Police

Ronald Pina, Bristol County District Attorney, 1978–1990

Raymond Veary, Ron Pina's chief deputy

Robert St. Jean, chief investigator for Ron Pina

Paul Boudreau, detective, Bristol County Drug Task Force

John Dextradeur, detective, New Bedford Police Department

Jose Gonsalves, corporal, Massachusetts State Police, lead homicide investigator in the Highway Murders

Maryann Dill, trooper, Massachusetts State Police, and Gonsalves's partner

The Victims

Robin Rhodes, 28, last seen in New Bedford, April 1988

Rochelle Clifford Dopierala, 28, last seen in New Bedford, late April 1988

Debroh McConnell, 25, last seen in New Bedford, May 1988

Debra Medeiros, 30, last seen in New Bedford, late May 1988

Christine Monteiro, 19, last seen in New Bedford, late May 1988

Marilyn Roberts, 34, last seen in New Bedford, June 1988

Nancy Paiva, 36, last seen in New Bedford, July 7, 1988

Deborah DeMello, 35, last seen in New Bedford, July 11, 1988

Mary Rose Santos, 26, last seen in New Bedford, July 16, 1988

Sandra Botelho, 24, last seen in New Bedford, August 11, 1988

Dawn Mendes, 25, last seen in New Bedford, September 4, 1988

The Families

Judy DeSantos, sister of Nancy Paiva

Joseph Botelho, father of Sandra Botelho

Diane Clifford, mother of Rochelle Clifford

James McConnell, father of Debroh McConnell

Charlotte Mendes, mother of Dawn Mendes

Madeleine Perry, mother of Deborah Greenlaw DeMello

Donald Santos, husband of Mary Rose Santos

The Suspects

Neil Anderson, Dartmouth, Mass., fishcutter, cleared January 1989

James Baker, Tiverton, R.I., diesel mechanic, cleared, June 1989

Tony DeGrazia, Freetown, Mass., stonemason, cleared, October 1989

Kenneth Ponte, New Bedford, Mass., attorney, cleared, August 1991

Paul Ryley, New Bedford, Mass., businessman, cleared, August 1991

The Others

Frankie Pina, Nancy Paiva's boyfriend

Henry Carreiro, radio talk-show host

James Ragsdale, editor, New Bedford *Standard-Times*

Maureen Boyle, reporter, New Bedford *Standard-Times*

Tom Coakley and John Ellement, reporters, *The Boston Globe*

Diane Doherty, witness against Kenneth Ponte

Paul Walsh, Ron Pina's election opponent in 1990

Paul Buckley, special prosecutor appointed by Walsh to review the case, 1991

Preface and
Acknowledgments

Such dreary streets, Melville had written in 1850 of New
Bedford, Massachusetts, at the height of the city's century-
long, whale-killing bonanza. Though nearly 140 years had
passed since the time of Melville, and the whales were
long gone, the streets of New Bedford remained dreary in
the late 1980s, lost in a gloom that seemed as permanent
a part of the city as its bumpy cobblestones.

In the town once made rich by oil from the largest
mammal in the history of the world, there seemed to be
as many cobblestones and historic buildings as there were
tenements; and there were almost as many tenements as
there were addicts—that is, drug addicts. The harpoon, at
least, had survived, miniaturized perhaps, but still firmly
lodged in the forearms of the unhappy, trapped people of
what was once the richest city in the world.

A pedestrian on Purchase Street in the spring of 1988
could not avoid the evidence—indeed, it was loudly whispered, spoken, sometimes even shouted, advertised by sidewalk pitchmen called runners, or sometimes "clockers":

"Power," "Power Ninety-five," "Master of Death"—
these were the street names of the small packets of white
or brown powder dispensed by shadowy figures down on
Purchase Street in New Bedford in the spring of 1988.
Crumpled, sweaty bills changed hands; a darkened space
was sought, a spoon produced, a match was lit, a needle
was filled and plunged.

Then came the explosion, or rather, implosion, as a human life shrank down to its lowest conscious level, a full retreat from the things that could no longer be suffered. And not just a few, either.

By the spring of 1988, nearly *1 out of 50* New Bedford citizens was an acknowledged heroin addict, while an equal or larger number were addicted to cocaine or its compulsive cousin, "crack." It was not surprising that New Bedford, once known as the whaling capital of the world, was now known as one of the world's biggest drug dens.

The new harpoon, the hypodermic, led directly to real-people crime—petty thefts, burglaries, muggings, shootings, indeed, untold wreckage in human lives. In time those crimes led to serial murder, and the destruction of the soul of a city.

There are three main highways into and out of New Bedford. Interstate 195 runs east from Providence, Rhode Island, slices through the northern half of New Bedford, then heads farther east in the direction of Cape Cod before fading out in a merger with another interstate headed south out of Boston.

A second freeway, State Route 140, heads north out of New Bedford on its way to Taunton, Mass., where it too joins another road to Boston. A third highway, U.S. 6, also known as the King's Highway, once linked all of southeastern Massachusetts to Cape Cod and Boston, back in the days when coachmen drove with whips. All three of these roads figured prominently in the serial murder case with which this book is concerned.

I first came to New Bedford in the spring of 1989, when the hunt for an unknown murderer was in full cry. Nine women were dead and two others had disappeared. The newspapers and television stations were saturated with coverage about the crimes, and most of all, the suspects. A special grand jury was in session, taking secret testimony.

One man had just been charged with the rapes of nearly a dozen women, and one of those women went on national television to accuse the rapist of being the murderer. The district attorney, Ronald Pina, gave a smug and knowing press briefing on the steps of the county courthouse, saying nothing of consequence but with winks and smirks suggesting broadly that the case was almost solved.

I came back in 1992 and again the following year. Ronald Pina was no longer district attorney, one suspect was dead, another's life in tatters, a key witness had died on the street, and the nine murders were still unsolved. The two missing women were still missing. But by that time, the killings were a thing of the past for most of New Bedford, a dark event receding into the shadows of the willfully forgotten. The crimes had started, were stopped after they were discovered, and then galvanized the city, and were then ignored as an aberration that somehow could never be explained, just as a controversial pool table rape case had convulsed the town a few years earlier. But the residue of bitterness lingered on.

Why hadn't the case been solved? There was an ample amount of physical evidence; the pool of potential victims was relatively small, and quite close-knit; indeed, the victims even seemed to be closely interconnected, some living together, others living next door to one another, or having, at one time or another, been coworkers or close acquaintances.

The answer, as I hope this book demonstrates, was not so much an absence of evidence, but rather the result of an inability of police and political officials to set aside their own personal agendas and instead focus methodically on the facts. Manipulation of the news media became commonplace, while the media themselves failed to ask critical questions at critical times. The case gradually became a political mess, and eventually the investigation was torn apart in the maelstrom of competing interests. A Federal Bureau of Investigation expert who was familiar with some of the details of the case minced no words when he shook his head sorrowfully and offered his opinion that the investigation had been destroyed by a toxic combination of arrogance and ineptitude.

Meanwhile, the killer proceeded on his deadly course, doubtless continuing his depredations somewhere else in America.

New Bedford is a small city, long and narrow, running north-south along the west bank of the south-flowing

Acushnet River, which widens into a large estuary before emptying into the aptly named Buzzard's Bay.

Over the three centuries of its existence, the city's off-river border has straggled loosely westward, edging up, away from the water, by the line of least resistance; year after year it has incorporated aimless courtyards and directionless alleys, most marked off by buildings composed of chip-slipping granite or rust-weeping brick, or later, by cheap, rough-hewn lumber. All together, these incarnations of investment represent the physicality of 300 years of hopes, betrayals, dreams, illusions, anticipations, lies, epiphanies, and misperceptions—a menagerie of petty evils and their complement of unrecognized virtues. We often speak of a city in terms of what it *looks* like; but the reality of a city lies in how it lives.

In truth, there have actually been *four* New Bedfords: the original version, the small wood-and-mud village founded by Quakers bent on escaping the dominance of their Puritan fellow colonists in the late 1600s; the whaling New Bedford, the bustling town of ropes, tar, miles of wharves stacked high with casks of boiled whale fat, where captains' wives kept lonely vigils in magnificent mansions, and captains' daughters were given anticipated whales as dowries; the third New Bedford, the textile town, where waterside mills churned cotton into fabric for the world; and fourth, the fishing New Bedford of today, whose trawlers scour the submerged slopes of the Grand Banks in search of bivalve mollusks known to the world as scallops.

Over the centuries, the people of New Bedford also changed even as their means of livelihood evolved. The first settlers were pious Friends, content to wrest their sustenance from the shallow offshore waters; most of them bore English surnames like Cooke, Allen, Waite, Howland, Hathaway, Potter, Rotch, or Russell, and had first names like Increase, Stalwart, Harmony, Faith, Charity, or Hope.

But later, as the hunting of whales began returning such magnificent profits, the Quakers were joined by others outside the Massachusetts Puritan mainstream, many of them Roman Catholic. The huge profits likewise attracted a wide assortment of world travelers to New Bedford, including harpooners from the Azores, the Cape Verde Islands, from Scandinavia, and even from the South Pacific.

As a result, by 1850, Herman Melville was able to write of New Bedford, that for sheer variety of culture and costume, there was no more eye-popping city in the world.

"In these last mentioned haunts you see only sailors," Melville wrote, "but in New Bedford, actual cannibals stand chatting at street corners; savages outright; many of whom carry on their bones unholy flesh. It makes a stranger stare." In Melville's time, the rush for whale oil was on, and it was no different than in modern times, when black gushers in Texas spawned the wildest boom towns of an age.

By 1860, as the whaling industry began to decline, and the textile mills began to ascend, New Bedford's population began to change again, this time with a large influx of French-Canadians who came to work in the newly created textile mills. Most of the new immigrants were people with names like Boudreau, LeRoux, Deschamps, or Michaud, or similar surnames. Large sections of the city, mostly in the middle-class north end—away from the dangers of possible hurricanes or tidal surges that frequently wiped out the south end—were dominated by French-Canadian food, language, and culture.

The textile mills were huge, noisy, dusty places where workers stood over dangerous machinery for hours on end, feeding cotton in and taking cloth out. It was low-paying, hard work that had none of the romance Melville found in chasing the whales. In almost every sense, New Bedford had joined the Industrial Revolution.

By the 1890s, the English, the Irish and the French-Canadians began to give way to the Portuguese, many of them relatives of harpooners, sailors, and navigators taken on by the whaling ships a generation earlier at the Azores. Twenty years later, by 1910, nearly two-thirds of the city's population was foreign-born, a great majority of them from either the Portuguese-speaking Azores, or the Portuguese-speaking Cape Verde Islands off the northwest African coast. By the early 1960s, New Bedford was the second

largest Portuguese-speaking city in the northern hemi-
sphere, after Lisbon.

Like their earlier French-Canadian and Irish counterparts, the newest immigrants were hardworking, religiously
devout, and intent on making their way upward in
America. Many anglicized the pronunciation of their
names in the hope it might smooth the way.

Thus, names like Ponte were pronounced "Pont,"
without the Romance "ay" at the end, or Jose, which became, for some, "JOEsey;" Mendes, changed to "MEN-
deez," Alves, "Alvs"; or Gonsalves, which was transmuted
into "Gone-Salves." Sometimes, people even changed
their names to the English translation of the name, such
as Blanco to White or Verde to Green. Many, if not most,
of the early twentieth-century immigrants were interrelated by both blood and marriage.

"Ironically, we all come from the same islands," noted
Henry Carreiro, a New Bedford radio personality. "So,
we're all cousins. I mean, if you live on an island for 500
years with less than 100,000 people, when *your* (last) name
pops up, you know that person's got to be in your family
tree." Later, when it appeared that virtually all of the victims were known to one another, a major dispute arose as
to whether that fact had any real significance. In a town
the size of New Bedford, just about everyone knew everyone else, at least by sight, especially in the same age and
social groupings.

But as in many places where relationships are close,
even interrelated and long-enduring, when feuds broke out
in New Bedford, they were as vicious as they were difficult
to end. Old grudges gained virulence, and were held for
generations; and for many, revenge was a dish that was
always appetizing, whether hot or cold. That still held true
in the late 1980s, when the events that were to draw so
much attention to the city were about to unfold.

The research preparation of this book took place in the
city of New Bedford and the surrounding areas of Freetown, Lakeville, Dartmouth, Fairhaven, Fall River, Taunton, and Marion. While there, I made the acquaintance
of numerous residents, nearly all of them warm, friendly,

gregarious people, who have suffered repeated, staggering blows, including a reduction of 30,000 jobs from 1988 to the present time, coupled with the stigma of having been the location of notorious criminal events. Yes, there is drug addiction in New Bedford—serious drug addiction. But there is also pride, and where there is pride, there is hope.

Many people in New Bedford generously provided me with their time and their insights in the preparation of this book. Prominent among them are James Ragsdale, editor of the New Bedford *Standard-Times* newspaper, who provided invaluable assistance; Maurice Lauzon, formerly of the *Standard-Times* library, who patiently assembled literally thousands of news clippings for my review; Maureen Boyle, reporter for the *Standard Times*; John Ellement, a reporter for *The Boston Globe*; Edward Harrington, a former mayor of New Bedford, who provided vital background; Judy DeSantos, the sister of Nancy Paiva, without whose assistance this book could not have been written; Bristol County District Attorneys Ronald Pina and Paul Walsh; and numerous police officers, both of the Massachusetts State Police and local Massachusetts departments, who cooperated with their time and opinions to explain what had gone wrong, and who therefore should best remain unidentified. Special thanks go to Helga Kahr for her valuable advice, to Michael Van Ackren for his support at a critical time, and to Michaela Hamilton of Dutton Signet for her steadfast belief in this project.

As in earlier books I have made every effort to use the actual words spoken by participants, either as revealed in tape recordings, in testimonial transcripts, or as specifically recalled by the individuals involved. In circumstances where the actual words were not available, but the content and flow of the conversation was, I have paraphrased the information as conversation but have omitted quotation marks.

So, New Bedford: the place that once ascended on harpoons and dying whales; the next-to-last stop on the pre-Civil War Underground Railway; the place where black men first volunteered to be killed for glory and pride in the Civil War; the place where millions in whale oil were once made, then lost; where the bruises of daily events continually proved that politics, at least in the Commonwealth of Massachusetts, was a hard-hitting, body-contact sport; the place where a town was both a perpetrator as well as a victim . . .

Gomorrah.

—Carlton Smith
December 1993

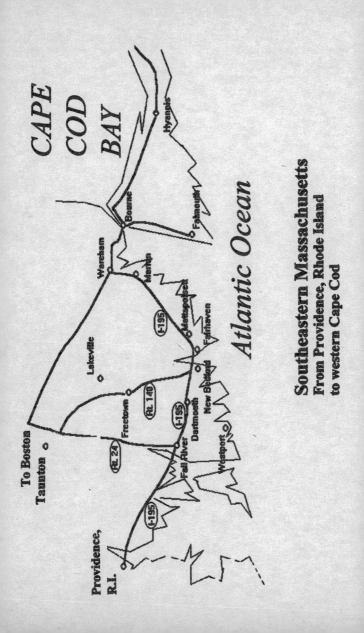

CAPE COD BAY

Atlantic Ocean

Providence, R.I.

To Boston

Taunton

Lakeville

Freetown

Rt. 24

I-195

Rt. 140

I-195

Fall River

Dartmouth

Westport

New Bedford

Fairhaven

I-195

Mattapoisett

Marion

Wareham

Bourne

Hyannis

Falmouth

Southeastern Massachusetts
From Providence, Rhode Island
to western Cape Cod

SUMMER 1988

"But think not that this famous town has only harpooners, cannibals, and bumpkins to show her visitors. Not at all. Still New Bedford is a queer place. Had it not been for us whalemen, that tract of land would this day perhaps have been in as howling condition as the coast of Labrador. As it is, parts of her back country are enough to frighten one, they look so bony . . ."

—HERMAN MELVILLE, *Moby Dick*

——— 1 ———
Remains

The woman wasn't sure she could make it much farther. She knew she shouldn't have had so much coffee. How long, how long, she wondered, until the next exit? Just the thought of pulling off and finding a restroom seemed to make it worse.

Outside, the trees rushed past as her car flew north on State Route 140 outside of New Bedford. She didn't want to stop; people driving around her would wonder why, and probably guess. It would be embarrassing. Women weren't supposed to use the woods for toilets.

But the pressure was becoming excruciating. Well, she thought, it's either off to the side of the road or it's have an accident. Succumbing, the woman slowed her car and pulled off on the shoulder of the four-lane highway. She opened the door of her car and clambered down the brushy embankment. She found a concealed spot in the scrubby trees. That's when she saw the sight that forever afterward would fill her mind every time she headed north on the road from New Bedford. The sightless eyes stared back at her, and the woman knew she would never forget the afternoon of Saturday, July 2, 1988.

Sergeant Alan Alves was tinkering around on his boat that afternoon when the call came in. Skeletal remains, the word was; just over the Lakeville town line into Freetown's jurisdiction. A woman driving north had stopped to walk her dog—how the cops laughed at that—along Route 140 and had stumbled over what was left of a human being.

Fifty yards more, just fifty. Why couldn't the person who left the body have driven just a little farther north? Now Alves would have to go to work on his day off.

Alves was the township of Freetown's only detective. He was widely regarded as a no-nonsense cop. A solidly built, darkly complected man with a pockmarked face and a bushy mustache, Alves's tough appearance seemed incongruous with his often humorous demeanor. Alves knew the streets about as well as anyone in southeastern Massachusetts, and he knew the drug scene. But what Alves was most noted for was his grasp of the subtleties of Satanism, or at least, devil worship as it was practiced in this largely rural portion of the country's second oldest state.

Alves pulled his car off onto the shoulder of the highway, where units from Freetown and the township just to the north, Lakeville, were already gathered. A call had already been made to the Bristol County district attorney's office, and experts from the Massachusetts State Police were on their way. The uniformed officers showed Alves the site.

It smelled awful. Alves guessed the skeleton had been there rotting away for several months. He was pretty sure the dead person had been a woman. The skeleton lay on its back, eye sockets pointed upward aimlessly. The arms and legs were thrust outward, as if the victim had been spread-eagled by the killer at the moment of death. The reason Alves thought the dead person was a woman was because of the panties bunched and dropped to the side, and the brassiere that was still twisted around the neck. Alves had the impression that the woman had been raped and murdered right here on the spot. *Or maybe, with some of these guys you could never tell, maybe she had been murdered, then raped,* Alves thought.

After the photographs, the light began to fade, so the scene was secured with yellow crime-scene tape, and plans were made to return the following day for a more thorough look.

A decomposing skeleton is an ugly thing, and it did not occur to Alves for even a second that the stinking, whitening bones he saw before him could ever have been connected to his beautiful, laughing friend, and sometime undercover informant, Debra Medeiros of Fall River. A self-admitted prostitute, Debbie was much too alive to ever be dead, at least in Alves's mind. But dead is what Debbie was, although it would be months before anyone realized the bones they were staring at that day were Debbie's.

Nor did anyone then realize that the ghastly remnants marked the start of one of the largest manhunts in Massachusetts' history—a frantic search that would take years, cost millions, and register the deaths of ten other young women besides Debbie, along with one suspect and a key witness.

It would be a manhunt that would destroy professional and public reputations, torture 11 families with agonizing doubts and bitter hatreds, and finally, irrevocably demolish what had once been one of the most promising political careers in the Commonwealth called Massachusetts.

But all of this was to come with hindsight years later, for Alves and everyone else. By then, though, it would be far too late.

2

Wired

While finding a dead body off the side of a major highway leading out of New Bedford was hardly an everyday occurrence, it *had* happened before.

Ever since the city had begun its slide into the drug abyss, occasional victims of overdoses, dope rip-offs, unpaid drug debts, or periodic outbursts of homicidal insanity, were unceremoniously dumped near some roadway, there to decompose undisturbed until finally discovered.

Indeed, the roads from New Bedford offered a multitude of places where a dead person could be gotten rid of quickly and easily, with no witnesses, with no ties back to the living; and with the added advantage of the unlikelihood of immediate discovery. Such sporadic incidents were part of modern life in most American cities, and New Bedford was no exception.

The major roads from New Bedford—I-195 and Route 140—are much like their federally financed counterparts in most other parts of the nation: long, smooth, elegantly engineered ribbons of asphalt or concrete, gently banked and marked, well-signed and shouldered, instrumentalities of transportation that are the envy of the world.

It is possible, for example, to leave New Bedford heading west on I-195 and be in Providence, R.I., within 40 minutes; or New York City within a matter of hours. Or one can drive north on Route 140 and be in Boston in less than an hour, or in New Hampshire in just a little over that.

Lined with dense stands of trees, heavy brush, sometimes extending miles between exits and on-ramps, the sides of the highways near New Bedford are thus quite attractive for the impatient cadaver caster. By the time the body is found, it is highly likely that the dumper will be hundreds of miles away, or even several states removed from the scene of the crime.

And if the would-be body dumper is too nervous to use one of the major highways, there are plenty of side roads throughout the countryside which can serve just as well. The back country around New Bedford is a sparsely populated region of isolated clumps of settlement, linked together tenuously with narrow, twisting lanes of blacktop and gravel that run through gloomy woods, heavy brush, past scattered farms, pastures, cranberry bogs, sharp outcroppings of granite, concealed ravines, meandering creeks, and sudden marine estuaries. All of them are excellent places to get rid of an unwanted corpse, if one is so inclined.

On the day after the skeleton was discovered on Route 140, Alves and State Trooper William Delaney returned to the scene for a closer look. Another state trooper, Kenneth Martin, supervised the recovery of the skeleton, and an ensuing search for related evidence. It was one of the hottest days of the summer, in a summer that would later be known as one of the hottest in years. The heat, of course, made the dead decompose far faster than usual.

Martin's task was often the hardest part of investigating a murder that took place outdoors. In almost every case, victims in outdoor crime scenes bring with them tantalizing clues to their last hours before death—usually in the form of microscopic fibers, often stray hairs, sometimes paint flakes, material under fingernails, and even small amounts of powdery soil residues. Careful inspection and sifting of the site where a murder victim's remains are found can, under some circumstances, yield a small collection of such "trace evidence"; the minute materials are sometimes the only way to prove the guilt or innocence of possible suspects.

Collecting this sort of evidence was Trooper Martin's most important job. He was the State Police forensics expert for Bristol County, the region of Massachusetts that included New Bedford and its surrounding townships. Carefully, Martin took samples of the mud found around the skeleton for later processing to see what might turn up, and checked for worms and insects whose generations of offspring might indicate just how long the skeleton had been there. Later, Martin would check the nearby brush for hairs and fibers; sometimes birds picked up tiny threads or loose hairs and wove them into their nests.

But Martin well knew that the odds of getting anything useful from an outdoor site diminished with each passing day. Every day it rained, more potential trace evidence washed away. In that sense, the forces of nature were an outdoor killer's greatest ally. It appeared to some that the skeleton might have been off the highway for as long as nine months.

As Martin worked, the skeleton itself went on its way to Boston, where pathologists from the State Medical Examiner's office would perform an autopsy. One thing about the skeleton was already apparent, however. Whoever the dead woman had been, she had recently suffered from a broken jaw. In fact, the bones of her mouth were still wired together.

The way things worked in Massachusetts, the one man most responsible for solving the crime of murder wasn't even present on that third day of July 1988, as Martin, Delaney, and Alves inspected the site.

In Massachusetts, the most important figure in any homicide investigation is the district attorney, and that year in Bristol County, that meant Ronald A. Pina, then in his third term as the area's top cop. Under the statutes of the Commonwealth of Massachusetts, the legal responsibility for investigating murder belongs to the D.A., not the police.

True, most of the actual work on an investigation was normally performed by state troopers like Delaney and

Martin, assisted, where necessary, by local cops like Alves. Essentially, the state police functioned as a sort of state-wide FBI, administered from a central headquarters in Boston, but operationally controlled by local D.A.'s like Pina.

Thus Pina was the man who had ultimate responsibility, even if the state police were the people who would gather the evidence. Still, finding a body by the side of the road, while not an everyday occurrence in Bristol County, was not so unusual that it required Pina's immediate presence on the scene.

Pina's absence was not a problem, at least as far as Delaney was concerned; in fact, many in the state police preferred it when Pina stayed away, Alves knew.

As he watched Delaney and Martin process the site for evidence, Alves was very much aware that there was bad blood between Pina and his state police contingent, stemming from a feud of longstanding duration; and Alves was likewise aware that it was only when a crime promised to generate a lot of publicity that Pina usually put in his appearance. So Alves thought Delaney was just as happy not to see the big boss, whom Alves suspected Delaney detested anyway.

Alves knew many state troopers held Pina in contempt. To them, Pina was just another politician on the make—hardly a real cop, but someone who had to see his name in the paper or his face on television as often as possible, someone likely to do just about anything as long as he thought it might make him look good in the news media. When there was a big case to be prosecuted, Ron Pina was sure to hog the limelight, as far as the cops were concerned. Hadn't he done exactly that with the Big Dan's pool table rape?

No, the way Alves saw things, Delaney and Martin were probably quite happy the district attorney hadn't shown up. But then, there were no television cameras present that day, either.

3

Four Men

Even as Alves, Delaney, and Martin were working along Route 140 that July 3, only a few miles away, four other men were preoccupied with the routine of their own lives; none then realized that the bones found by the side of the road would eventually affect them in ways too terrible for any of them to imagine.

One was a young East Freetown stonemason and occasional construction worker named Tony DeGrazia. That afternoon, just a few miles north of the site of the skeleton, the 26-year-old Tony couldn't decide whether he was more happy than nervous, or the other way around. On this day before the Fourth of July, Tony had asked his longtime girlfriend, Kathy Scanlon, to marry him, and Kathy had said yes.

Kathy was a beautiful young woman, and in Tony's eyes, perfection. Her soft brown hair, spectacular figure, and dancing eyes thrilled Tony, who deep down couldn't believe his good fortune. That made him very happy. For someone like Kathy to choose to be with *him* seemed unreal, Tony often thought, and that was what made him nervous.

The truth was, Kathy and Tony were about as different as Beauty and the Beast, and Tony always secretly feared that one day Kathy would awaken and see him for what he *really* was. But then, Tony realized, this was only his self-hatred talking, that little man inside, who kept trying to keep him down.

Tony remembered the time he had first really gotten to know Kathy, ten years earlier. It still seemed like a dream, or at least, an answer to a prayer. Tony had been 16 then, living on his own, sleeping wherever he could find a place that seemed safe. It was, Tony said, better than going home. In the summer of 1978 he'd found himself a tool shed in the back of a vacation home, near Long Pond in East Freetown. When the nights were clear Tony would leave the shed, take a blanket, and curl up in the woods.

One night it rained, and he awoke, shivering and covered with a swarm of biting mosquitos, as an older woman tried to rouse him. He knew the woman, and the woman knew him, Tony realized. It was Mrs. Scanlon, little Kathy Scanlon's mother. Lorraine Scanlon invited Tony to sleep on the screened-in back porch of their house a few hundred yards away. Tony gratefully accepted; by the end of the summer he was almost a part of the Scanlon family, and falling in love with Kathy, who was then 14.

Sometimes, when Tony looked back on that summer, it seemed like the happiest year of his life. The Scanlons fed him, gave him clothes, taught him things—sometimes basic things, like how to wash, comb his hair, and brush his teeth. Mostly, they just accepted him, without judgment, with humor, understanding that he was lonely, frightened, and confused; that he was just a child thrown into a cruel, adult world by no choice of his own. Eventually the Scanlons allowed Tony to live in a trailer in their backyard, and by the end of the year, Tony was calling the Scanlons "Ma" and "Pa."

The years passed, and as Tony found his grown-up footing, and his own place to live, he watched with awe as Kathy grew into a spectacular beauty. Kathy returned Tony's interest in her; she was attracted to his powerful form, his dark, sometimes brooding nature that could be swept aside with the power of her smile. There was something about Tony that called out to her: she would never forget the night he had come in from the rain, a lonely, tragic figure, as vulnerable as he was proud, someone who wanted love so bad it was pitiful. Tony was wild, sometimes, she knew; he did crazy things, got into fights and scrapes and other troubles with the law.

But underneath, Tony was good, a kind, gentle person who struggled mightily to overcome his horrifying childhood. And Tony believed deeply in God; he carried his rosary beads in his back pocket no matter where he went, and he attended church and confession faithfully throughout all the years Kathy had known him. The person closest to Tony was a priest, Father Robert Harrison, at St. John Neumann Catholic Church along Long Pond in East Freetown. And if Father Harrison was Tony's strength, Kathy Scanlon knew she was his inspiration.

Kathy also knew that Tony's heart would break if she refused to say she would marry him. So she agreed, even though something told her it wasn't going to work. No date was set; but on that night, July 3, 1988, while Delaney, Alves, and Martin were picking up the last fragments of a human being, Kathy moved in with Tony at his small lakeside house, and both of them prepared themselves to face the future. It was Kathy's twenty-fourth birthday.

About 15 miles to the south, a brash, outspoken, often volatile 38-year-old New Bedford lawyer named Kenneth Ponte was contemplating his imminent retirement to the sun-drenched Florida Gulf Coast. He was finished with New Bedford, Ponte told his friends and family; he was going to move to the land of sand, warm breezes, and palm trees, and put his old life behind him forever.

The second son of a highly respected former official of the City of New Bedford, Kenny's life had lurched off to a rough start, but then had stabilized. Many people in New Bedford knew all about Kenny's battle with heroin as a teenager and young adult. But Ponte had been able to escape the habit, leaving behind so many others who had been sucked in.

Eventually, he'd graduated from college, then law school; an influential state senator had helped him win a pardon for crimes he had committed while an addict, and Kenny had passed the bar examination and become a lawyer in his hometown. He'd even become an honorary dep-

uty sheriff of Bristol County. Now Kenny was getting
ready to move on to even better things, with the help of
his rich friend, Paul Ryley.

Like Ponte, a third man, a 36-year-old New Bedford
fish cutter and occasional handyman, Neil Anderson, had
no awareness of the police activity then underway along
the side of Route 140.

Anderson lived from week to week, with his mother in
a small house on Willis Street, only a few blocks away
from Ponte's own house on Chestnut Street; and if on
that Sunday afternoon, Anderson had looked at his heavy
motorcycle boots, he would have had no idea as to how
interested police would eventually become in those boots,
and indeed, all of his activities that summer of 1988.

And 15 miles to the east, in the small town of Tiverton,
Rhode Island, a 46-year-old diesel mechanic was similarly
oblivious of the discovery of the skeleton along Route 140.
James Baker was a man of definite views about some
things, including drugs. As far as Baker could see, drugs
were destroying people's lives. Everywhere Baker looked,
the evidence was all around. Heroin, cocaine, marijuana,
uppers, downers—all of it was rotting away people's souls,
and Baker detested it.

None of these four men knew each other, and indeed,
there were very few similarities in their lives. A stonemason, a lawyer, a fish cutter, and a diesel mechanic. But all
had in common at least *one* thing, and that was an attraction to the city of New Bedford's red-light district, an
area known as Weld Square. In the end it was an attraction
that would alter their lives forever.

4
Dextradeur

On the second floor of an old ramshackle stone building in downtown New Bedford, up a flight of stained and narrow linoleum stairs, lies the dusty, cluttered office of the city's embattled detective squad. There, during the first week of July 1988, a man named John Dextradeur contemplated his large and seemingly ever-expanding caseload, and couldn't see much reason for optimism.

Dextradeur had been a cop in the city for almost 20 years; he'd already had one heart attack as a detective for the department, and he was more than familiar with the ordinary routine of human foibles that marked the lives of many, perhaps even most, of the nearly 100,000 residents of the city that paid his salary.

As one of the larger cities in the Commonwealth of Massachusetts, New Bedford had a police force of just over 230 officers—about one cop for every 430 residents, a low ratio for many East Coast cities, and one that meant Dextradeur's department was very nearly overmatched by the criminal element.

From the dilapidated three-story headquarters in the center of the city, New Bedford's limited numbers of finest ranged across an intensely urbanized warren that was about ten miles long and perhaps three miles wide.

Because New Bedford developed long before the automobile, the city was filled with narrow, crooked alleys, dead-end streets, pedestrian-only byways and fortuitously located but unexpected passages, along with obscure and darkened stairwells enabling anyone equipped with fast feet and a knowledge of the city to make a quick escape from the law.

New Bedford was therefore a haven for purse-snatchers, smash-and-grabbers, pickpockets, strong-arm robbers, and a never-ending cavalcade of petty dope dealers and dealees. The cops had long ago learned to use their radios to put their cars in strategic positions to maximize coverage, much like basketball players playing a zone defense. Still, a person afoot beat a police cruiser on many days of the week—too many.

As a result, the days and nights of veteran cops like Dextradeur were filled with matters to be investigated: street fights, domestic battles, threats, thefts, strong-arm holdups, assaults, stabbings, shootings, rapes, and occasionally worse. It was enough to make anyone cynical about the potential of human nature, and Dextradeur was not immune.

There was always a surplus of things to be looked into, and a shortage of people to do the looking. Every detective on the New Bedford force had an apparently inexhaustible supply of open cases, a backlog made worse by the creaking slowness of the courts; too often even the solved cases were dismissed simply because too much time had elapsed between the crime and the courtroom.

Sooner or later, though, the perpetrators and the victims came back around again, with new crimes, although occasionally the roles of victim and perpetrator were reversed. Dextradeur did not then know it, but just such a situation was about to present itself, and it would tie back to several of those cases that were clogging the open-file bin that was the bane of his existence.

The police of the city of New Bedford were only one level of the state's police hierarchy. At the local level were cops who worked for townships, like Freetown's Alves; next up were city cops, both uniformed patrol officers and detectives like Dextradeur. Both the township police and the city police performed similar functions and had similar responsibilities, even if being a cop in a city like New

Bedford was a hundred times more frenetic than in a rather more bucolic setting like Freetown.

In addition to the local police departments, the Commonwealth of Massachusetts had another police agency—the Massachusetts State Police. Organized along the lines of an old colonial militia, the state police had two primary functions. One was to patrol the state's highways; the other was to investigate major crimes—like murder—within the boundaries of each local elected district attorney's territory.

Police organizations are notoriously clannish all over the country, and those in the Commonwealth of Massachusetts are no different. Efforts by well-meaning politicians and administrators to consolidate or break down barriers to cooperation and communication are invariably resisted. Cops usually have a hard time trusting each *other*, let alone officers from a strange department; added to these barriers to communication were ego obstacles; many officers of the state police, for instance, considered themselves the elite cops in the state, and only rarely deigned to concern themselves with the troubles of cops on lower levels like Alves or Dextradeur.

As a result, information collected on one level of the system does not routinely flow to another level of the system, and that is just what transpired during the first week of July 1988, as Detective Dextradeur contemplated his open-case files—files that contained several pieces of information that eventually became of great interest to Ronald A. Pina, district attorney for Bristol County.

5
Pina

Ron Pina was 44 years old that summer of 1988, and whatever else one might say about him, he had a style that was all his own.

Born the only child of a successful New Bedford contractor, Antonio Pina, and his seamstress wife, Ron Pina had been groomed from childhood to do great things, to carry the banner of his ethnic community, the hardworking Portuguese-Americans of southeastern Massachusetts, into the mainstream of America; with the grace of God and a little money, Pina hoped to be seen as a Portuguese-American version of a Kennedy.

It was only later—much later, as Ron Pina's future haplessly unraveled before his eyes—that most Portuguese-Americans in southeastern Massachusetts concluded that their former great hope was first of all an illusion, and worse, had sold them out.

Blessed with a long, angular, trim frame, coal-black hair, full, sensuous lips and intense dark eyes, Ronnie Pina—as many still called him even as he neared his middle forties—was as handsome and elegant as he was articulate.

After growing up in New Bedford, Pina graduated from Providence College in Rhode Island, and then went on to Boston College for a law degree. He married a former Miss Massachusetts, and almost immediately embarked on a career in politics. Pina served several terms in the Massachusetts legislature, and soon became one of then-Governor Michael Dukakis's top allies.

As many in New Bedford were later to observe, at least initially Ronnie Pina was seen as the true champion for a long-ignored minority, who by his actions and public stature might somehow finally legitimize aspirations and allow so many of whose roots were in the Azores or Lisbon to feel fulfilled in the possibilities of America. So, at least in the beginning, there were tens of thousands of New Bedford residents who cheered Ron Pina as one of their own.

Such acceptance, lionization, and adoration can be intoxicating stuff, particularly to the young, and there are many in New Bedford who still say Ronnie Pina stayed far too long at the punchbowl. Outwardly, Pina was self-confident, at home in his gifts of articulation, aware of his good looks and his powerful connections. Whatever doubts possessed Pina, he kept them well-hidden; but precocious as Pina was, there were those who couldn't help feeling he would be a better person when he finally failed at something.

In 1970 Pina was just out of law school, and he quickly won a spot in the Massachusetts House of Representatives. By the mid-1970s, he was among the inner circle of idealistic reformers associated with then-Governor Dukakis.

Soon Pina carved out a spectacular reputation as the charismatic, liberal *enfant terrible* of the Massachusetts legislature, bent on cleaning up political corruption, confronting entrenched interests, legislating consumer protection laws, mandating environmental regulations, insurance reform, or a host of similar measures seen in Massachusetts as progressive lawmaking. Pina was particularly adroit at manipulating the Massachusetts news media, which rarely cared if Ronnie made any real sense, but *were* interested in the sort of conflict with other talking heads that Pina, playing the role of Outrageous Young Legislator, often provided for the evening news.

By 1976 Pina considered running for lieutenant governor on a ticket with Dukakis; his relationship with Dukakis had advanced that far. In the end, however, Pina was thwarted by the ambitions of another career politician, Thomas P. O'Neill, Jr., the son of then U.S. House

Speaker "Tip" O'Neill. But for Pina, losing out to the younger O'Neill might have been a blessing in disguise, at least initially.

As Dukakis was heading for a defeat by Republican Edward J. King in 1978, Pina realized that his time in the Massachusetts legislature was about to expire; conservatives were on the march in tax revolts across the country, and Ronald Reagan was looming large on the political horizon; as a result liberal, progressive reformers like Pina were about to become an endangered species.

Thus, in 1978, Pina ran for a new, $38,000-a-year, soon-to-be full-time job: district attorney of Bristol County, a swatch of territory that encompassed the most populated areas of southeastern Massachusetts, and where Portuguese-American voters were in the majority. His name, his family connections, and his earlier, highly publicized experience as a member of the state's legislature helped him win the job easily.

But if in 1978 Pina at least temporarily exited from the legislative arena, his political instincts—and more particularly his deftness in orchestrating news media coverage—were hardly in remission.

Whether he intended to or not, Pina soon became known as a rather flamboyant prosecutor, one who seemingly relished seeing his name in the headlines and his image on the evening news. Some later contended that Pina quickly realized that as the chief crime fighter in the most populated, drug-affected area of southeastern Massachusetts, he was in control of a cornucopia of good publicity, with all its potential for his political future.

6

The Politician

As the late 1970s merged into the early 1980s, Pina's irrepressible desire to play to the news media sometimes got the young district attorney in trouble. At least one rival soon called him a "grandstander, a publicity hound"; and even neutral critics readily conceded that the aroma of naked political ambition sometimes wafted from the offices of the district attorney.

Until the Highway Murder case, unquestionably Ron Pina's largest claim to fame (or infamy, depending on which side one was on) were the two Big Dan's rape trials from the middle 1980s.

In that notorious case, a somewhat intoxicated woman had been raped by four men while held down on a pool table in New Bedford's north end. At least five other people in Big Dan's tavern at the time did nothing to interfere.

Later, there was a question about just what the uninvolved five *actually* saw, or could reliably testify to, but as it was reported throughout the world—mostly by news leaks from Pina's office—it seemed there was an entire barroom filled with a cheering section of men urging the rapists on.

Whatever the true facts, as it was publicized, the Big Dan's rape instantly ignited women all over the country. Pina was sought out by news media from New York, Los

Angeles, Chicago, Atlanta, even from other countries. He became fast friends with Geraldo Rivera, and granted scores of interviews. In each, Pina came across as the sorrowful but sincere district attorney: sensitive to the needs of the victim, seemingly slightly uncomfortable with all the media notoriety, but committed to justice.

Nationally, it played very well, and in liberal Boston—crucial to any politician's statewide ambitions in Massachusetts—Pina gained a great deal of favorable name recognition. The pool table crime later served as the rather loose foundation for a movie which won an Academy Award for actress Jodie Foster, *The Accused*.

But in New Bedford, the Big Dan's case was an entirely different story. Feelings ran so high in the community over the rape cases that Pina and others began receiving death threats. Half the city blamed him for bringing charges against the Big Dan's Four; the other half approved of the trials, but blamed Pina for making New Bedford look bad in front of the nation by being so perversely public about it.

In the beginning, most of the reaction came from those who were outraged that the rapes had taken place; but soon thoughtless remarks were made in the newspapers and over the airwaves about Portuguese immigrants and Portuguese culture, and inevitably there was a backlash.

"There was a lot of stupid talk, and it tore this community apart," Pina's chief deputy, Ray Veary, recalled years later. "It had friends not talking to one another. It got very ugly here." Fights broke out in barrooms and on the streets between proponents and opponents of the charges, while children of native-born Americans taunted the children of immigrants, calling them animals and worse, and saying they should all go back to Portugal, that they didn't *deserve* to live in America.

Almost overnight the case became a symbol: a woman's right to be safe from rape, against perceptions of prejudice against Portuguese immigrants; as a simultaneous symbol of two different deeply felt things, to two different groups, the case moved well beyond whatever the facts might have been at the time of the crimes.

At the end of the first trial, tried by Veary, the defendants and the prosecutors were literally trapped on the top of the courthouse while thousands of angry people ran around the building, shouting curses and screaming threats and fighting one another. "It was awful, just awful," Veary recalled. To the present day, there are many in New Bedford who still blame Pina for dividing the city over Big Dan's.

But underneath his carefully constructed public persona, Ron Pina was a sensitive man, acutely conscious of how others were perceiving him. Yes, he wanted to seem commanding, in control, capable; that was, after all, the essence of being a politician. No one wanted to vote for someone who looked down at the floor, or was painfully shy, or who fumbled for an answer under pressure. Sometimes Pina could be acerbic, or sound arrogant; but these were ways Pina used to hide his sensitivity, his vulnerability, and to override that quiet, always-present, tiny voice of self-doubt.

So there was a hidden aspect of Pina, one which usually only emerged in his moments of introspection, often taken out on the sea in the cockpit of his small sailboat, *Cyrano*, or with his teenaged daughter, Kari, or in other similar places or situations where others who competed with him or wished to judge him did not tread. His marriage to the former beauty queen, the mother of his child, had disintegrated as Pina had moved up in politics, and the truth was, Ron Pina was a man who craved love and acceptance, an addiction that often made him a lonely man, even when he was surrounded by others.

But this side of Pina was not one that was well-known to those who worked for him, particularly among the state police who had been assigned to his office. To the troopers, Pina was just a politician—and a peculiarly insensitive and selfish one at that.

Early in his tenure as district attorney, Pina had actually been in a fistfight with one of the troopers; the officers had responded to a particularly gruesome murder, in which a mentally disturbed mother had killed her infant son with a chainsaw.

When the ashen-faced cops returned to the office, Pina had made a flip remark about the crime, as much to protect himself against the horror of the act as anything else. One of the troopers, overcome by his own emotions, ignited at Pina's remark and instantly decked him; and while apologies were given all around, the incident did little to convince the troopers that the man they worked for was anything more than a shallow, publicity-hungry politician who was as arrogant as he was insensitive.

And after another dispute, Pina had effectively fired all the troopers assigned to his office, when he decided all were plotting against him to help another lawyer—the brother of one of the troopers—to be elected district attorney in his place. The troopers were disloyal, Pina decided; therefore, he couldn't trust them. He ordered them out of his office, and the troopers retreated to their barracks in Dartmouth just west of New Bedford, while intermediaries tried to heal the breach.

Eventually, of course, Pina realized that he simply couldn't function as district attorney without the troopers, even if he *didn't* trust them. Pina backed down and invited the troopers to return; but one result of the fracas was legislation granting district attorneys more power over who would and would not be allowed to work as investigators.

Pina's offices were on the fifth floor of the Times Building in downtown New Bedford, and were connected to a nearby wing of rooms that housed the local branch of the Massachusetts State Police. A person going from Pina's wing to the troopers' wing had to walk down a corridor, up a short flight of stairs, and make a right turn to another corridor on another level; the separation of elevation seems to stand as a metaphor for the nature of the troubles between Pina and his investigators.

The way things worked in Massachusetts, each district attorney—there were 12 of them statewide—was assisted in his prosecutorial endeavors by officers assigned to him by the state police headquarters in Boston. The troopers were assigned to investigative groups called Crime Prevention and Control Units, or CPACs. Troopers went from patrolling the highways to the CPACs based primarily on seniority. There were no other special qualifications required, such as advanced training in investigative techniques; most troopers learned on the job. Almost as soon as the CPACs were started, the jobs in each unit became highly sought after by the troopers.

Why? Because the average salary of a state trooper assigned to patrol the highways was around $40,000, and members of CPAC teams could earn, with overtime, as much as $70,000.

As this system of dual control—between police headquarters in Boston and the local district attorneys—developed, district attorneys gradually became empowered to select individuals from the list of state troopers qualified to fill the available investigative jobs. As a result, it isn't surprising that many of those state troopers who held CPAC jobs were also political supporters of their appointing district attorney, who had the power to make or renew their appointment. All of this made the district attorneys acutely sensitive to the troopers' job performance, and the troopers acutely sensitive to the district attorneys' political needs.

In an ideal world, making the troopers' job security contingent on their pleasing the district attorney who selected them might seem a good way to get both sides to work together.

But on the other hand, the detectives assigned to a CPAC unit tended to follow the directions given to them by their district attorney, few questions asked, whatever their own professional judgment might have otherwise told them. In a state with a long history of organized crime infestation, this is not a good situation, as many thoughtful troopers will attest.

Moreover, the dissonance between the troopers' professional judgment and their personal financial interest was one of the most glaring inadequacies of the Massachusetts system for investigating major crimes such as homicide; inevitably, it led to jealousies, frictions, and resentments that would prove to be a major drawback as the next few years unfolded.

But Pina's relationship with the state police assigned to

him was different than most other Massachusetts D.A.'s. For one thing, Pina was paranoid about his troopers; he could never quite convince himself that the troopers in his office really had Ron Pina's interests at heart. Pina *never* asked the troopers to support him during election campaigns; for him, it was enough if they would only keep quiet and remain neutral. He knew in his heart that the troopers didn't like him.

Pina believed that if the troopers wanted to do him in politically, all they had to do was deliberately botch an important investigation, and thus make him look bad. To Pina, the troopers' union was his mortal enemy, and had been ever since his days in the legislature as an ally of Michael Dukakis. For evidence, Pina cited Dukakis's experience in 1978, when the state police union had backed Edward J. King's candidacy for governor, in the process making Dukakis look like he was soft on crime. As a result, Pina was extraordinarily sensitive to *any* signs that the state police weren't doing their job exactly the way Pina thought it should be done.

Pina also believed that the state police were not competent, at least as investigators. He didn't blame the individual troopers so much as the state police organization; most of all, he blamed the troopers' union. The union, Pina believed, was so powerful in the hallways of the State House of Representatives that it could get pretty much anything it wanted. Dukakis's loss to King proved that, Pina believed.

One of the things the union wanted was a scrupulous adherence to a seniority system. The seniority system in turn kept the investigative CPAC positions reserved for those who had risen high enough on the seniority list to qualify for the jobs—regardless of training, ability, or experience. The "staties," as some referred to them, were in Pina's mind good for writing traffic tickets, but that was about it.

"They're poorly trained, they are not investigatively trained," Pina said later, after he was out of office. "I'm not knocking people. This is part of my speech on wanting more training. I know I'm probably gonna get in trouble here, but let me pull that rock back.

"The state police are basically individuals who are highway patrol. They're on the highway. Their prime directive is speed traps and things like that, and to maintain the Commonwealth highways. When you reach a certain seniority level, you can then say, 'I want to be a detective,' and put in for the district attorney's office. Now this was more of a promotion, but you weren't trained to *do* anything. I mean, you didn't get a special course to be a detective.

"So if you were a regular trooper and you did well, and now you got some seniority, for example, you could get on the list and come into my office. You'd be there for a while, then you'd take the corporal's exam." If a trooper passed the corporal's test, they'd be transferred back out to the highway, going back down to the bottom of the seniority list of corporals.

"You know how many corporals move in and out of the D.A.'s office?" Pina asked. "So, spending any extra money on you to train you or to teach you things, like at the FBI school, well, it's gonna be a waste of time. Because as soon as you take the corporal's exam, now you're back on the highway." Eventually, after other corporals had moved up, or retired, and seniority was regained, a corporal might return to investigative work. But then the whole thing started all over again, according to Pina, when a corporal took the *sergeant's* test.

"You take the next test, you're a sergeant now, you can try to transfer back in," Pina said, "but it's not gonna happen tomorrow. You're talking a year or two years . . . So it's all this weaving back and forth." As a result, investigations lost a lot of continuity and experience, at least in Pina's view.

Worse, as far as Pina was concerned, was what he felt was the unresponsiveness of the investigators to his requests. Some of this was personal, Pina knew, but much of it was institutional because of the dual control over the troopers.

This was one of the fundamental problems in the investigation of the Highway Murders: while Pina, as district attorney, was charged under the state law with the responsibility of investigating murder, the detective work was the

job of the troopers—who responded to a completely different set of bosses in Boston. The bosses in Boston had 12
district attorneys to worry about, not just Ronnie Pina,
who wasn't one of their favorite people to begin with.

When Pina attempted to go around the bosses, and talk
directly to the investigators, the sergeant in charge of
Pina's CPAC would chastise the troopers, at least according to Pina. The military structure of the state police
emphasized the formal chain of command. That meant all
communications and written reports had to be sent to the
higher-ups in Boston before they were routed back to
Pina—if they ever came back. Sometimes, he recalled, it
took months for reports to make the round-trip journey,
and even then, no one in the district attorney's office was
sure that there wasn't additional information that simply
hadn't been passed on.

And there were even deeper, more personal reasons for
the antipathy between Pina and his investigators. One of
them involved Sheila Martines, the district attorney's
bride-to-be.

——— 7 ———

The Trunk Case

Only a few months before the skeleton was found on
Route 140, there had been another embarrassing public
flap between Pina and the police, this one over Pina's fiancée, Sheila Martines.

Sheila was a well-known television personality in Providence, Rhode Island, where she hosted an afternoon magazine show. Beautiful, witty, a high-energy personality,
Sheila had parlayed an earlier journalism career on radio
and in newspapers to the television business. Over the
years she had become quite well connected in the broadcast industry. She and Pina had begun dating each other
in 1987, and most of those around Pina—who had a reputation for skipping from relationship to relationship—were
struck by how serious the district attorney was about the
attractive, 34-year-old broadcaster.

Then, one morning in April 1988, Sheila disappeared
while driving to work on I-195.

The following day, a distraught and disheveled Sheila
was discovered in an isolated, rural area of Bristol County.
She claimed she had been kidnapped by a knife-wielding
man while stopped on the side of the highway, driven
around all night, molested, and then locked in the trunk
of her own car.

But the investigating troopers noticed that there were
only three sets of footprints around Sheila's trunk: Sheila's,
those of the man who first heard her cries for help and

28

released her, and those of the cop who had first come to the scene. Some troopers speculated that Sheila had locked herself in the trunk, for some reason. They made jokes about spirit abductions.

When the troopers asked to interview Sheila a second time to clarify matters, Pina had refused to let them. While many in New Bedford gleefully seized on the incident and Pina's reaction as evidence he was covering up for Sheila, others saw a deeper motive: Pina loved Sheila, and wanted to protect her from the troopers, whose motives and integrity he deeply distrusted.

Under Pina's prodding, a hue and cry was raised across the county, composite sketches of the kidnapper were distributed, and squads of troopers began scouring the highways in search of a criminal most thought existed only in Sheila's mind.

This touchy situation almost immediately grew worse when someone in the state police leaked the three-footprint facts to the news media, apparently in an effort to make Pina look foolish. The so-called Trunk Case, as the affair quickly became known, was merely the latest development in the long-running feud between the D.A. and the state police.

Suggestions were made that Sheila had simply partied too much, and was too embarrassed to give that as the reason she never made it to work. Both Pina and Sheila denied that rumor, of course, and asserted that the three-footprint story was bogus. But Sheila quit her job shortly after the incident, and entered a hospital for treatment. Pina's closest advisers, meanwhile, urged him to distance himself from Sheila, but Pina refused. *No way*, he said. *I love her*.

Very few realized it at the time, but others in New Bedford and Bristol County were also losing patience with Pina in that summer of 1988.

One was James Ragsdale, the editor of the local newspaper, the *Standard-Times*. Although the newspaper had supported Pina for district attorney three times, both Ragsdale and the paper's publisher were having doubts about Pina. Most of those doubts had to do with the seeming inability of the police and the district attorney to do anything to stop the flood of drugs which was threatening to drown the city in crime.

In the aftermath of the "Trunk Case," an anonymous caller had telephoned Ragsdale, offering to provide him with medical information about Sheila Martines. Ragsdale suspected a setup, but nevertheless expressed cautious interest in learning more. Rumors were then flying that Sheila had been using cocaine the night before her reported kidnapping, and Ragsdale thought the newspaper should check the stories out.

Within a few days, however, Ragsdale was telephoned by a furious Pina, who accused Ragsdale of being scum and invading Sheila's privacy. Ragsdale defended the paper and himself by observing that since drug abuse was one of New Bedford's worst problems, the newspaper needed to follow tips wherever they led—just as he expected Pina's office to do the same. Ragsdale was well aware that drugs were no respecter of income or social station in New Bedford; his own son had been convicted of possession of cocaine.

But Pina wasn't buying Ragsdale's explanation.

"You don't *want* me to follow cocaine, wherever it leads," Pina told Ragsdale, according to the editor.

"Yes, I do," said Ragsdale.

"No, you don't," said Pina, who then suggested that the trail would head directly into the *Standard-Times'* newsroom.

Ragsdale said he didn't care where the trail headed. He hung up the telephone and went to talk to the paper's publisher. Ragsdale recounted the conversation he'd just had with Pina.

"Do you have a problem with that?" Ragsdale asked. "Not me," said the publisher.

"Me neither," said Ragsdale, and the stage was set for a confrontation between the local newspaper and Pina that would affect the course of the Highway Murder investigation over the following two years, as Pina indeed attempted to follow cocaine wherever it led—even if that path was nowhere near the real killer.

— 8 —
Judy and Nancy

Five days after the skeleton was first discovered along the side of Route 140, a 33-year-old New Bedford woman was walking through the city's south end with two of her children. One of Judy DeSantos's kids looked up and remarked to her mother: "Oh, look, there's Auntie Nancy."

Judy DeSantos glanced over at the low-income apartment on Morgan Street, not far from the city jail. Sure enough, there was her older sister, Nancy Paiva, sitting on her front porch, wearing her robe and drinking a cup of coffee. Judy didn't say anything, and neither did Nancy.

The two sisters, once so close, were feuding. They had barely talked to each other for nearly eight months—not since Judy had played a part in seeing Nancy's two children taken away from her and placed with other relatives.

Unlike Nancy, Judy, her children, and her husband Tony lived quietly in New Bedford's north end. Tony was a factory assembler, while Judy worked part-time for the city's election office. So closely was she tied to hearth and home, Judy didn't even know how to drive. That, along with many other things in Judy DeSantos's life, would soon change.

Nancy was three years older than Judy. The two sisters were about as different as one could imagine. Where Judy was heavy for her size, Nancy was short and skinny; where Judy tended to hang back because of her shyness, Nancy was outgoing, entertaining, assertive, and "quite pretty," as Judy would later describe her. When they were little girls growing up in New Bedford, Nancy always took the lead, cajoling Judy into taking chances.

"She was the optimist, I was the pessimist. I still am a pessimist," Judy said later, after Nancy was dead. "She would trust everyone and I would trust no one. I was shy. If you yelled at me, I would cry." Nancy would yell right back.

"Well, we played the normal kids' games. We went roller skating, things like that," Judy recalled. "Growing up, we played with the dolls and normal girl stuff that you do. It was a loving household, it was a two-parent family. I remember the time when she made me climb a tree. And then wouldn't help me get out of the tree. That always has stuck with me, because I was afraid. But she was never afraid. She did well in school, went on from school, she married right away when she got out of high school."

Unlike Judy, Nancy "made friends easily." Nancy was Judy's idol, in some ways; "She was who I wanted to be," Judy said.

But while most of Nancy's twenties were normal— "Nancy was the woman who made the cookies for the bake sales at the schools, and Nancy would load up her car and bring the kids to apple picking or whatever, there were always kids at the house and she would have slumber parties," Judy recalled—by Nancy's early thirties, things started going wrong.

A divorce was followed by a boyfriend who first fathered one of her two children, and then left her for another woman. One day, Nancy accompanied a friend to see someone at the Bristol County House of Corrections—the county jail—and there met a smooth-talking, dominating man named Frankie Pina.

Frankie was no relation to Ron Pina. In fact, they were about as far apart socially, psychologically, and economically as possible. Frankie was from the Boston area, and had a long arrest record for petty crime—burglary, robbery, assault, fraud. He was a prisoner in the jail when Nancy Paiva first met him. Nancy fell for him.

At first Judy thought Frankie might be all right. He

often called Judy's house to talk to Nancy, who sometimes stayed at Judy's overnight. Frankie told Judy that he'd had some troubles, but after he got out of jail he was going to straighten his life out. He really loved Nancy, Frankie said, and he wanted to help take care of Nancy's kids. Judy believed him. It seemed to her that Nancy was happy with Frankie's attentions.

Frankie got out of jail in mid-1985, and almost immediately moved in with Nancy and her two daughters, Jill, then 14, and Jolene, then 10. Judy didn't see as much of Nancy after that. At one point Nancy declared bankruptcy; Kenny Ponte became her attorney. Later Nancy worked for Kenny as a part-time secretary, and after that, Nancy got a job in a video-rental store.

But then the relationship between Nancy and Frankie started going downhill. It was some time after Frankie moved in that Jill told Judy an attorney from Boston had driven down to visit Frankie, and that Frankie had beaten Nancy up in front of the lawyer; the lawyer, who was *not* Kenny Ponte, hadn't done a thing to stop it. Nancy hinted to Judy that Frankie was up to something illegal or possibly dangerous with the Boston lawyer, whoever he was. Judy later came to believe that the mysterious lawyer might have had something to do with Kenny Ponte, although there was never any evidence of that.

As 1985 turned into 1986, Nancy often went to stay with Judy to keep away from Frankie. Nancy told Judy that Frankie was stealing her money and her food stamps. Judy began giving Nancy money to help her out. Soon relations between Frankie and Judy went into the deep freeze, especially after Judy tried to convince Nancy to dump Frankie. But for some reason, Nancy always went back to Frankie, and the cycle began again.

Meanwhile, Jill and Jolene went back and forth between Nancy's house and Judy's, bringing tales of Frankie's brutal behavior. By that time Frankie's beatings of Nancy had also gained the attention of the New Bedford Police, who were frequently called to Nancy's house to keep Frankie away from Nancy. Still, Nancy would never file any complaints against Frankie, and allowed the police to think of her as Frankie's wife, "Nancy Pina." It wasn't until later that Judy understood why.

That day came in early November 1987, when Nancy sold her microwave oven to Judy for $150. Judy knew the microwave had cost Nancy $500; she figured that Frankie had been stealing from Nancy again, and that Nancy needed the money to pay pressing bills.

"So I said, 'All right,' and I gave her eighty, because that was all I had. I told her I'd go to the bank in the morning, and I'd give her the rest of the money. But what happened was, in the morning, no microwave. But I got a call from Frankie . . ."

"You gave Nancy money for that microwave?" Frankie asked Judy.

"Yeah," said Judy, "and now I want the microwave."

"Well, you're not getting the damn microwave," Frankie told Judy, "you're not getting it, you hear me? Do you want to know why she's selling it? Do you wanna *know*?"

In the background Judy could hear Nancy crying, begging Frankie: "Don't tell her, please don't tell her, don't, don't, don't tell her . . ."

"Your sister is doin' *heroin*," Frankie told Judy. He laughed. "That's where your money went, for heroin!"

Judy sat at the table, numb. "I had a cup of coffee and I was shaking," she remembered later. "I started telling Frank I was gonna kill him. Then my husband took the phone, because he didn't know what was going on. He started saying, 'Leave my wife alone' and that sort of thing. I told him, 'I'm going over there, I'm gonna kill the son-ofabitch, I don't care, I'm gonna *kill* him.'" But Judy didn't kill anyone. Instead, she convinced her sister to go into a drug treatment center.

"I said, 'Nancy, you need help. Let me help you, I'll take the kids. You gotta get rid of Frankie.' Now, I think, that's probably a mistake that I made." Someone reported Nancy to the state's Department of Social Services, which threatened to take Jill and Jolene away from Nancy if she didn't get the drug treatment. A goal of the treatment was to help Nancy get away from Frankie, Judy said.

"But I think we did it wrong. You know, I kept saying,

'You gotta get away from him, you gotta get away from him. It's *him*.' And everybody kept saying the same thing. But I think sometimes the more you say it, the worse you make it.

"Now, I can see that. They threatened to take her children away from her, so that's why she entered the treatment center, which is a wrong thing to do. You don't say 'We're gonna take the one thing you love, the only thing in life that you have,' and use that against someone. So she really didn't get the help. In two weeks, she was out and, Frankie was back."

Afterward, Nancy rarely talked to Judy; while Judy, for her part, was convinced that when Nancy did call, it was only because Nancy wanted something from her, and Judy had resolved to force her sister to confront her problems with so-called tough love, and if that meant denying Nancy money or other forms of support, so be it. Later, Judy found out that Frankie beat Nancy to keep her away from her sister. For the better part of eight months, the two sisters, once so close, barely spoke to each other.

Thus, on July 7, 1988, Judy resolutely ignored Nancy as she and the kids made their way up the street. But that was the last time Judy ever saw her sister.

——— 9 ———
Whispers

Nancy Paiva's descent into the hell of heroin came to an end sometime that same evening.

The exact circumstances of Nancy's disappearance remain obscure. What is known is that sometime during the afternoon, Nancy was sitting in a south end New Bedford bar called Whispers, along with Frankie Pina, and several other people.

According to some of those present, an argument between Nancy and Frankie ensued, with Frankie ordering Nancy to leave the bar. Nancy left. An acquaintance later told Judy DeSantos that she saw Nancy walking up the street toward her house around 7 P.M., with tears in her eyes. It was raining. That was the last time anyone saw Nancy Paiva alive.

The Whispers Pub was a notorious hangout in New Bedford's south end. Later, it would be alleged in federal court that the establishment was the center of a cocaine ring that handled sales of nearly $5.2 million *each year*.

Almost all of these sales went to New Bedford residents—including, it would later be learned—to many of the victims of the Highway Killer. Cocaine was so easy to procure in the bar that a line of would-be buyers often formed, heading down the stairs to the basement to wait their turn to purchase the drug. It was just after leaving Whispers that Nancy was last seen.

*   *   *

Two days later, after the afternoon Nancy left Whispers, Sergeant John Dextradeur of the New Bedford Police Department was on his way back to the detectives' squad room, when he saw something that disturbed him. Dextradeur dropped what he was doing and walked over to the front desk to eavesdrop.

The man at the counter was Frankie Pina, and Dextradeur knew him well. In fact Dextradeur had once arrested Frankie for armed robbery, and those charges were still pending.

Now Frankie wanted to file a complaint with the police, and Dextradeur was *really* bothered.

"I don't know why," he said later. "I just felt that it was out of character for Mr. Pina to be casually standing at the front desk of the police lobby speaking to an officer. Usually when Mr. Pina was at the desk in the lobby, he was there in handcuffs, against his wishes."

Learning that Frankie was reporting "Nancy Pina" as a missing person made Dextradeur feel even more uncomfortable.

The last time the detective had seen Frankie—in April 1988—Frankie had been with *another* woman, who appeared to have gone missing as well. Twenty-six-year-old Rochelle Clifford had been with Frankie on April 27, 1988, but had seemingly vanished shortly thereafter.

That earlier disappearance was irritating to Dextradeur, because Rochelle Clifford was a key witness in *two* open cases Detective Dextradeur had in his files, one a rape, and the other an assault; if Dextradeur could only find Clifford, he might be able to resolve those two cases and get busy on something else. But for two months Rochelle Clifford had been nowhere to be found, and here again was Frankie Pina, now talking about a *second* woman connected to him, who was also missing—the woman he lived with, in fact. To Dextradeur, that seemed to make Frankie two for two. It was enough to make a detective think.

Even as Frankie was known to the cops in New Bedford, so was Nancy Paiva—actually, of course, as "Nancy Pina," although Nancy and Frankie had never been married. The way the police knew Nancy was as Frankie's regular victim: countless times police had been called to "Nancy Pina's" Morgan Street apartment to keep Frankie from beating Nancy, or at least rescue her after he'd already started.

Now, with Frankie reporting the woman he beat so often as newly missing, as well as Frankie's earlier connection to Rochelle Clifford, Dextradeur was immediately suspicious of Frankie. Dextradeur wanted to know more, so he told Frankie he would *personally* investigate Nancy's disappearance, even though handling missing persons cases was not his job. Actually, what Dextradeur had in mind was investigating *Frankie*.

Dextradeur and Frankie moved out to the front steps of the police station, and talked for more than an hour about Nancy, Rochelle Clifford, and Frankie's most recent criminal activities. Frankie, in fact, was about to go to jail again on yet another assault charge.

As Dextradeur put it later, "I just felt uncomfortable with the whole thing ... It was really strange. It was just that I was sitting there talking to a guy that I can't gather any respect for, knowing his background. And he's showing me this great love and concern for this girl that he used to beat the hell out of so regularly."

Why was Frankie suddenly worrying about Nancy? Had Frankie done something to Nancy, and was he now trying to cover it up by acting worried? Had he likewise done something to Rochelle Clifford? Dextradeur assured Frankie that he would give Nancy's disappearance an all-out effort.

The next day, Judy DeSantos learned of Nancy's disappearance for the first time. She found out from Nancy's daughter Jill, who heard from Jolene. "Jolene says Mom hasn't been home for three days," Jill told Judy. "Do you know where she is?"

It wasn't unusual for Nancy to stay away from Frankie, Judy knew, but almost always before, she had gone to stay with Judy, or sometimes with friends. Judy called around to see if anyone had seen Nancy, but no one had. She waited for two more days, thinking Nancy might turn up, but Nancy didn't. By this time Judy was really worried about her sister.

She thought about calling the police, but was intimidated by the idea of talking to the authorities. She thought the police might think she was being hysterical. But through a friend, Judy learned the name of a detective in the department. Judy called and reported that her sister, Nancy Paiva, was missing. Judy also told the police that her sister was addicted to heroin. That was a mistake, Judy decided later, because then the detective told her that Judy just had to understand that "junkies disappear all the time."

Judy knew that wasn't true about Nancy, however. No matter how badly addicted Nancy was, she always made an effort to maintain contact with her children, or with Judy herself. It just wasn't in Nancy's nature to disappear without leaving word with someone. But because Judy was intimidated by the confident attitude of the police, and secretly ashamed of Nancy's addiction, she at first meekly accepted the department's cavalier verdict about her sister. She sat down by the telephone and waited for Nancy to call.

10

Missing

On the evening of July 15, 1988, Donald Santos drove his wife Mary Rose into the downtown core of New Bedford from their apartment in the south end, and dropped her off at a tavern across the street from the Greyhound bus station.

Mary Rose Santos was 26 years old, a somewhat heavy young woman with a pleasant, smiling face. The tavern, called the Quarterdeck Lounge, was a rough place of low ceilings, grime, music, and cheap beer. It was one of three taverns in New Bedford owned by a woman named Faith Alameida, and as matters unfolded, would be one of the four or five places that linked the 11 victims of the so-called Highway Killer to each other.

For one thing, Mary Rose Santos was well known to Nancy Paiva and Frankie Pina, who had been frequent patrons of all three of the Alameida taverns, along with many of the other victims; Nancy Paiva, in fact, had once worked for Faith Alameida's Town Tavern, a place also frequented by Mary Rose Santos and her husband Donald.

For another, Mary Rose had a drug habit, just as each of the other victims also suffered from drug addictions. But it would be months before these and still other interconnections between the 11 known Highway Murder victims would become fully understood.

Just why Donald Santos dropped his wife of eight years off at the tavern remains unclear. Investigators later determined that sometime around 1 A.M. Mary Rose left the tavern to visit a friend who lived nearby. A short time after that, Mary Rose, the mother of two young sons, simply vanished. Police later determined that Mary Rose had supposedly been headed toward the city's red-light district when she was last seen.

A day or so later, Donald Santos reported Mary Rose missing to the New Bedford police. The report went into the department's missing persons unit, where it was promptly filed and forgotten—for the moment.

The day after Mary Rose disappeared, Frankie Pina was back in court, this time appealing an earlier assault conviction. The case was assigned to a court in Fall River, Massachusetts, a small city lying about midway between New Bedford and Providence, Rhode Island. While awaiting his hearing, Frankie was booked into the Bristol County House of Corrections. From the jail, Frankie maintained daily telephone contact with Detective John Dextradeur, who kept assuring Frankie that he was doing everything he could to locate Nancy.

Meanwhile, Judy DeSantos also continued looking for her sister. She called numerous people who knew Nancy, and asked them to tell Nancy to call her if they saw her. Soon Judy was getting reports from all over New Bedford from people who said they had seen Nancy at one place or another. Because she didn't know how to drive, Judy prevailed upon friends to take her to those locations, or go themselves to see if Nancy was there. But none of the reports panned out.

Donald Santos, however, took a slightly different tack in searching for his wife, Mary Rose. He went to the newspapers.

In a story published about a week after Mary Rose Santos disappeared, Donald Santos told Maureen Boyle, a reporter for the New Bedford *Standard-Times*, that Mary Rose was missing.

"I'm worried sick," Donald Santos told Boyle. He said he'd spent hours driving around the streets of New Bedford looking for his wife. At night, he continued, he would fall asleep clutching Mary Rose's photograph. Santos told Boyle he believed that his wife was dead. Their two sons, five and seven, missed their mother terribly, Donald Santos said. The five-year-old son, Donald Santos added, wanted to know whether he could die, too, so he could see his mother again.

Boyle's story was placed on an inside page of the newspaper, but it did not escape the attention of Judy DeSantos. Learning of another woman's disappearance galvanized Judy. She called the police again, and this time was connected with John Dextradeur.

Judy explained that her sister was missing, the same as Mary Rose Santos. Dextradeur wanted to know who Judy was, and Judy explained that she was Nancy Paiva's sister. Dextradeur said he'd never heard of Nancy Paiva. After a few minutes, Dextradeur and Judy got the situation straightened out. The woman Dextradeur thought was Nancy Pina was really Nancy Paiva.

Nancy had *never* been married to Frankie, Judy told the New Bedford detective. Her name was *Paiva*, not Pina. Well, Dextradeur demanded, why hadn't Judy called sooner? Judy was embarrassed to admit that she had been afraid to talk again to the police, especially after the police had first told her that "junkies disappear all the time."

Now Dextradeur told Judy that Frankie had reported "Nancy Pina" missing almost a week earlier. Judy got mad at Frankie all over again for his failure to call her about Nancy's disappearance—anyway, she thought, what made Frankie so sure Nancy wasn't at *Judy's* house?—and on his insistence that Nancy was his wife. But both Judy and Dextradeur were agreed on one thing: it seemed completely out of character for Frankie to have called the police to report Nancy's disappearance.

After all, Nancy had left Frankie for brief periods before, and Frankie hadn't bothered to call the police on those occasions, even when he had no idea where she might have gone. Why was Frankie calling police *this* time? "Don't you think that's strange?" Dextradeur asked Judy. Judy thought it *was* strange. Judy thought Dextradeur was extremely suspicious of Frankie's role, whatever it might have been, in Nancy's disappearance.

Judy arranged to meet with Dextradeur. The detective at first didn't believe the two women were sisters because of their different appearance. And, Dextradeur explained, Frankie had told him that Nancy was from the Cape Verde Islands—meaning, Judy thought, that Frankie had implied to Dextradeur that Nancy was part black. Just why Frankie had given this misleading description of the woman he wanted Dextradeur to find was puzzling, to say the least.

Judy, however, had an idea. She wanted to get into Nancy's public housing project apartment to see if there were any indications there of Nancy's whereabouts. Now that Frankie was in jail, Judy thought she could get into Nancy's apartment without interference. Maybe there would be some notes or letters that would shed light on Nancy's disappearance. She met Dextradeur in front of Nancy's apartment, and while Dextradeur stood on the sidewalk, Judy tried the apartment key she'd obtained from Jolene, who by now was living with other relatives. But the key didn't work. Someone had tampered with the lock. Looking through the windows, Judy could see that *somebody* was living there; if it wasn't Nancy, and Frankie was in jail, who was it?

By this time, Dextradeur was in something of a quandary. He was, after all, a sergeant in the detective unit assigned to handle major crimes, like assault and rape. It wasn't his job to deal with missing persons. That job belonged to the department's juvenile division, whose efforts were confined to locating little kids, not adults.

Still, Dextradeur had a bad feeling about these disappearances. First, Rochelle Clifford had vanished; then Nancy Paiva, followed by Mary Rose Santos. It seemed to Dextradeur that something more was going on than the usual transience of drug addicts.

All of the women, for instance, had young children, while two of them had fixed abodes. At least two of the three were connected with Frankie Pina, and Mary Rose Santos at least knew who Frankie and Nancy were, Dextradeur discovered, and occasionally spent time in the three taverns owned by Faith Alameida, as well as in the Whispers bar, where Frankie and Nancy were seen on the after-

noon of Nancy's disappearance. But when Dextradeur
tried to point out these connections to his superiors, he
was told to get back to work on the tasks he was assigned
to do, not add to his already heavy workload by trying to
take on missing persons work as well.

As the rest of July unfolded, Dextradeur became increasingly worried and frustrated. He was still getting calls
from Frankie from jail, as well as from Judy. Then, in late
July, Dextradeur heard of still another reported missing
person who seemed to match the background of the first
three. Robin Rhodes was 28, and the mother of a seven-
year-old boy. She had last been seen by her family in
April 1988.

On further inquiry, Dextradeur learned that like the
first three women, Robin was a known drug user who
frequented the three Faith Alameida taverns, and possibly
the Whispers bar, as well. And it appeared that she had
once worked at the same fish-processing plant that had
employed Donald and Mary Rose Santos. To Dextradeur,
there seemed to be powerful links between the four cases.
In vain, Dextradeur pleaded for his department's higher-
ups to assign more manpower to the problem, but was
refused. The attitude remained unchanged: junkies disappear all the time. As a result, Dextradeur began following
leads on his own time.

Meanwhile, State Trooper William Delaney still had
the problem of the unidentified skeleton found by the motorist alongside Route 140 earlier in the month. Yes, there
was a spate of missing persons in New Bedford, Delaney
realized, but those were *recent* missings, not someone last
seen nine months ago, as the experts kept saying the remains on Route 140 represented.

That was the situation when, on the next to last day of
July, a second skeleton was found, this one about six miles
west of the New Bedford city limits on the westbound side
of U.S. I-195.

——— 11 ———
"That's My Sister"

Just as in the case of the first skeleton found on July 2, 1988, the latest discovery was made by a motorist who stopped to relieve himself in the tree line back from the roadway. What was almost immediately striking about the new skeleton was the similarity in the disposition of the body to the earlier victim.

Both victims were found on their backs, with feet toward the highway. That suggested to some that the killer had carried them over his shoulder in a fireman's carry, then unceremoniously rolled them forward off his shoulder and onto their backs before making a quick departure. In turn, that suggested that both women were killed at some other location. Because both roads were leading *out* of New Bedford, it was logical to speculate that the women had been killed somewhere inside the city limits. Unlike the first victim, however, there was no clothing found at the newest scene, and there was no obvious cause of death, like the earlier brassiere around the neck.

The state police assigned to Ron Pina's CPAC unit were hardly experts in serial homicide investigation, but it didn't take a Sherlock Holmes to figure out that the two cases of skeletal remains were quite likely connected. Again, Trooper Ken Martin took samples of mud and dirt for the purposes of assembling any trace evidence. A search was made of the surrounding woods, but nothing of significance was recovered. Later that day, as the sheet-covered body bag of the skeleton was being wheeled out toward the roadway, Judy DeSantos happened to be driving by with her husband and kids on her way back from swimming at a public pool in Fall River.

From the backseat of the car, Judy watched the activity off the north side of the road. The car radio had already reported the discovery, so Judy knew exactly what was going on. That was when she turned to her husband and children. "That's my sister they're taking out of the woods," Judy told her family. The kids looked at her as if she were flipping out.

That day, the state police decided they needed more help to identify the remains, which some thought might have been in the woods off the road for two to five months. A call was made to the Federal Bureau of Investigation, and arrangements were made to ship the two skeletons to Washington, D.C., where they would be examined at an FBI laboratory.

Meanwhile, another state police investigator, Corporal Jose Gonsalves, was assigned to work with Trooper Delaney on the two cases, with Delaney retaining responsibility for the first skeleton and Gonsalves taking over the second.

But just as in the case of the first skeleton, the estimate of the death date for the second skeleton was wildly overestimated. Judy DeSantos was right: the skeleton being removed from the woods that day *was* that of her sister, Nancy Paiva. But it would be another four months before anyone besides Judy would figure that out.

—————— **12** ——————

The Weld Square Dance

As the summer of 1988 unfolded in New Bedford, there was yet one more person whose activities that season would eventually gain the intense interest of the police in the months to come. This was a huskily built, dark-haired man with a flattened nose, whose peculiar predilection was the beating and raping of young women who earned their living as prostitutes in the city's red-light district, an area known to all as Weld Square.

Weld Square was not really a square, but rather a neighborhood in the middle of the city, where Weld Avenue, connected to an off-ramp from I-195 as it passed through the city, crossed Purchase Street, one of the city's main commercial thoroughfares. The Weld Square neighborhood was filled with seedy apartments, rundown or abandoned businesses, vacant lots, dark alleys, and sidewalk squadrons of drug pushers, and there a great many prostitutes plied their trade. The neighborhood's handy proximity to the interstate highway just a quick on-ramp away made it a favorite attraction for motorized vice.

The "Weld Square dance," as some news media later called it, was little different than commercial prostitution practiced in most other parts of the country. Essentially, prostitution as practiced in New Bedford was a trade conducted on wheels.

Prostitutes, most of them women with heavy drug habits, congregated during evening hours at intersections in

47

the Weld Square neighborhood. Drivers pulling off the interstate simply drove through the area; it was easy to catch the eye of a strolling woman, pull over to the side of the street, make a "date," and drive to some nearby secluded location. That, after all, was exactly what Flat Nose had done with a 34-year-old woman named Bethany in late April 1988, and with many others during the season of killing.

Bethany later recalled that a man in a dark blue pickup truck pulled over and offered her a "date." She recalled that the man in the truck had very distinctive features: a nose flattened against his face and a right arm which seemed to be slightly impaired. Bethany agreed to give the man in the truck fellatio for $20. Bethany suggested that the man drive to a place behind New Bedford High School, but the man said no. Instead he drove out toward the New Bedford Municipal Airport some three or four miles away.

As he drove, the man with the flat nose told Bethany a little about himself. He said his name was Kurt, and that he was a former prizefighter. That was how he'd gotten the smashed-in nose, Kurt said. Now, he said, he worked for a construction company, and Bethany saw a check on the truck dashboard from what appeared to be Kurt's employer. Kurt wanted Bethany to show him her arms—to inspect her for possible needle tracks, a prime source of AIDS for many prostitutes—and then said he'd been watching her and thought she might be an undercover policewoman. Bethany denied this, and then realized Kurt had been drinking pretty heavily.

After parking the truck, Bethany started giving Kurt the oral sex he'd asked for. Suddenly Kurt grabbed her by the hair and pulled her head up. He made a fist and told her she'd better do exactly what he wanted or he'd punch her in the face and mess it up.

Bethany was scared. She was sure Kurt would beat her face in if she resisted. Kurt made her take off her pants, and then raped her. Afterward, Kurt drove her back to downtown New Bedford and let her out of the truck. Bethany immediately told one of her friends what had happened. Neither woman reported the attack to the police.

For a short while, though, the word about the ex-boxer with the flat nose made the rounds among other prostitutes in the city; Flat Nose was someone to stay away from. But despite Bethany's description of her unpleasant experience, many of the women in Weld Square either didn't get the message, were high on drugs, or had simply forgotten about Flat Nose by the time the heat of the summer arrived in 1988.

Bethany and her friend saw Flat Nose driving around the Weld Square area several times in late May, and again in June, July, and August of 1988. Although Flat Nose was now driving a black 1987 pickup truck, Bethany was sure it was the same man: the face was so distinctive.

Yet she still did not go to the police. Who would have listened to her, anyway? A drug user and convicted prostitute? In this, Bethany's confidence in the police was little different than it was for most of the women in the Weld Square area in the summer of 1988.

Caught between the perils of their drug addiction and the prospect of being arrested by the police for prostitution, the Weld Square women simply took their lumps from violent customers like Flat Nose and told themselves to be more careful the next time.

A year later, it was hard for those not familiar with the ravages of serious drug addiction to understand this. An investigator with the state police tried to explain to a grand jury:

"With regard to you, sir," said the investigator in response to a question from a grand juror, "I know you're saying there's a gap from when she reported it. It's unfortunate that these girls—they're heroin addicts, they're addicted to drugs. And if they don't get their drugs every day, that's a life-and-death situation to them.

"They know if they go to the police department and say, well, 'I was raped by this guy,' unfortunately, some of them may be charged with soliciting themselves, and they know they're going to be locked up for a period of time. They're going to be 'dope sick,' as they say, and they're not going to get their heroin. That's why they don't come forward sometimes, and give their information as soon as maybe someone who wasn't a prostitute would. Do you understand what I mean?"

So Flat Nose continued to roam about the Weld Square area with impunity, picking up women pretty much on a weekly basis, driving them to darkened areas, punching them, choking them, raping them, and generally terrorizing them with threats of homicidal violence. Usually Flat Nose appeared to be drunk, and once he was finished, he seemed desperate to get away, often thrusting his truck door open and literally kicking his victims across the seat and out into the street before roaring off. At least a dozen women were assaulted in this fashion by Flat Nose between June and September 1988, and not one reported their experience to the New Bedford Police Department—at least, at the time.

One night in late July or early August, a woman named Margaret Medeiros found herself walking down Purchase Street near Weld Square when a man driving a blue-and-white Ford Bronco truck beeped his horn at her and waved her over. Medeiros, known as Peggy to her friends, was new on the streets of New Bedford. She knew very few of the people who hung out in Weld Square, and certainly had not heard anything about the man with the flat nose who was behind the wheel. She did notice that the Bronco had Rhode Island license plates, so she was immediately suspicious that the driver was a cop.

Flat Nose told Peggy that he wasn't a cop, that he was from Tiverton, Rhode Island, just across the state line. Where do you want to go? Flat Nose asked her. Some-place nearby, Peggy told him, and then she asked Flat Nose what he wanted.

A blow job, Flat Nose told her.

That'll be 25 bucks, Peggy said.

Flat Nose steered the Bronco over the tracks down to the waterfront. Pulling up into a darkened area, Flat Nose guided her into the Bronco's rear seat, then sat down and began to unzip his pants, but Peggy said he'd have to give her the money first. When he heard Peggy say those words, Flat Nose suddenly lunged toward her and grabbed her around the neck with both hands. He was incredibly powerful. Peggy couldn't breathe. Flat Nose's eyes were demonic as he twisted the muscles in her neck, and Peggy was sure she was going to die.

"I'm gonna do to you what I did to those other bitches," Flat Nose hissed as he choked her. Crazily, Peggy noticed a tiger tattoo on Flat Nose's right forearm. She put her hands up to Flat Nose's wrists and tried to pull his hands away, but he was too strong. She began to black out. Her arms were losing their strength and her grip on his wrists was weakening. Desperately she kicked at Flat Nose with her last remaining ounce of energy. One kick seemed to have some effect, so she tried again. On the second kick, Flat Nose removed his hands and bent over, holding his groin. Peggy guessed she'd nailed him in the testicles. Quickly Peggy jumped back into the front seat, threw open the passenger-side door, and ran away from the Bronco.

Incredibly, the following night Peggy saw Flat Nose again, driving the same Bronco. Even more incredibly, he beeped his horn again, and again waved her over. Peggy couldn't believe that Flat Nose didn't recognize her. She kept walking, and Flat Nose moved on.

About two weeks after the discovery of the second skeleton—the remains that Judy DeSantos was convinced were those of her sister, Nancy Paiva—State Trooper Delaney gave a short press briefing about both skeletons.

The victims were both short, slightly built, brown-haired women, Delaney said, just over five feet in height; of course, that description applied to thousands of women in the Bristol County area, so it wasn't much help.

But Delaney also noted that both victims had extensive dental work, and both appeared to have been dropped at their respective locations in the same fashion. In addition, Delaney noted that the first woman had recently suffered a broken jaw. There was always the hope that the information about the broken jaw might jog someone's memory.

In the meantime, Delaney said, he'd sent a teletype requesting information on possible missing women fitting the criteria to other states, and received about 20 different responses. But then Delaney added that he'd asked the state police computer systems for a listing of *all* missing women in Massachusetts alone who were between four-eleven and five-five in height, and was presented with a list of 1,724 names. Nearly 2,000 names was just way too many.

To narrow things down, Delaney said, he'd asked all local Bristol County police departments for any reports on missing women that might fit the characteristics of the two victims. Delaney told the reporters that he intended to start with the Bristol County list when it was assembled. Then, he said, he intended to track down the group's dental and medical records, and send them to Boston for the medical examiners there to check for possible matches to the two skeletons. Once police figured out who the dead women were, work could begin to determine who might have killed them, and why.

But in this there remains something of a small if painful mystery.

Just after seeing the police pull the second skeleton out of the woods along I-195, Judy DeSantos began trying to assemble her sister Nancy's medical and dental records for Detective Dextradeur of the New Bedford Police. After doing some detective work of her own, Judy learned the name of Nancy's dentist. She called Dextradeur, telling him that she would get Nancy's records. Dextradeur told her it wouldn't be necessary, that he'd go himself.

The following day, Dextradeur called and said he'd gotten the records and turned them over to the state police. Dextradeur also told Judy that it would take about two weeks to compare the charts to the recent victim. Judy marked the date down on her calendar: August 14, her daughter's birthday.

On that day—the day after Delaney told the news media that he wanted dental records—Judy called the New Bedford Police Department to find out the results of the check of Nancy's dental charts. She was told that there was no information on whether Nancy's charts matched the teeth found with the second victim, the one Judy was somehow sure was that of her sister.

Why wasn't there any information? If Delaney had Nancy's records, had they been compared with the latest skeletal remains? If they had, did that mean Nancy's charts didn't match? Why else would Delaney be asking for *more* records? Why couldn't the police answer this simple if vital question?

It was maddening to Judy to be enmeshed in the disinterest of the police bureaucracy, most of which treated her as if *she* were some sort of crook, at least judging by their indifference or outright hostility. But at this stage, Judy was still timid about confronting the police.

"Whatever they said to me," Judy recalled, "I would say, 'Okay, all right.' I'd hang up. I didn't want to upset anyone. I figured that they knew what they were doing . . . you know, you put all your faith and trust in them. These are the people you're brought up to believe in, your police officers, your firefighters, your dentists. And then you find out, hey, they're human."

Beneath her timidity, however, Judy had a disquieting thought. Did Delaney ever *have* the records at all, despite Dextradeur's assurance that he'd given them to the state police? Or if Delaney had them, what had he done with them? Had he even bothered to look at them, or send them on to the experts, or whatever it was that was supposed to be done?

Like most people, Judy didn't understand that in those days, the state police rarely gave the time of day to the city police; cops were cops were cops, at least to Judy, and what she said to one she assumed would go on up the ladder. But that was not the case.

Eventually, the city cops told Judy to call back again in two more weeks.

But by the time the two weeks was up, Dextradeur had been forced to go on a medical leave. He was suffering from hypertension, probably due to frustration and too much work. Hypertension did nothing to ease Dextradeur's already battered heart. When Judy called early in September to ask about the charts once more, no one at the city department seemed to know anything about Nancy's dental records, or much care.

Thus, even while Trooper Delaney was casting his net during August and September for dental charts to match the two skeletons, a complete set of records from a known missing person that could have identified one set of remains was available to police.

And as a further result, Judy DeSantos continued to search for her sister for the next four months, even while one level or another of the police had all the information needed to resolve the mystery of Nancy's whereabouts. It was not a great testament to police efficiency, and stands as one of the main reasons Judy later became so angry at the police.

Because, as Judy later recounted, the reports of Nancy's whereabouts continued. Judy found herself sitting near Weld Square on the off-chance that she might see her sister; once, she thought she recognized Nancy at a telephone booth. She ran over to the booth and turned the woman around, but it wasn't Nancy. It was embarrassing, Judy said later; the strange woman thought Judy was attacking her.

On another occasion, Jill Paiva called Judy, weeping hysterically. Jill told Judy that someone had telephoned to say that the police had just found Nancy dead in a tenement hallway, with a needle still in her arm. The report was completely false.

But Judy spent far more time in the south end of New Bedford than by Weld Square; she knew Nancy rarely went into the Weld Square area, because she wasn't a prostitute.

"I knew she was hanging around down at Whispers," Judy said later, "down in that area. I approached people who knew Nancy, and asked them to keep a lookout for her." As August and September unfolded, then October, the calls kept coming in.

"Oh, I just saw your sister getting into a car heading north on Purchase Street," the caller would start out, and then Judy would either drop everything herself or ask a friend to go check out the report. Judy tried to cling to the hope that her sister's heroin habit had suddenly grown insurmountable, and that she was living on the streets somewhere, ashamed to contact any of her family or friends, while she rode the snake of her addiction. But deep down, Judy was sure Nancy was dead. Nancy would have called her by now, Judy was sure. Almost.

——— 13 ———
Summer's End

Throughout the rest of August and into early September, Judy made several new attempts to get into Nancy's apartment on Morgan Street. She was becoming more and more certain that the answer to Nancy's disappearance was to be found inside. Several times she went to the apartment with Dextradeur, but, as before, the key wouldn't work. Still, Judy was sure *someone* was living inside. It appeared that someone was rifling Nancy's mail, and stealing her welfare checks.

Late in August, Frankie was released from jail. Somehow, Frankie at least could get in and out of Nancy's apartment. One afternoon late in the summer Frankie stopped at a house in the south end where Jill Paiva was living. Jill was still worried about her mother's disappearance, but Frankie told her that Nancy was fine, that she'd checked herself into a drug treatment facility.

When Jill doubted Frankie, he picked up the telephone and dialed a number.

"Hello," he said into the telephone, "I want to speak to Nancy Paiva." Then Frankie told Jill that her mother was in a recreation session and couldn't come to the telephone just then. As Jill reached for the phone, Frankie hung up. Frankie wouldn't tell Jill the number he had dialed.

Soon Judy was calling every drug treatment facility and halfway house in two states, looking for her sister.

Later, Judy told this story to John Dextradeur, who told her that Frankie had made the story up, and that he had done so to give Jill some hope. Judy was furious once more with Frankie.

Meanwhile, Dextradeur was becoming more and more frustrated with his own police department. No one, it seemed, took his suspicions about the missing women very seriously, not even the state police. That was when Dextradeur took his leave; he didn't want to die of frustration.

Dextradeur would be out of the picture for about a month. Just after he took his leave, Judy finally managed to get into Nancy's apartment. She got in with Jolene, who found a way to get in through a window.

"Me and Jolene," Judy recalled later. "By this time, John Dextradeur's had his heart (illness), nobody else cares, so I get into the house and, you know ... I find a telephone with some blood spots, splatterings, and a shoebox, my father's shoebox, full of hypodermic needles." The discovery of the beloved shoebox jammed with syringes made Judy want to weep.

The apartment was filled with other people's clothes. It was obvious that someone had been living in the apartment during Nancy's absence. The blood-splattered telephone unnerved Judy. She was sure this was evidence that something horrible had befallen her sister. She immediately left the apartment and called a friend, who told her to notify the police right away.

Soon two police cruisers drew up in front of the apartment, and officers went in to search. A few minutes later they emerged to tell Judy they couldn't find anything that she had just described.

"What do you mean?" Judy asked. She was furious. She went back into the apartment and showed the officers the shoebox.

"What do you call *that*?" she asked. Judy believed that the police wanted her to tell them exactly where it was, and that somehow the police were suspicious of *her*.

Later, the public housing authority managing the apartment complex protested the police inspection, saying that the police had entered the apartment without legal author-

ity. That made Judy mad; after all, it was her sister who
was the legal tenant of the apartment, and her sister was
missing, for Pete's sake.

Next Judy discovered some of Nancy's mail scattered
in a park across the street. She went to the welfare office
to get Nancy's checks stopped. It was clear that someone
was stealing the checks and forging them. Once the checks
stopped, the housing authority ordered Frankie evicted
from the apartment. Judy went back with Jolene and Jill,
forced the door open, and carted out all of Nancy's belongings. Judy felt that if she took all of Nancy's things,
Nancy would be forced to seek her out, if she was still
alive.

As they carried things out, Judy discovered a Polaroid
photograph of her sister, naked from the waist up, grin-
ning at the camera. Her upper torso was literally covered
with black-and-blue bruises. Judy quietly slipped the photograph into her purse. She decided to keep it forever to
remind herself of the hell Nancy's life had become. Now,
Judy felt, she had hard evidence for her hatred of Frankie.

Later, Judy, Jill, and Jolene went through all the things
they had removed from Nancy's apartment. Much was
strange to Jill and Jolene. There was a great deal of clothing they'd never seen before. Judy packed up everything
that didn't belong to Nancy and threw it away. But that
one innocent act by Judy, preventable had the police taken
Dextradeur's warnings seriously, or Judy's contribution of
Nancy's dental charts, might have made solving the Highway Murders far more difficult.

Without knowing who the clothing and other articles
actually belonged to, the possibility exists that some items
found in Nancy Paiva's apartment might have belonged to
other victims of the Highway Killer.

Certainly, there is evidence that at least two other victims of the killer had been in Nancy's apartment just before their deaths.

The failure to identify Nancy Paiva from the dental
records provided by Judy DeSantos in August 1988 thus
effectively prevented investigators from conducting the
timely, thorough examination of Nancy's apartment that

was required. That search, in turn, might have been crucial in solving the case.

In the years to come, the missed opportunity was recognized as a devastating breakdown of the investigation, and would be one of the main things the police fervently wished they had the opportunity to do over again.

14

Misery

For Tony DeGrazia, the dream was ending: Kathy was leaving, the marriage was off.

He and Kathy had spent the summer together in the little house on Long Pond. One of their friends owned a boat, and they spent the afternoons waterskiing and partying. It seemed like an idyllic summer, but Tony wasn't happy. His fears had been right, after all. For the first time, Kathy was seeing him up close, every day, and he could tell she didn't like what she was seeing.

It was the nightmares, Tony guessed. Kathy knew the whole story, and kept saying she understood, but he could see that she was—well, frightened. It was the nightmares, or the sleepwalking. Tony cried, and Kathy was sympathetic; but sympathy wasn't love. Near the end of September, Kathy moved out. Within a month she was involved with another man, and Tony was almost as miserable as he'd ever been in his life.

FALL 1988

"What could be more full of meaning?—for the pulpit is ever this earth's foremost part; all the rest comes in its rear; the pulpit leads the world. From thence it is, the storm of God's quick wrath is first descried, and the bow must bear the earliest brunt . . ."

—HERMAN MELVILLE, *Moby Dick*

——— 15 ———
Lost

By the fall of 1988, the discovery of the two skeletons along the highways leading out of New Bedford had long faded from the news. Most of the state had its attention focused on presidential politics. Massachusetts' governor, Michael Dukakis, was the democratic nominee for president.

District Attorney Ron Pina was squarely behind his old ally, even going so far as to hold a press conference with other Democratic district attorneys in which wanted posters of Republican nominee George Bush were passed around, posters holding that Bush was "wanted" for failing to stop crime. Two years later, Pina would try in his own reelection campaign to portray himself as a Batmanesque "Crime Fighter," a tack that subjected him to wide ridicule among the voters, given what had happened by then. But politics, as always, was a bully pulpit for someone like Ron Pina who enjoyed being out front, leading the way.

By early October, John Dextradeur was back from his medical leave. By now Dextradeur was utterly convinced that something was going on, relating to missing women. On his return to duty, Dextradeur discovered two *new* reports of missing women that seemed almost identical to the earlier cases.

One, Sandra Botelho, had last been seen on the night of August 11 when she left her north end apartment to get "bread." Checking further, Dextradeur learned that Botelho had an arrest record for prostitution—in fact, she'd been in court on such a charge just a week before her disappearance; additionally, Sandy was known to have a cocaine habit.

Then, while Dextradeur had been out of action with his heart attack, 25-year-old Dawn Mendes had likewise disappeared. Like Botelho, Dawn had a prostitution background and a cocaine addiction.

Even more striking, it appeared to Dextradeur that Botelho and Mendes had known one another, and that both women had probably known Nancy Paiva.

That made six women missing: Rochelle Clifford, Nancy Paiva, Mary Rose Santos, Robin Rhodes, Sandra Botelho, and Dawn Mendes. And the striking thing was: *all* of the women appeared to have known one another, and had spent time in many of the same taverns, bars, and housing projects. All were drug users, and all but Nancy Paiva favored cocaine.

Nevertheless, Dextradeur was still unable to interest his superiors in the possible links. Even the dental records on Nancy Paiva that Dextradeur had given to the state police carried no weight. The state police were fairly sure that the skeleton found on I-195, the one Judy DeSantos seemed convinced was her sister, had been off the side of the road far too long to be Nancy Paiva. Dextradeur wasn't sure whether anyone had even checked the records, so sure were the troopers of their judgment.

The more Dextradeur thought about the situation, the more distressed he became. For a man with a heart condition, being distressed was not good. Finally Dextradeur decided to do something about it. Contacted by reporter Maureen Boyle of the New Bedford newspaper, the *Standard-Times*, Dextradeur confided his concerns.

"Fears Build for Missing Women," Boyle's story read on October 3. Boyle went on to name Sandy Botelho, Mary Santos, Dawn Mendes, and Nancy Paiva as women missing from New Bedford.

"All lived, frequented, or were last seen in the Purchase and Pleasant Street areas," Boyle noted, thus implicitly linking the four she named to the Weld Square subculture. "Three are known drug users or addicts. Mrs. Santos was visiting a drug-using friend the night she disappeared."

Boyle backhandedly revealed her source for the story when she quoted Dextradeur, who said that no evidence had surfaced "yet" to link the four cases.

"News of the missing women has sent chills through those frequenting Purchase Street," Boyle continued, "raising fears that one of the men circling the area known for prostitutes may be a killer.

"One woman said two others were missing, but police have not been officially notified yet.

" 'It's scary,' said one woman, a heroin addict. 'No one knows what's going on.' "

One of those who also did not know what was going on was District Attorney Ronald Pina. Years later, Pina would say he had only the vaguest awareness that anything was wrong, at least at first. As a general rule, he pointed out, the state police rarely consulted with their counterparts in the city department just four blocks away. Just because the city had a problem didn't mean it was anything the state police needed to know about; if the state police didn't know about it, then he wasn't likely to know, either, Pina said.

Pina recalled attending a meeting in his office sometime in October, in which the two skeletons and the four missing women were briefly discussed. The state police told *him*, Pina recalled, that the two dead women were probably victims of drug overdoses. It doesn't seem very likely that the troopers really believed a woman with a brassiere tied around her neck was a likely candidate for a drug overdose, but that's the way Pina chose to remember events much later. But then, Pina had other things on his mind that fall.

For one, he'd just married Sheila Martines. The ceremony, attended by nearly 200 well-wishers who represented the range of Bristol County's social and economic elite, was held in the Seaman's Bethel in New Bedford's historic old town—the same church described in *Moby*

Dick, in which a character named Father Mapple mounts a prow-like pulpit to relate the story of the stubbornness of Jonah, and thereby foreshadows mad Ahab's tragic end. One of Pina's closest friends and political pals, Fall River Mayor Carlton Viveiros, was Pina's best man.

16

The Trees

November 8, 1988, was Election Day, and about 2 P.M., as Ron Pina's longtime ally Michael Dukakis was going down to defeat at the hands of George Bush, a state public works crew pulled to a stop along the shoulder of a highway cloverleaf interchange at I-195 and Reed Road, about six miles west of New Bedford.

Like many of the interchanges on I-195, the space between the on-ramp from southbound Reed Road onto eastbound I-195 enclosed a heavily wooded circle—mostly short, thin pines, grass, and thick brush. The bank of the curved roadway was designed to ease vehicles around the tight turn, and also provide for drainage into the circle's interior. That in turn meant that much of the trash and garbage thrown out by thoughtless motorists found its inevitable way into the wooded circle area. The garbage was one reason public works crews made regular stops—to clean up the mess.

The crew began working its way into the circle's trees when one of its members was brought up short by a grisly sight. There, just inside the tree line, were the remnants of a human being.

Within a very few minutes of the discovery of the skeleton, Massachusetts State Police Corporal Jose Gonsalves knew he was probably looking at the handiwork of a serial murderer. After all, Gonsalves reasoned, the new remains made three such finds in the preceding four months—all off to the side of major highways leading into and out of New Bedford. One victim—well, Gonsalves thought, that could happen anywhere. Two was suspicious, but not conclusive. At three, the odds were quite strong that police were looking for a repeat killer.

That the latest victim had been murdered could not be seriously disputed. The evidence was in the trees.

There among the branches was one of the strangest sights Gonsalves had ever seen. Strewn through the pines and brush were articles of clothing—everything from a tank top to panties, from jackets to jeans. One thing was for sure—it was highly unlikely that the dead person had first taken off her clothes, tossed them high into the tree branches, and then lay down to die alone. Gonsalves had a sudden vision: after having dragged the victim into the trees, Gonsalves imagined the killer returning to his vehicle, retrieving the victim's clothing, then throwing the clothes into the trees and brush in some sort of frenzied outburst. How else could the various clothing articles have gotten so high up, and so far apart?

What did the disposal of the clothes say about the killer? Was this apparent outburst due to a suddenly acute sense of self-loathing? Was it evidence of remorse? Or was it disgust with the victim, some sort of psychological clue to how the killer saw his prey? Did it mean he hated the victims, hated everything about them, including, even, their clothes?

As certain as he was that the latest skeleton was related to the July discoveries, Gonsalves also knew there were some differences: where the first victim had only minimal clothing, and the second none at all, in this latest scene there was practically a whole wardrobe. Gonsalves knew that the clothes might be quite helpful in identifying the newest victim. And in that he was wrong, but in another way, still accidentally right, much to nearly everyone's later surprise.

Several years later Judy DeSantos could still remember that particular Election Day. After all, Judy worked in the city's election office, so voting days were always hectic, never mind when the state's governor was a nominee for president. But all of the turmoil of the office immediately faded from her mind when she received a call from her niece Jill, saying that the state police had called and wanted Judy, Jill, and Jolene to come into their office and look at some things to see whether they could identify them.

The following day Judy and her two nieces found themselves in the state police portion of District Attorney Ron Pina's suite of offices in downtown New Bedford. Corporal Gonsalves and his detective partner, Trooper Maryann Dill, showed them several articles of clothing. Nancy's two daughters immediately identified a striped tank top and a pair of panties as having belonged to their mother. Two jackets (why would Nancy have been wearing *two* jackets, and in the heat of July?) both daughters also identified as having been Nancy's. Judy looked at several small pieces of gold jewelry and recognized them as having been in Judy's and Nancy's family. All of the clothing, Gonsalves and Dill told Judy and her nieces, had been found at the scene discovered the day before at I-195 and Reed Road.

Now the state police wanted to know who Nancy's dentist had been, so that Nancy's dental charts could be compared with the teeth found with the latest skeleton. Thus, Judy learned for the first time that the charts she had told Dextradeur about months earlier had never found their way to the state police; or if they had, they had never been examined. Judy was stunned.

To Judy, identification of the clothing meant only one thing—the skeleton discovered on Election Day was probably that of her sister, Nancy Paiva. Later, as detectives Gonsalves and Dill drove Judy and her nieces home, Jill and Jolene fell into an emotional dispute about some of the clothing, arguing whether it was really Nancy's. Judy felt like bursting into tears, and Jill and Jolene's squabble, as much a part of their own reaction to the trauma of seeing their mother's clothes in a police station, nevertheless suddenly seemed unreal to Judy. Dill looked at Judy sitting in the backseat, smiled at her quietly, and told her that things would be all right. Judy knew they wouldn't, but was grateful to Dill for trying to help.

*   *   *

Jose Gonsalves—known to nearly everyone in New Bedford as "Joe-sey Gone-Salves," rather than the more traditional Jose—was a tall, rangy man in his early forties. Close-cropped, graying hair was slowly giving way to an emerging bald spot high on the back of his head, but Gonsalves was a man who looked like he had once been a terrific athlete, and whose still-lean frame packed a powerful build. Even in his neatly arranged office he still wore a large caliber semiautomatic pistol clipped to his belt. The walls of Gonsalves's office were decorated with the usual interdepartmental memoranda, calendars, and the like, along with a child's computer drawing of a smiling, uniformed trooper in the drill-instructor, Smokey-the-Bear hat worn by all those assigned to "the road," as the troopers called highway duty; the computer printout was clearly labeled with an arrow: "Daddy," it reported.

Gonsalves was not one of those police officers given to excitability. He preferred to work methodically, building fact upon fact. He innately distrusted quick bursts of sudden insight, and was suspicious of those who talked too much. He felt he understood Pina, or at least the circumstances that led Pina to mistrust the troopers; and he was clear enough about the events of the preceding years to see both the good things Pina had done, as well as some of the bad. He credited Pina with trying to run a professional office, and Pina's attempts to keep politics and the police separate.

But he also saw Pina as someone who wasn't particularly well trained in the techniques of investigation, especially interrogation. Pina's quick mind and impatience too often worked against the district attorney, at least in Gonsalves's view, and blinded Pina from possibilities that lay just beneath the surface. Nor was Pina as receptive as he should have been to others' ideas, Gonsalves thought.

Beneath his poker face, and his phlegmatic approach, Gonsalves tried to keep a solid vein of sardonic humor well hidden, but it occasionally burst forth when absurdities couldn't be denied. On those occasions, when something was manifestly ridiculous, Gonsalves's eyes would crinkle and a wry grin would struggle through the controls.

"Oh, wow," Gonsalves would say, "oh, wow," before looking away so that no one could see him laughing.

Gonsalves's partner, Dill, was a woman in her early thirties, with short dark hair. Over the years she spent working with Gonsalves, she learned to understand how Gonsalves thought. When both officers were together, they often communicated with silent looks; later, both would sort out their impressions. Both officers were very good at developing information from sources, and by the time the Highway Murder investigation was well underway, Gonsalves and Dill would learn a great deal about the underbelly of one of the eastern seaboard's toughest cities. Both would also conclude that the Highway Murderer, whoever he was, had picked up every one of his victims at random while they were practicing the trade of prostitution. That was a point of view, as time wore on, that would *not* be shared by Ron Pina.

Although Judy expected the identification of the Election Day skeleton to come quite quickly, a surprising problem soon developed: it appeared that the skeleton was *not* that of Nancy Paiva. For one thing, the Election Day skeleton had a partial dental plate, but Nancy's dental charts showed nothing of the kind. But even more detailed examination of the teeth and their spacings—as unique an identifier as a fingerprint—likewise showed the Election Day skeleton was not Nancy.

Well, if it wasn't Nancy, who was it? And how did Nancy's clothes get into the trees? And where was Nancy? All of these were the big questions for Gonsalves and Dill as November neared an end.

Publicly, at least, Gonsalves refused to be drawn into speculation as to whether the three highway deaths were related; indeed, since he and Delaney and Dill were so far unable to identify any one of the three, it would be foolhardy to say anything substantive.

Already, Gonsalves knew, the news media was becoming intensely curious about what were soon being called the Highway Murders. Boyle's report on the missing New Bedford women was adding to the curiosity. But still, Gonsalves worked hard to remain his usual phlegmatic self, keeping low key, trying to say little of significance.

Behind closed doors in the district attorney's office, it was a different matter. Whatever he might tell the press, Gonsalves was convinced the cases were related; and he believed that there were yet more bodies to be discovered. In mid-November, after a two-hour discussion with Dextradeur, Gonsalves's superior, Sergeant Gale Stevens, agreed with him. Arrangements were made to bring in three specially trained dogs from the Connecticut State Police to search among the woods along I-195. Gonsalves guessed that the killer, whoever he was, had a feeling for that roadway, and that a search would bring still more victims into the light.

——— 17 ———
The Dogs

Among the many talents possessed by dogs is an acute sense
of smell. While other creatures have similar talents, millions
of years of evolution have so developed the dog's olfactory
gift that it is possible for a dog to distinguish the most minute
traces of a particular substance—particularly when the dog is
trained to alert its human companion that a specific scent is
present—but *only* that scent. Thus, using dogs required selec-
tion of a dog trained for the required task. Josie, a three-
year-old German shepherd, was just such a specialist. She
was trained to sniff out human corpses, which normally give
off a strong odor of ammonia as they decompose.

The state police began their search on November 28,
working westbound along the north side of I-195 between
Faunce Corner Road and Reed Road—the area where the
July 30 remains had been discovered. It by now seemed
clear to Gonsalves that the killer had an affinity for dropping victims off the side of major highways leading out of
New Bedford. Gonsalves had the idea that if there were
more victims to be found, it was reasonable to assume that
they might be found between the July 30 site and the
Election Day remains at the interchange with Reed Road.

For nearly five hours on Monday, November 28, Josie
and her handler, Connecticut State Trooper Andy Rebmann, worked in and out of the brush and trees along the
north side of the highway. Two other similarly trained
dogs wove in and out of the trees as well.

73

As talented as the dogs were, their handling required special sensitivities by their human partners. Because of their training and conditioning, dogs expect to be rewarded by their handlers when the required scent is detected. Working for too long without finding the requested scent frustrates the dogs, thereby making them harder to control. Five hours without finding anything was just about the dogs' limit.

The following day, November 29, 1988, the search was begun again. A little after 2 P.M., as Rebmann and his dog were moving through the brush along the north side of the westbound I-195 on-ramp from Reed Road, Josie "alerted"—that is, indicated by her behavior that she had detected the required scent.

"Just show me where," Rebmann said, and Josie led him into the brush, tail wagging furiously. There, concealed under a tree, lay the fourth set of skeletal remains found in the previous five months. The site was literally just across the highway from where the Election Day victim had been found only three weeks before.

The discovery of the new remains, so close to the skeleton found on Election Day, created a minor sensation in New Bedford. For the first time, District Attorney Pina publicly noted the killings.

"The fact that they're all in the same area would lead you to believe that a person has done more than one killing," he told the *Standard-Times'* Boyle the day after the new skeleton was found. "I fell pretty confident that they are all connected somehow." And, Pina added, "There may be more than just the four women."

That same afternoon, November 30, 1988, state police met with New Bedford detectives to pool their information. They had little to pool, because none of the four skeletons so far discovered had been identified. It was hard to share information when nobody had much to share. The main topic was the six women reported missing from New Bedford—Rochelle Clifford, Nancy Paiva, Mary Rose Santos, Robin Rhodes, Sandy Botelho, and Dawn Mendes.

Gonsalves by now believed that Dextradeur's fears for the missing women were exactly right. That was small comfort to Dextradeur, however. Late in October, Dextradeur took his retirement from the police department.

Memory Banks

Dextradeur's involuntary absence from the police conclave of November 30, 1988, would later become a problem as the Highway Murder investigation proceeded, primarily because the information he held in his brain was not provided to all the investigators at one time, but instead dribbled in, piece by piece over the following year, as he remembered things and as bits of paper made their way into the hands of Ron Pina.

This gradual discovery of the ramifications of Dextradeur's information, coming under circumstances of greater and greater pressure to solve the crimes as 1989 and 1990 unfolded, may in turn have given the Dextradeur information more weight than it would otherwise have deserved. Ultimately, Pina came to see Dextradeur's information as far more important than did the state police.

Pina later asserted that as far as he could tell, in the beginning of the investigation, no one from the state police ever talked to Dextradeur. That wasn't true, of course, but it does reveal something of the ineffective communications between the D.A. and his investigators. Pina believed no one talked to Dextradeur because the state troopers generally held the city police in low regard, and thereby automatically discounted the merits of Dextradeur's information.

"Dextradeur had worked hard on the case," Pina recalled, "and nobody had talked to Dextradeur." It was only later, Pina insisted, when he and others took the investigation into their own hands, that the full dimensions of Dextradeur's information were developed. The state police insist that Pina was wrong, that they *did* know what Dextradeur knew, although they acknowledge Dextradeur was not present for the information-sharing meeting of November 30, 1988. What is clear is that nobody at the meeting knew everything that Dextradeur knew, whatever its real importance.

In those days, the information-retrieval system of the New Bedford Police Department was still firmly rooted in the precomputer past, to the times of old when what police knew and believed about a possible crime was largely confined to the flesh-and-blood memory banks of individual detectives. Once the detective was gone, however, the memories tended to go with him.

Dextradeur, for example, knew several things about the missing women. He knew about Rochelle Clifford, for example, because Rochelle was both a victim and a witness in two separate cases he had been investigating—a rape, and an assault. He knew that Rochelle was missing under uncertain circumstances, just like Nancy Paiva, Mary Rose Santos, Sandy Botelho, Robin Rhodes, and Dawn Mendes.

But Dextradeur was probably the only person who had any real feel for what possibly linked the six cases together; he was certainly the only person who knew of a positive, clear link between Nancy Paiva, for example, and Rochelle Clifford.

Indeed, Dextradeur was aware that Rochelle Clifford had been living at Nancy Paiva's apartment with Nancy and Frankie Pina *just before* her disappearance in late April 1988. Nancy didn't like Rochelle, according to Jill and Jolene, Nancy's daughters, but put up with Rochelle at Frankie's insistence. In the end, however, Nancy threw Rochelle out of the apartment just before she was last seen. What wasn't known was exactly when this happened.

Nevertheless, the case of Rochelle Clifford and her movements in the spring of 1988 would eventually lead Pina directly toward the man he remains convinced was deeply involved in the Highway Murders, Kenneth Ponte; but to understand how Pina reached this conclusion, it is

necessary to understand what *Dextradeur* then knew about
Rochelle Clifford—information that Dextradeur, because
of his illness, was unable to provide to the assembled police
that day on November 30, but which eventually came into
Pina's hands.

In the spring of 1988—at almost exactly the time the
Highway Murders first began—Rochelle Clifford was a 28-
year-old, pretty, diminutive young woman with dark ex-
pressive eyes and dark hair. Rochelle also had a serious
drug problem, using both cocaine and heroin, according
to her friends and acquaintances; she had a long record
of arrests and failed attempts to make it through drug
treatment programs.

Sometime in late 1987, Rochelle had delivered a baby,
but the child was taken from her by authorities because of
her drug habit. Later Rochelle had drifted into the New
Bedford street scene. Rochelle's mother in Falmouth, down
on Cape Cod, had limited contact with her. At one point
Rochelle moved into Nancy's apartment to live with Nancy
and Frankie, briefly, before Nancy ordered her out; on another occasion she stayed briefly with a doctor in nearby
Dartmouth; and on a third occasion she'd left Ken Ponte's
home telephone number with a dentist. It thus appears that
Rochelle, like many others in the fullness of addiction, slept
where she could, as various places became available.

In any event, in the spring of 1988 a strange series of
events unfolded that were ultimately to have a critical
bearing on the investigation of the Highway Murder case,
although Dextradeur had no way of knowing that, at the
time the events were occurring.

The Clifford matter had begun on Easter Sunday, April
3, 1988, with a bizarre encounter between a New Bedford
man named Roger Swire and a local lawyer—Kenneth Ponte.

As Swire related the story to police that day, he had been
walking down the street with his girlfriend in the north end
when another man—Ponte—had suddenly jumped out of a
car and supposedly accosted him at gunpoint.

Ponte, Swire said, flashed a deputy sheriff's badge in
his face, pointed the gun at him, and accused him of raping
Rochelle. Rochelle was sitting in Ponte's car nearby, and

Ponte had marched Swire over to the car and asked Rochelle if Swire had been the man who raped her. Swire said Rochelle agreed that Swire was the culprit, even though he wasn't. That, at least, was Swire's side of the story.

Later the same day, the police had returned to the same location, and found Ponte and Rochelle still present there. Ponte denied threatening Swire with a gun; Rochelle again said that Swire had raped her. Ponte asserted that he was a deputy sheriff, and therefore authorized to make arrests, so he hadn't done anything wrong. The police officer merely took the report, shrugged, and passed it on to Detective Sergeant Dextradeur to sort out.

In some ways, the incident was typical of Dextradeur's caseload: accusation and counteraccusation, probably seasoned by lies of omission if not commission.

The following day, April 4, 1988, Dextradeur had tried to get more information from Ponte, the lawyer.

Ponte told Dextradeur that he'd only been trying to *help* Rochelle Clifford, and that the two of them had been cruising the north end in Ponte's car looking for the man who Rochelle said had raped her. They'd found Swire, and Ponte had told Swire to stay away from Rochelle. That was the whole story, said Ponte. But Dextradeur didn't think it was the whole story, not by a long shot.

Dextradeur wanted Ponte to come to police headquarters for an interview, but somehow, Ponte never got around to it. Meanwhile, the two cases—the alleged rape of Rochelle Clifford and the alleged assault (the threat at gunpoint) by Ponte against Roger Swire, remained unresolved in Dextradeur's open-case files. Dextradeur realized in May of 1988 that he needed to talk to Rochelle Clifford if he were to make progress on either case.

But as the rest of April 1988, unfolded, Rochelle Clifford was nowhere to be found. Dextradeur kept after Ponte on Rochelle's whereabouts, but Ponte wasn't able to help him. Rochelle's mother, Diane Clifford, of Falmouth, Massachusetts, also told Dextradeur that she didn't know where Rochelle was. Diane told Dextradeur she hadn't talked to Rochelle for several months.

Then, on April 27, 1988—three weeks after the Easter

Sunday incident between Ponte and Swire—Dextradeur
went to a possible trouble spot in the south end, where a
man was seen with a shotgun. On the way back to the
office, Dextradeur saw a woman who looked like Rochelle
Clifford walking with a group of people. Dextradeur recognized one of the men in the group as Frankie Pina. He
stopped his car and halted everyone for questioning.

After questioning Frankie briefly, Dextradeur pulled
Rochelle aside and asked her about the two open cases,
that is, about the reported rape as well as the reported
assault by Ponte. Had Swire really raped her? Rochelle
nodded. Yes. Had Ponte really threatened Swire with a
pistol? Again, Rochelle said yes. Would Rochelle be willing to be a witness against both men? Rochelle told Dextradeur she would testify if it was necessary.

But Dextradeur was still suspicious about the whole
thing. With all of his instincts, he seriously doubted that
Ponte had threatened Swire with a gun merely because of
Rochelle's claims that she had been raped. He guessed
there was something else going on between the two men,
and that Rochelle was somehow involved—or, at least,
knew what the truth was.

As he pressed Rochelle for more information, Rochelle
grew more and more nervous. Dextradeur told Rochelle
he wanted to see her at police headquarters the following
day, and while Rochelle agreed to come, that afternoon—
April 27, 1988—was the last time anyone definitely saw
Rochelle Clifford alive; and the date would later become of
critical importance in the Highway Murder investigation.

A few weeks after both Rochelle and Kenny Ponte had
promised to come see him, but did not, Dextradeur heard
new information about Ponte, Swire, and Rochelle. It appeared that someone had burglarized Ponte's downtown
New Bedford house, taking several items, including, possibly, a handgun.

Was this the same pistol Ponte had allegedly used to
threaten Swire? If so, why was it taken? To blackmail
Ponte, perhaps? Or had the burglary actually taken place
before the supposed Easter Sunday threats? Was that the
real reason Ponte had accosted Swire? Dextradeur didn't

know, but the word on the street was, Ponte was claiming
that the burglars had been Swire, Rochelle, and possibly
Swire's girlfriend. Maybe that was why Rochelle was so
nervous about Ponte when Dextradeur had quizzed her on
April 27—Rochelle was afraid that if the truth about the
encounter emerged, she would be implicated in a burglary.

The only way to clear up the matter was to find Rochelle Clifford, and talk to her again. But Dextradeur did
not know in late April and early May of 1988 that Rochelle
was probably no longer capable of talking. By late May,
her body was almost certainly freshly dead, lying in a
gravel pit some ten miles west of New Bedford, where it
would not be discovered until nearly six months later—
when Detective Sergeant John Dextradeur was retired
from the New Bedford Police Department.

Although Dextradeur's information about the movements of Rochelle Clifford and Kenny Ponte in the spring
of 1988 was later to be crucial in Pina's effort to investigate the Highway Murders, in retrospect, the true relevance of the information has to remain uncertain.

If one assumes that the Highway Murderer was someone who knew the victims personally, as Pina and others
eventually concluded, then Dextradeur's information *was*
important, and did point toward Ponte, among others; but
if, as the troopers believed, the killer was someone unknown to the victims, Dextradeur's information had relatively little value.

What difference did it really make if Kenny Ponte,
Roger Swire, or Frankie Pina was seen with Rochelle Clifford, or Nancy Paiva, or anyone else, for that matter, if
the killer was a prostitution customer who had picked up
the missing women at random? None, of course. Indeed,
trying to resolve all the riddles of these relationships would
be a giant wild-goose chase, productive of froth and foam,
but little else. That was largely the attitude of the state
troopers at this, the true beginning of the Highway Murder investigation; and in that, it was an attitude almost
completely rejected by Pina himself, as we shall see.

---- **19** ----
"I Think We Got One ..."

The day after the big police meeting, on December 1, 1988, Josie the dog and her friends were busy again, this time along the east side of Route 140—the northbound highway where the skeleton with the broken jaw had been found the previous July 2. Just before 3 in the afternoon Josie alerted once more, just over the Freetown-New Bedford line, about two miles south of the July 2 discovery. District Attorney Pina himself came to the scene. Returning from a meeting in Boston, he saw the police activity by the side of the road and stopped.

"I see all the cars there and I saw our troopers," Pina recalled later. Pina drove across the grassy center divider of Route 140 and pulled up to the state police standing on the side of the road.

"What's up?" Pina asked.

"I think we got one," the trooper told Pina. Pina got out of his car.

"The dogs are going back and forth and then they're showing me how the dog is keying in on an area," Pina remembered. "Well, I went over there and I saw her ..."

The latest victim was fully clothed. She lay in the brush and weeds, an article of consumption to a killer, a human being reduced to a thing. A sack of spare clothes lay nearby.

Viewing the victim in the posture where her killer had left her affected Pina deeply. It was one thing to sit in an

81

office, Pina thought, hearing about murders, another thing entirely to see the actual result of such violence. Robbed of life, a murder victim, found by the side of an isolated road miles away from friends and family, far from the normal pathways of living, has a pathetic, vulnerable quality, no matter what their living past. The victim—clearly another woman, according to the experts—spoke to Pina in an emotional way.

"I saw the condition she was in," Pina said later. "I saw the position she was in and I'll never forget that as long as I live."

For ten years Ron Pina had been district attorney in Bristol County. He'd attended autopsies, and learned that it wasn't really necessary—at least not for his part of the job. But seeing the skeletonized remains of the unknown woman off the east side of Route 140 on December 1, 1988, somehow ignited Ron Pina. It was more than his job; it was more than politics. What was he good for, if it wasn't to catch the person who would do such a thing?

Hey, what am I doing here? Pina thought to himself. *I mean, if this, if this is what I'm supposed to do and this is my job, I'm gonna do it.* It was at that point, Pina later recalled, that he became committed; others, however, later came to see Pina as obsessed.

Just how much of Pina's fervent desire to catch the dead woman's killer had to do with his anger and shock at the killer's actions, and how much had to do with Pina's by-now nearly reflexive penchant for publicity would remain in dispute for years after that first day of December in 1988. While it might be uncharitable, some of those intimately familiar with Pina's previous posturing concluded that, at that exact moment, Pina realized that the Highway Murders might be his ticket to national fame and fortune, and possibly, higher political office. Whatever his motivation, it didn't take Ronnie long to talk again to the news media.

"It's just crazy," Pina told Maureen Boyle later that afternoon. "It's the same thing, a body off the road. It would seem to be a pattern. It looks like it's one person or persons."

What sort of pattern? Boyle asked. The highways, Pina
noted: *all* of the five victims had been found off the side
of the major highways going into and out of New Bedford.

Boyle pressed Pina further. What's being done? she
asked. Pina told her that investigators had reviewed 14
unsolved homicides in Bristol County, as well as several
in Rhode Island. And, Pina said, he intended to ask the
Federal Bureau of Investigation to do face reconstructions.
Face reconstructions? Pina explained that sometimes experts could examine a skull and attempt to reconstruct
what the flesh on such a skull might have looked like in
order to help identify the victim—just as in the movie
Gorky Park. "We want a face to put on these women,"
he said.

The state police told Boyle that the latest victim might
have been dead about a year, but that an autopsy would
be necessary to know for sure. There was, the troopers
told Boyle, no obvious cause of death—unlike the earlier
victim on July 2, when a brassiere around the neck had
obviously been used to strangle the victim.

Indeed, the presence of clothing on the victim's body
was a significant difference from the four earlier victims.
Did the fact that the latest woman was still dressed mean
a different killer from the first four? Did it mean anything
at all?

Or was it possible that a single killer—by now so into
his hate frenzy—couldn't care less that clothing found with
his victim might help with her identification?

The assessment of that issue, Gonsalves knew, depended on *who* the victim was, as well as when she had
been killed. Serial killers, he knew, often proceeded
through dimensions of control of their victims. Taking
control of clothing was an indication of such control.
Sometimes removal, or even theft, of the clothes indicated
a victim who had been killed by someone experienced in
killing; in other cases, leaving the clothes could be con-
strued as an oversight by a killer, showing that the killer
had *less* experience in killing.

But alternatively, leaving a dressed victim might show
contempt for the *police*—an indication that the killer had
so little belief in the efficacy of the police that it was safe

to leave the clothes behind. That in turn could mean that the killer was *quite* proficient at murder. To Gonsalves, Pina, Joe Delaney, and Maryann Dill, that was an unnerving thought. No one communicated any of these possibilities to Boyle.

At that point, however, events were about to accelerate.

—— 20 ——
Not the General Public

On the same day she reported on the latest discovered skeleton, Boyle talked to a Weld Square woman who told her a horrifying story.

Several months before all the skeletons began turning up, the woman told Boyle, she'd been picked up by a man who drove her to the same general area on I-195 where the skeletons were later found. The night was dark and rainy, the woman recalled. The man drove his white pickup truck into a wooded area, then suddenly produced a knife and demanded that she take off her clothes.

After removing some of her clothes, the woman took a chance and jumped out of the truck, running for the trees. The man started the truck and tried to run her over. The woman hid in the brush until the man drove off, then tried to pick her way through the trees to I-195. Just as she reached the roadway, the man leaped out of the drainage ditch with his knife, tackled her, and threw her to the ground. Burying the knife in the mud next to her head, the man succeeded in raping her. The woman was sure she was about to die. But for some reason, the man retrieved his knife and ran back to his truck and drove off. "I never came so close to death in my life," the woman told Boyle.

Here, then, was a real lead on the possible killer: a man in a white truck, described as being in his thirties with dirty blond hair and scars on his face, driving a white pickup truck, wielding a knife, raping a woman from Weld Square in the same area where the skeletons were later found. Boyle's report created a new sensation; it also helped link the skeletons to the Weld Square subculture irreversibly, at least in the public mind.

That was a link almost immediately strengthened by District Attorney Pina.

"DA Probes Weld Square Links to Killings," read the headline in the *Standard-Times*. In an interview with Boyle, Pina said the deaths appeared to be connected to drugs or prostitution as practiced in the Weld Square area. Pina added that police had recovered a fingerprint from one of the victims, and the print had been tentatively linked to a woman who had a history of drug use and prostitution activity in the Weld Square neighborhood.

The subtext of Pina's remark, however, was a message to the rest of New Bedford that the murders were the natural outcome of lives of vice. "There is no cause for the general public to be alarmed for their safety," Pina added.

Pina's attempt to narrow the focus of concern about the murder to those associated with Weld Square had two immediate effects. First, it relieved the "general public" of anxiety that a mad killer might get *them*; after all, according to the district attorney, to avoid being murdered all one had to do was stay away from drugs, prostitution, and Weld Square.

Second, it sent out an alarm to those women who were still to be found in the Weld Square area, and helped lay the groundwork for better cooperation between the habitués of Weld Square and the police. Telling a potential murder victim they are a target does wonders for communications.

But Pina's constriction of the danger zone to Weld Square also had a secondary consequence: once the "general public" realized the murders had little to do with them, it became a sort of sideshow—something to be observed, or commented on, for the average person, not their affair, but instead the inevitable result of succumbing to sin and degradation, a sort of divine retribution for doing bad.

The same day Pina was tying the murders to Weld

Square, medical experts in Boston succeeded in identifying the first of the five victims—the skeleton found on November 29 under the trees off to the north side of the westbound on-ramp to I-195 from Reed Road, the fourth actually discovered. A partial fingerprint led investigators to police records for Dawn Mendes—the woman reported missing to the New Bedford Police Department in September, while Dextradeur was on his earlier medical leave. The identification of Dawn Mendes empirically validated for the first time Dextradeur's fears for the missing women.

"I-195 Body is City Prostitute's," the *Standard-Times* headlined. Boyle went on to document the prostitution connection: Mendes, 25, and the mother of a five-year-old, had an arrest record for prostituting, and was possibly last seen in the Weld Square area. Dawn had last been seen by her family on September 4, 1988, when she left to go to a baby shower at a relative's nearby apartment. To get there, however, Dawn would likely have passed through Weld Square, and police concluded that it was in that area that Dawn had somehow met the killer.

The following day, Boyle tried to soften the portrayal of Dawn Mendes by interviewing Dawn's mother, Charlotte Mendes, and trying to cast a softer light on Dawn and her life.

"Maybe I'm one of the lucky ones," Charlotte told Boyle. "At least I know what happened." Dawn's mother described her as devoted to her five-year-old and close to her family—a much different portrait than that called to mind with the unadorned prostitute label.

"I'm not happy that she's gone," Charlotte continued, "but now she won't have to walk the streets, she won't be beaten and abused. She's at peace now, and hopefully they'll find who did it."

Over the next several days, Josie the dog and her cohorts were back out on the highways leading from New Bedford. By this time, the Highway Murders had gained wide regional notoriety. News media from Boston, Providence, and other places streamed into New Bedford, setting up cameras to record the dogs as they continued their

search. Relations between the media and the police grew
tense as the reporters and cameramen crowded into the
search areas. At one point a dog got a whiff of a reporter
and alerted, bounding into the traffic lane on I-195, where
it was barely missed by a passing truck. The police said
they would arrest anyone who ignored warnings to stay
back from the search area.

Meanwhile, Gonsalves and Dill began rounding up
more dental records for Dextradeur's remaining missing
five, and sending them to Dr. Douglas Ubelaker, an expert
on skeletons at the Smithsonian Institution in Washington,
D.C., who often did consulting work on forensic pathology
for the Federal Bureau of Investigation.

On December 7, 1988, Ubelaker was able to make positive identification of two more skeletons—the July 2 remains, and those discovered July 30. Judy DeSantos had
been right after all. The victim she had been sure was her
sister Nancy Paiva *was* Nancy Paiva.

The July 2 victim, the first to have been discovered,
turned out to have been Debra Medeiros, a drug user and
occasional prostitute last seen in New Bedford in late
May 1988.

When he heard about the Medeiros identification, Sergeant Alan Alves of Freetown was shocked. Medeiros, he
knew, had been one of his most reliable informants. Now
Alves, the area's expert on both Satanism and Santeria
(sometimes practiced by a few residents in the New Bedford community) began to wonder whether the murders
were the work of devil worshippers. Stranger things had
happened in New Bedford, he knew.

As if to give Alves's ruminations credibility, the day
after Debbie Medeiros's remains were identified, the *Standard-
Times* reported that more satanic markings and artifacts
had been found in the Freetown State Forest just north
of I-195. The story didn't quote Alves, but noted that a
1979 triple murder case involving satanic symbols in the
forest had involved New Bedford prostitutes . . .

21

"Ron Pina Should Shut His Mouth"

Ever since the discovery of the Election Day remains, Judy DeSantos had been waiting to hear the dreaded news that her sister was dead. First days passed, then weeks. Despite the dental charts she had given to Dextradeur, who had assured her they had been passed on to the state police, there was no news. Later, Gonsalves was to tell Maureen Boyle that the dental charts for Nancy found by Judy were out of date, so that it was impossible to determine whether the charts matched *any* of the victims.

The enduring puzzle, however, was why Nancy Paiva's clothes and jewelry were found near a skeleton that her dental charts did not match. In other words, how did Nancy's clothes and jewelry come to be near a body, the Election Day remains, that *wasn't* hers?

But when the July 30 skeleton was eventually identified as that of Nancy, it appeared, at least initially, that Nancy's killer had taken Nancy's clothes from the earlier I-195 place, and put them at the Election Day site at Reed Road, possibly in an effort to confuse the police as to each victim's true identity.

But why? Why was it so important for the killer to shift the clothing with Nancy Paiva's remains and the Election Day skeleton, when he hadn't bothered to do the same with Debbie Medeiros or Dawn Mendes, or with the latest discovery, the fully clothed body just found on Route 140? It didn't make much sense. What was so important about Nancy?

Judy learned of Nancy's identification on December 6, when Gonsalves and Dill called her to tell her that a positive identification had at last been made. After four months of having her hopes repeatedly raised and dashed, of chasing all around New Bedford to check out putative sightings of her lost sister, Judy at first didn't know what to think. After a few minutes, however, she knew: she was plenty mad—all over again.

Why hadn't the identification come far sooner? Hadn't she tracked down Nancy's dental charts, just as Dextradeur had suggested? Didn't the New Bedford police ever talk to the state police? Wasn't this just more evidence of police indifference to drug addicts? Gonsalves warned her that Nancy's identification would be released to the news media. Judy might want to be prepared for an onslaught of reporters, perhaps even make herself scarce, Gonsalves suggested.

As Gonsalves had predicted, Nancy's identification opened the floodgates of publicity. Soon reporters tracked down Nancy's daughter Jolene. Jolene was furious with Pina for publicly linking their mother with Weld Square and thereby tarring her with the stigma of prostitution. Nancy Paiva had never spent any time in Weld Square, Jill and Jolene insisted. Nor had she ever been arrested for prostitution. But all the publicity about the murders, taken together, seemed to imply that Nancy had been both a hooker and an indifferent mother. Nothing was further from the truth, Jill and Jolene protested through angry tears.

"It hurts," Jolene told reporters. "My mother's gone . . . I never thought that my mother would die like that. My mother wasn't a prostitute, so Ron Pina should shut his mouth."

But the following day, Pina's office identified Debra Medeiros as a prostitute who frequented Weld Square, and the focus returned to sex-for-sale. Soon, in scenes reminiscent of the Big Dan's controversy, Jolene was being cruelly taunted in school by other children.

With the identification of three of the five victims, investigators for the first time had something concrete to work with. Determining the last-known places and times for Debra Medeiros, Nancy Paiva, and Dawn Mendes was critical to seeing what, if any commonalities might be present in each of the murders. Commonalities, in turn, might be vital in determining who might have killed them.

That the five murders were related and probably the work of a single man seemed obvious; Pina repeatedly stressed the similarities in the crimes. But for some reason, Pina seemed reluctant to use the phrase "serial killer" to describe the homicides. A reporter for *The Boston Globe*, John Ellement, buttonholed Pina in Boston one day in early December and tried to get Pina "to say the magic words," as Pina later recalled.

Ellement by this time had already talked to several experts who had assured him that the five known murders bore all the earmarks of a serial killer—victims drawn from a vulnerable population, all similar in age and stature, all found in roughly identical settings, apparently killed over a period of months for no apparent reason—but Pina steadfastly refused to utter the phrase. That didn't stop Ellement from quoting the other experts, however, and in the space of less than a day, media coverage of the murders exploded.

"Well," Pina said later, "that was it. All hell broke loose from the *Globe* story on. What the *Globe* writes, so goes the rest of the world. The (Boston) *Herald* responds and then the camera crews follow *The Boston Globe*, and New York follows that ... So they started descending on the place and at that point, it got crazy, because you really couldn't think or work anymore. The press got in there, their hands were everywhere, they were calling everybody, people were giving interviews off the record, privately ... and as you tried to collect information, you'd read it in the paper. And it really drove me up a wall because ... when you're trying to do an investigation, it's not exactly something (you want to tell everyone about), it's gotta remain secret . . ."

But in addition to confounding the investigation with a barrage of rumors and confusion, the media coverage also generated a strong upsurge in information called into the investigators. To handle the volume and encourage more calls, Pina and the state police set up a special telephone line for tips. Pina also put out the word that investigators believed that the killer was someone who lived in the New Bedford area, was familiar with the highways around the city, and likely was a frequent visitor to Weld Square.

Pina likewise announced that the Federal Bureau of Investigation would be asked to develop a psychological profile of the killer, based on the evidence found at the death scenes.

What Pina didn't say was that the evidence found at the scenes was so fragmentary, so limited, that it would never be possible to develop anything more than a generalized profile of a man who liked to kill women. That, unfortunately, might apply to so many men in the New Bedford area as to be almost useless. A spokesman for Pina said investigators were reviewing previous reports linking specific men to violence against prostitutes and female drug users in an effort to generate a list of possible suspects. Undercover policewomen were assigned to pose as prostitutes in the Weld Square area in the hope that the killer might reveal himself by acting strangely.

Four days later, on December 10, 1988, a Saturday, two hunters making their way across an abandoned gravel quarry-turned-illegal-refuse-dump about half a mile north of the Reed Road exit from I-195 discovered a sixth skeleton under a small grove of trees. This skeleton was partly clothed. The hunters immediately called the state police, who arranged to have emergency lights brought to the scene. The weather was bitterly cold, with snow threatening.

This time Trooper Kenneth Martin, the forensics expert, wanted to be absolutely sure if there was any trace evidence at the site that he would find it. Dogs were brought in to search the surrounding area, but no other remains were found. It was obvious that the latest victim had been strangled, but by this time police were learning to be cautious in what they said publicly. They declined to say just how the victim had died.

But there were some subtle differences between the gravel-pit victim and the others. For one thing, the latest location was down a long, winding dirt road that led off Reed Road into the gravel quarry. That was a difference, because all the other victims had been found right next to the highways, not down two different lonely roads. If the killer of the other five felt most comfortable getting rid of the bodies quickly—ergo, why else would he have used areas right next to the highway?—was the killer of the latest victim someone completely different? Why the difference in setting? "They may be linked," Gonsalves told Maureen Boyle, "and they may be not."

Three days later, police arrested Neil F. Anderson of Dartmouth and charged him with rape. The word spread like wildfire through the community and news media alike: Anderson was also a suspect in the murders.

22

"It's Not the Right Guy"

Anderson was a 35-year-old former truck driver, welder, and fish cutter, as well as the father of two children. As it happened, Maureen Boyle's story in the *Standard-Times* ten days earlier—the one about the Weld Square woman who told of being attacked in the rain by the scarred, blond man with the knife—led directly to his arrest.

After the story appeared, the woman who told the story to Boyle noticed a man glaring at her from inside his truck. With a shock she realized that the man was the same person who had attacked her! Doubtless he too had read the account of the rape by the side of the road; that was probably why he was glaring at her, the woman concluded. Quickly she made a note of his license plate before the man drove away. Within a few minutes she was on the line to the police, turning over the information and the plate number.

When police checked the plate's registration, the name returned was that of Anderson. When the woman identified Anderson from his photograph—he'd been arrested twice in earlier years for assault—police decided to pick him up for questioning. They also searched his house and his truck, looking for evidence that might tie him to the murders, and clothing described by the rape victim. Trooper Martin, the forensic expert, wanted to see whether Anderson's house and truck might yield trace evidence, such as fibers or paint, that might link Anderson to the murders. During the search, the police seized knives, ammunition, brass knuckles, and a whip belonging to Anderson.

While Pina declined to call Anderson a suspect in the killings, others in his office freely acknowledged that he was one of a number of men under investigation. The publication of Anderson's photograph in the newspapers also clearly tied him to the investigation, and soon, several other women called police to say that they, too, had been raped by Anderson. To police, Anderson denied being the murderer, and in court, Anderson pleaded not guilty to the rapes.

On the streets, meanwhile, the news of Anderson's arrest did little to reduce the growing anxiety over the murders. Some people who spent time in Weld Square even flatly denied that Anderson was the killer.

"It's not the right guy," a woman who identified herself as a prostitute told a reporter for *The Globe*. And another woman agreed, saying, "I don't believe he did it." That woman said she'd gone to elementary and junior high school with Anderson, and that Anderson just wasn't capable of committing murder.

Judy DeSantos also reacted with caution to Anderson's arrest. "I don't have any feelings either way," Judy told *The Globe*. "I only found out a week ago my sister was killed. That hasn't sunk in."

All the publicity about the murders and the rapes was meanwhile making New Bedford city officials cringe.

"Murders Cast Harsh Light on City," the *Standard-Times*'s Carlos Cunha reported. All the reporting about Weld Square, drug users, and prostitutes made it seem as though New Bedford was a hellhole of the worst order. It all depended on how you looked at it, Cunha reported.

"It is a charming, easily reached waterfront city. It boasts a good quality of life, loads of history, dabs of culture, and an interesting ethnic mix—not to mention the richest fishing port in the U.S. and some of the best discount shopping to be found anywhere," Cunha noted.

"Then again, it's a sleazy, seedy, rundown, working class, welfare-funded warren with a hopelessly polluted

harbor and a metropolis-sized crime and drug problem—
the likely setting for such sensational stories as the Big
Dan's gang rape and the ongoing saga of skeletal finds
along the highways. The two possible faces of New
Bedford."

Lately, Cunha continued, the second face seemed to be
gaining ascendancy over the first, largely because of the
reporting of outsiders drawn to the city because of the
murders. Some city officials began to speak of Pina privately in caustic terms: it seemed to them that the district
attorney was, once again, beating up the city to gain national publicity for himself.

Amid this low-level grumbling, the Smithsonian's Ubelaker continued to work trying to identify the three remaining skeletons. On December 19, Ubelaker was able
to conclude that the skeleton found by the hunters in the
gravel pit on December 10 was that of Rochelle Clifford.
Rochelle's identification in turn gave the investigators a
couple of intriguing leads.

It did not take long, for example, to check back through
the New Bedford police records to unearth two important
names: Frankie Pina and Kenny Ponte.

Both men had been linked with Rochelle Clifford the
previous April, when Dextradeur had tried to sort out the
conflicting stories of rape and assault that had initially puzzled the New Bedford detective. Kenny had been with
Rochelle the day of the supposed assault against Roger
Swire. Frankie had been with Rochelle on April 27, 1988,
when Dextradeur had questioned Rochelle about both incidents. Ubelaker's best guess was that Rochelle had been
murdered sometime the previous spring—about the time
that Dextradeur had been investigating the parallel cases,
and, obviously, shortly after Dextradeur had seen her with
Frankie Pina.

Then, further checking revealed another seemingly significant fact: Kenny Ponte had represented Nancy Paiva
in a bankruptcy proceeding, and Nancy had actually
worked part-time for the lawyer.

Where were Frankie and Kenny? Frankie, at least, was
easy to find: he was in jail again. He claimed to barely

know Kenny Ponte, and again denied any romantic involvement with Rochelle. He described Rochelle as a street person, a friend of Nancy's, who happened to use Nancy's apartment to store her belongings and take showers. He said he'd last seen Rochelle sometime in May or June of 1988 after Rochelle had been released from a drug-treatment facility in Quincy, near Boston. He said he and Nancy believed that Rochelle had gone back to the Cape Cod area.

When investigators began searching for Kenny, however, they discovered that he had shut down his law practice in late September, and had moved to Florida in October or November. For some of the investigators, the timing of Kenny's move to Florida seemed important: after all, the spate of missings seemed to stop shortly before Kenny moved away. The investigators also noted that Kenny had been charged in district court with the alleged assault against Swire, and that he was due to appear in New Bedford District Court on the charge in January.

Just why Kenny moved to Florida in the fall of 1988 remains a rather fuzzy matter. Kenny himself maintained that he'd long wanted to live in Florida, where his family had some modest property investments. Indeed, he'd been talking about moving south for more than a year before he actually did so. But just how Kenny proposed to earn a living in Florida was rather more obscure.

It does appear that in moving out of New Bedford, Kenny was influenced by a relatively new friend. That friend was Paul F. Ryley, a former Massachusetts prison guard, a businessman, and like Kenny, an honorary deputy sheriff for Bristol County.

Kenny, in fact, helped Ryley with some legal work in connection with a substantial estate—nearly $620,000, all in cash—in which Ryley was to be the executor for an elderly great aunt, Margaret Sundelin.

Kenny had helped videotape Mrs. Sundelin's last will and testament in January 1985, and as a result of the new will, Ryley's share of the inheritance was increased by about $90,000. Ryley also had previously obtained power of attorney over Mrs. Sundelin's ten different savings accounts, which gave him access to all of the money.

When Mrs. Sundelin died in April 1987, Ryley's efforts to probate the estate, with Ponte's assistance, were almost immediately contested by some of Mrs. Sunderlin's other relatives, who claimed cousin Paul had exerted undue influence on Mrs. Sundelin by keeping her a virtual prisoner in a house he owned in New Bedford.

As 1987 turned into 1988, Ryley embarked on a series of business trips, of which more later. It appears that some of those trips were to the state of Florida, and it also appears that Kenny Ponte's plans to move to Florida were made in conjunction with Ryley's interests in the Sunshine State. Indeed, Ryley told others that he and Ponte intended to go into the real estate business in Florida together, with Ryley using Mrs. Sundelin's capital, and Ponte providing the legal and management skills. But Ryley told a lot of people a lot of things, and not all of them were true.

Two years later, in 1990, an attorney appointed by the court to investigate the handling of the estate discovered that virtually all of the money was missing; lawyer Michael A. Kehoe speculated that the money had all gone to Florida—with Paul Ryley. What wasn't clear was whether any of the allegedly missing money made its way into Ponte's hands, although there would be anecdotal testimony suggesting that some did.

In any event, before leaving New Bedford in the fall of 1988, Kenny sold his house on Chestnut Street in the central part of the city. On paper, at least, the sale netted him about $26,000—just about exactly the amount Kenny owed in back debts to federal and state tax authorities, according to *The Boston Globe*. The man who bought Kenny's house, a New Bedford lawyer named Norman McCarthy—a longtime friend of Kenny's—promptly listed the same house at an asking price of $127,000, *The Globe* reported. Later, when reporters and others persisted in prying into Kenny's financial affairs, it appeared that there were no reliable records to show just where Kenny got his money.

For their part, the police contended that Kenny had no

visible means of support while in Florida. There is little
that inspires police suspicion as much as someone with no
regular, visible income, but who still manages to prosper.

Still, as far as Kenny was concerned, prosperity was
hardly his condition, at least by the beginning of 1989.
The deals with Ryley hadn't materialized. Kenny found
himself living in one side of a cinderblock duplex in a
rather rundown section of the middle-class town of Port
Richey. While the weather was wonderful, his shrinking
bank account was cause for major anxiety.

In the week before Christmas, news media attention
turned to the families of the victims. In addition to the
expected expressions of grief and loss, however, came a
new undercurrent—complaints about the police. Several
family members said they blamed police for not taking
the disappearances seriously, and soon several community
activists were openly suggesting that the lifestyles of the
victims—drugs and prostitution—had made authorities indifferent to their plight. A candlelight vigil was held in
downtown New Bedford, during which several hundred
people walked from the courthouse to District Attorney
Pina's office.

To counter those charges, Pina granted an extensive
interview to *The Globe*.

"This is not the first time Pina has found himself a
central character in a very public criminal case," reporter
Tom Coakley noted. "There was the Big Dan's gang-rape
case here five years ago. And in April, there was his controversial role in the wake of the reported kidnapping of his
fiancée, now his wife.

"The sordid nature of the latest crimes has intensified
public interest and scrutiny," Coakley added. "The young
daughter of one of the dead women complained after Pina
told reporters that at least three of the dead women frequented a New Bedford area known for drugs and prostitution. 'My mother wasn't a prostitute, so Ronald Pina
should shut his mouth,' the girl protested.

"'The press wants to know,'" Pina told Coakley,
"'and I didn't want a mass population fear that there is
someone out there that everybody should be afraid of—a

mass hysteria. I feel in my heart for these people . . . particularly the little girl. We have our victim-witness people
working with the family. She is just having a very, very
tough time.

" 'It gets very frustrating, when you think about the
killings and the families," Pina continued. "It isn't fun
(identifying) bodies . . . and you've got some nut or nuts
out there you want to find.' "

And in another story, Maureen Boyle reported that investigators were working hard on the case. None of them
had taken a day off in seven weeks, Boyle reported. A day
or so later, after activists again criticized the police for
failing to react quickly enough to the disappearances of
"throwaway people," the state police shot back that they
had spent more time and money on the murders than any
case in the history of the county.

Two days after Christmas, a Tufts University specialist
made a fifth identification—the Election Day remains
found with Nancy Paiva's clothing on November 8, 1988.
Deborah Greenlaw DeMello, 34, had walked away from a
Rhode Island work release facility in June of 1988 while
she was completing a sentence for a prostitution violation.
Like Rochelle Clifford, Nancy Paiva, Dawn Mendes and
Debra Medeiros, Deborah DeMello was a drug addict.

The latest identification answered one question, but
posed a host of others. Did Deborah DeMello know
Nancy Paiva? Was that how Nancy's clothes and jewelry
came to be in the place where Deborah's skeleton was
found? Frankie Pina now told the investigators that De-
Mello had never stayed at Nancy's apartment. Jolene, however, thought Deborah's picture seemed familiar. More
checking seemed to show that acquaintances of Deborah
DeMello saw her in New Bedford around July 11, 1988.
By that time, of course, Frankie Pina was supposedly in
jail—wasn't he?—and Nancy had already disappeared.

But had Deborah DeMello somehow gained access to
Nancy's apartment? After all, Judy DeSantos was certain
someone was living in the apartment after Nancy disappeared and Frankie was supposed to be in jail. Was that
someone Deborah DeMello? Was that how Nancy's
clothes—and jewelry—found their way to the site of Debo-

rah DeMello's remains? Had Deborah been *wearing* Nancy's clothes? Her jewelry? Or had the killer, as first supposed, actually gone back to Nancy's site, reclaimed the clothes and jewelry, then taken the articles to the DeMello site for disposal? Would a killer have done that, even with *jewelry?*

Or, an even more disquieting possibility: perhaps the killer had been *inside* Nancy's apartment in order to take the items himself to the DeMello site. Did that explain why there were *two* jackets at the DeMello scene? Why? To confuse the police? But at such a risk of discovery? How would the killer know there was no one in the apartment?

Just about any way one thought about the situation, the possibility existed that the killer was far more familiar with Nancy's apartment than had previously been supposed. That in turn could help narrow the focus of suspects rather considerably.

Well, what about Frankie? Was Frankie really in jail, as everyone thought, during the middle of July 1988? The records weren't clear; Dextradeur was sure Frankie had been locked up, because he recalled Frankie calling him from jail. But Dextradeur couldn't be sure that Frankie wasn't jailed sometime *after* July 11, 1988, when Debbie DeMello was last seen.

Frankie was known for his violent ways with women. Frankie knew Rochelle Clifford, and as far as anyone knew for sure, was among the last to see her alive. Frankie lived with Nancy Paiva in the apartment, which Rochelle had stayed in, at least for a while, before she disappeared. Frankie had access to Nancy's clothes and jewelry for a short time after she disappeared, just after she'd had an apparent argument with Frankie. Deborah Greenlaw DeMello's skeleton was found near Nancy's clothes and jewelry, and it was therefore possible Deborah DeMello might have been at Nancy's apartment; and it was also possible Frankie and Debbie had had contact with each other.

But if it was true that Deborah DeMello had been seen alive on July 11 and that Frankie had been in jail, Frankie *couldn't* be the killer. And if one of the missings, Sandra

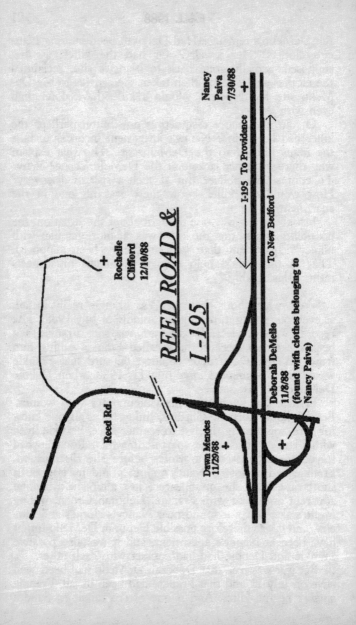

REED ROAD &
I-195

Rochelle
Clifford
12/10/88
+

Reed Rd.

Dawn Mendes
11/29/88
+

Deborah DeMello
11/8/88
(found with clothes belonging to
Nancy Paiva)
+

I-195 To Providence

To New Bedford

Nancy
Paiva
7/30/88
+

Botelho, was also a victim of the Highway Killer, Frankie was supposed to have been in jail then, too. Most important, would Frankie have killed again—actually *four* more times—after having already attracted police interest by reporting Nancy's disappearance? That seemed highly unlikely.

Finally, it did not appear that Frankie had a reliable means of transportation, and whoever the killer was, it seemed obvious that he had a working car or truck. All of this together seemed to let Frankie Pina out of the picture. Still, Trooper Delaney was given Frankie as a high priority for investigation. In every discussion with the police, however, it appeared that Frankie was both cooperative and candid. The police concluded that Frankie, despite his background, was probably not involved in the murders.

But was it someone who knew Frankie, and thereby knew the other women as well? That could pose a large problem for the police. Frankie was well-traveled throughout eastern Massachusetts; his voluminous criminal record was evidence of that. He knew hundreds of people all over the state—many of them shady characters, and therefore hard to find, and certainly not disposed to cooperate with police. What if the killer were someone who knew Frankie casually, someone who had used that connection to seem safe to the victims? That couldn't be ruled out.

Then investigators discovered something new: in addition to knowing both Rochelle Clifford and Nancy Paiva, Kenny Ponte had been lawyer for Donald and Mary Rose Santos, and had also represented Sandra Botelho's boyfriend, Craig Andrade. Were there *other* connections between the missing and dead women and Kenny Ponte? In a small city like New Bedford, it was certainly possible. Thus, at that point, just as Christmas approached, Kenny Ponte and Frankie Pina were running neck and neck for being the most likely to know something about the murders—whether they were aware of what they knew, or not.

Winter
1888–1989

"To this, in substance, he replied . . . he had a particular affection for his own harpoon, because it was of assured stuff, well tried in many a mortal combat, and deeply intimate with the hearts of . . ."

—HERMAN MELVILLE, *Moby Dick*

23

The Saint

While Ron Pina and the state police were striving, with their various media interviews, to present a public image of dedicated, confident professionals wholly committed to finding the killer, the backstage reality was quite different.

Doubtless much of the problem dated back to the time six years earlier, when the brother of the man in charge of the state troopers ran against Pina for district attorney. Pina said then that he didn't trust the troopers' loyalty, and although things had been patched over, residual bitterness remained.

In the aftermath of the 1982 election fiasco, when Pina had effectively fired all of the troopers assigned to his office—after the fistfight with one of the troopers, in fact—Pina had hit on a new scheme to get more control over the investigative process. He decided to hire his own chief investigator. The man Pina picked for the job was a former state trooper and local politician named Robert St. Jean. St. Jean, inevitably, became known as "the Saint," or sometimes, simply, "Saint." However the troopers felt about him, Pina was sure that St. Jean was loyal to *him*.

The way Pina worked things out, the Saint was essentially one of the district attorney's two main arms of the investigation. The other arm, the office's attorney, was headed by Ray Veary, a longtime Pina political ally, and a man generally regarded throughout Bristol County as one of the brightest lawyers around. So, while Pina handled much of his office's political and public relations, Veary and St. Jean had most of the day-to-day control over the office's functions.

St. Jean's major job was to try to manage the state troopers like Gonsalves, Maryann Dill, Joe Delaney, and the 20 or so others assigned by the state police to Pina's office. To do this, the Saint had to work with the sergeant assigned to head the CPAC unit. The relationship between the Saint and his former colleagues, however, wasn't always smooth. Sometimes, in fact, things became downright unfriendly.

In addition to the Saint, Pina had another investigative arrow in his quiver to call upon when the state police weren't willing to satisfy him, and that was the Bristol County Drug Task Force. In one of his efforts to find alternatives to the troopers, Pina had formed the task force from officers drafted from each of the surrounding city and township police departments, including New Bedford.

While members of the task force primarily worked out of their own departments, Pina's control of the group, exercised through the Saint, effectively allowed him the use of what amounted to a separate police force, and a completely separate intelligence unit.

While the task force approach brought its own political problems—the New Bedford department, for example, was forever trying to reclaim its two officers, for various reasons—the task force essentially gave Pina a limited capacity to circumvent the state police if he needed to.

The task force members, however, were primarily trained to do one thing: track and arrest drug dealers. Just like dogs trained to sniff out drugs, and drugs only, the task force was of limited utility when it came to rooting out serial murder. The drug police were simply not trained to investigate random, psychopathically generated crime. In the world of drugs, behavior is normative; that is, causes and actions can be understood by the application of rationality: people commit crimes to get money to buy drugs, or people get money by selling drugs. That's pretty much the whole story, and it applies to almost every event in the drug world. Not so with serial murder.

Inevitably, when the task force did become involved in the Highway Murders, it burrowed deep and produced, ta da!—drug connections. But then, in a city with the highest per capita heroin addiction rate in the country, a city where crack cocaine was endemic, in a murder case in which virtually all of the victims and many of the suspects were involved with drugs, that the task force in the end produced what appeared to be a drug conspiracy completely unrelated to the murders, was hardly a surprise. But all of this was to come later.

It was sometime in mid-December that Pina decided that the murder case needed the personal attention of the Saint. One result of that decision was that Bill Delaney, the trooper who had first started with the case after the discovery of Debra Medeiros's remains on July 2, was transferred to another caseload. Delaney blamed Pina for his removal, creating still more friction between Pina and the troopers. The way Pina saw it, Delaney was angry because the transfer promised to cost him the extra pay that came with overtime.

As St. Jean worked his way into the case, the connections seen earlier by Dextradeur became apparent to him as well. The Saint was familiar with Kenny Ponte, because of Kenny's juvenile arrest record, and because of his later work as a lawyer.

Later, the accounts of St. Jean and Ponte diverged substantially. Ponte claimed the first inkling that his name was being mentioned in connection with the Highway Murders came when a New Bedford lawyer, Joseph Harrington, called to tell him that the district attorney's office wanted to talk to him.

Harrington advised him not to talk with the police, Ponte said later, but he decided to do it anyway. Kenny said he called the office and asked to speak with Pina himself. He figured that Pina was a fellow lawyer, and besides, Kenny had supported him in his political campaigns. They could have a friendly and informal lawyer-to-lawyer discussion, Kenny thought.

Instead, it was St. Jean who came to the phone.

Pina later claimed it was Kenny's initiation of contact

with St. Jean that provided an initial trigger for his investigation's interest in the former New Bedford lawyer. That is probably not true, given the information that investigators had already developed on Kenny by the time the conversations occurred. Still, it seemed to some that Kenny was overly curious about what was happening. In any event, in mid-December, a series of telephone conversations between Kenny and the Saint ensued—usually with Kenny initiating the calls.

The Saint later told Pina that while some conversations with Kenny were calm and completely rational, others were wildly emotional, with Kenny often weeping and making nonsensical statements. The wild mood swings baffled St. Jean, and added to his suspicions. And Kenny was providing information about the victims—sometimes, weird information that seemed to come out of left field.

As telephone calls proceeded, St. Jean and Ponte discussed the lawyer's relationship with Rochelle Clifford, Nancy Paiva, and several other possible victims. The matter of Roger Swire and the supposed assault was discussed, along with the burglary of Kenny's house. Kenny's representation of Nancy came up, as well as Nancy's job in his office. Kenny confirmed that he had known Mary Rose Santos, and that he had also represented Sandra Botelho's boyfriend. Further, Kenny himself thought that he might have once met Dawn Mendes.

Why was Kenny calling? St. Jean wasn't sure, but was suspicious. It just seemed to St. Jean that Kenny Ponte knew too damn many of the dead and the missing. Certainly, he was evidencing an intense emotional reaction to the murders, perhaps beyond all proportion for someone who was not involved.

Carefully, St. Jean inquired as to when Kenny had left town, and why; and when would he be back?

But as St. Jean probed, Kenny continued to oscillate between cooperation and emotional indignation, because, as the discussions unfolded, Kenny began to sense that St. Jean was suspicious of him. Kenny became convinced St. Jean was taping the telephone calls, although Pina's office later denied that.

As December faded, St. Jean became increasingly uneasy about Kenny. When it came down to specifics about Rochelle Clifford, for example, Kenny seemed evasive— just as Dextradeur had thought Kenny was being evasive earlier in the year. Finally, St. Jean decided to test Kenny by asking him a direct question. "Kenny," said the Saint, "did you kill those girls?" Kenny indignantly denied it, but St. Jean wasn't satisfied.

This isn't working, the Saint told Kenny. I've got to be able to see you in person. He wanted Kenny to return to New Bedford so he could look him in the eye.

The way Kenny recalled it, St. Jean asked him when he planned to come back to New Bedford. Kenny said he jokingly told St. Jean that he was *never* coming back to New Bedford, meaning that because he'd spent his whole life trying to get out of New Bedford, why would he want to go back?

Well, said St. Jean, what about Christmas and New Year's? He'd be coming back for the holidays to see his family, wouldn't he? Kenny agreed that it was likely he would return for the holidays, and an interview was tentatively set for December 28.

But then Kenny decided to spend Christmas at the beach. Who was St. Jean, anyway, to cajole him to come back? Kenny was light on money, and air fare was expensive. The way Kenny figured it, if St. Jean wanted him back in town, the district attorney's office could foot the bill. Otherwise, he was going to enjoy the sun.

On December 28, St. Jean called Kenny. I thought we were going to have a meeting today, St. Jean told him. Kenny said that if St. Jean wanted to send the plane fare, he'd come up. That was when, according to Kenny, St. Jean lost his temper.

"He said, and I quote exactly, 'Ken, you'd better get your ass up here and talk with us, or I'm going to see that you'll get screwed in the media.'" Whether St. Jean really said this, or Kenny later made it up, can't be determined with accuracy, unless St. Jean *did* tape the discussions, as Ponte insisted he did. But if the Saint did say the words, it was a threat that was to prove as prophetic as it was disastrous.

24

The Leak

While St. Jean wasn't sure that Kenny had anything to do with the murders, he *was* sure that Kenny had more to tell him about the victims. Because, by this time, St. Jean and other investigators had done still more checking on Kenny. One thing they discovered was that, in addition to the Easter Sunday incident involving Roger Swire, Kenny had been stopped by police a second time in New Bedford—on June 7, 1988.

In that second encounter with the New Bedford police, Kenny had been accompanied by another young woman, Jeanne Kaloshis, while both were in a parked car on New Bedford's drug-infested South First Street—coincidentally, the same area of the city frequented by none other than Nancy Paiva, Rochelle Clifford, and Dawn Mendes—all victims tenuously linked to Kenny Ponte.

On that day in June 1988, the police had questioned Kenny about his activities while they arrested Jeanne on a charge of possessing drug paraphernalia—syringe needles. Kenny claimed that "this woman"—Jeanne—had "lured" him into the area; he seemed miffed at Jeanne for somehow involving him in something that was untoward.

When police asked to see Kenny's permit for the gun, he told them he had left it at home. The police took his name, but let him go on his promise that he would drive home to get the permit, and return to show it to them. But Kenny never came back. The following day, the police charged Kenny with possession of an unlicensed weapon. The day after that, a magistrate in New Bedford District Court ordered the complaint against Kenny dismissed.

This was certainly a curious incident, at least to St. Jean. Like Rochelle, Jeanne was a convicted drug user. In fact, she had been in a drug-treatment facility with Rochelle, and considered Rochelle one of her best friends.

The forensic experts were pretty sure that by June of 1988, Rochelle Clifford was already dead. Why was Kenny then hanging around with Jeanne? Indeed, why was he keeping company with either woman, each a convicted drug user, and why was he packing a pistol on both occasions?

An obvious key was Jeanne Kaloshis. Where was she, and what did she know about Kenny and her old friend Rochelle? And were there other women in the drug/prostitution community who might have things to say about Kenny Ponte? Investigators began pulling out the names of women arrested in New Bedford on prostitution charges. A list was compiled, and plans were made to interview them one by one to see what they might have to say about Kenny or Frankie or Neil Anderson or anyone else, for that matter. But at this point the investigation was about to come apart at the seams.

On January 6, 1989, the *Boston Herald* reported that investigators in Pina's office had been talking to a New Bedford attorney in connection with the murders. The story named Ponte, and also reported that investigators had searched Kenny's former home and office—and added that a dog trained to sniff out human remains had alerted to a spot on the office carpet.

Reported simplistically and without explanation, that was tantamount to a suggestion that a human being had died on the floor of Kenny's office.

What wasn't reported was that it was highly unlikely that a search dog could have detected the odor of a corpse on Kenny's old carpet.

One of the strongest odors given off by a decomposing corpse is ammonia, which is why dogs trained to sniff out compounds containing ammonia are able to find remains.

It wasn't very likely that a corpse had decomposed on Kenny's office floor long enough to impart the odor of ammonia, however. It *was* possible that the carpet might have once been cleaned with ammonia. And as events later showed, there was even another possible explanation for the dog's behavior.

The lack of precision in the reporting aside, the story ignited a media firestorm that would rage for nearly two years, and in retrospect, was probably the single worst thing that could have happened to the Highway Murder investigation.

With publication of the story, all hope of gaining Kenny's cooperation died immediately; additionally, naming Kenny had the inevitable effect of shaping the accounts of future witnesses, of building in a bias against Kenny Ponte. As the next 18 months unfolded, both of these developments were to decimate the efforts to solve the case.

Kenny heard about the *Herald* story from a friend in New Bedford. He immediately called Pina. St. Jean came on the line. According to Kenny, the Saint was laughing. Kenny accused St. Jean of planting the story in the paper. St. Jean, still laughing, denied it. Kenny cursed St. Jean, called him a badge-carrying moron, and hung up.

Later, Pina claimed to have been as furious at the leak as Kenny Ponte. "It blew my mind," Pina said, "because it just blew the whole thing up. It was *done*. I mean, any opportunity I would have had to at least have the guy (Kenny) in a room with me, to sit there and listen to him, was gone."

Pina knew the leak about Ponte had come from somewhere inside his office. The most logical suspect was of course the Saint, who after all had been having the conversations with Kenny, and who also had a long-standing relationship with the *Herald* reporter who wrote the story, Alan Levin. But St. Jean denied being the leak.

"I asked him until I was blue in the face," Pina said later. "I don't think Bob would have blown the investigation ... It came out of the office somewhere, a trooper. You know, Al Levin was the guy (who wrote the story). Al Levin is someone I've known for a long time, and if you ask him, it didn't come from me."

That's exactly what the state troopers thought, however: that it was Pina himself who had leaked. In any event, the leak became yet another incident of bad blood between Pina and his investigative forces, especially as the damage became apparent.

It is interesting to note that, at the time, Pina took little action to pour cold water on the Ponte speculation. The day after Levin's story appeared, Pina told Maureen Boyle of the *Standard-Times* that the number of suspects in the murders had been reduced to less than ten, and confirmed the searches of Ponte's home and office, and the dog's actions.

"Highway Killing Probers Search Former Area Lawyer's Office, Home," read the page-one headline in the *Standard-Times*. A subhead gave even more damning information: "Ex-New Bedford Man Reportedly Frequented Weld Square."

Boyle continued: "Investigators probing the Highway Murders of six women have searched the home and office of an attorney who abruptly left the area two months ago." The use of the word *abruptly* made Kenny's move to Florida look like a guilty act.

The other newspapers and television stations joined in. In an interview with John Ellement of *The Boston Globe*, Pina confirmed the searches, and added that it appeared that Kenny had "a personal relationship" with some of the victims.

For its part, *The Globe* quickly had someone knocking on Kenny's front door in Florida. "Ponte denied any knowledge of the investigation," the paper reported. "Ponte said, 'I have no knowledge of what you're talking about and have no comment. Now, please get off the property.'"

25

Homework

At his house in Port Richey, on Florida's Gulf Coast, Kenny Ponte couldn't believe what was happening to him. At first he thought it was some sort of horrible joke being played on him by St. Jean.

One by one, Kenny's friends called him to read the newspaper stories and tell him what the television was saying. As the calls mounted, the idea—or hope—that the whole thing was a joke began to fade. The tales his friends told began to add up to an ugly picture; worse, the more he found out, the more sure Kenny was, one way or another, somehow, that he would find himself in the middle of the frame. This was not at all how his retirement in the sun was supposed to be working out—*not at all*.

How could St. Jean think he had anything to do with the killings? He was no murderer. He wasn't even violent, Ponte protested to his friends, his voice rising in volume until he was shouting. Pina and St. Jean were out to ruin him!

But the news media was just beginning with Kenny Ponte.

Within a few days, the details about the Easter Sunday incident involving Rochelle and Roger Swire were in the papers. Swire looked like the hero in the retelling.

"Lawyer Was Seen With Victim," headlined the *Standard-Times*. Maureen Boyle had located Swire and got his side of the story. Swire made Ponte look guilty. He told Boyle that he had seen Ponte with Rochelle at least six times, including three times on one day.

"Then I never saw her again," Swire added, ominously. Swire added that Rochelle had apologized to him for accusing him of raping her; just how Rochelle had made this apology "about a week later," when Swire was also claiming that the last time *he'd* seen Rochelle, she was with Ponte while the gun-toting Ponte was supposedly chastising Swire about the rape, wasn't made clear. The obvious conclusion (apparently missed by Boyle) was that Swire had seen Rochelle by himself after previously seeing her with Ponte. Boyle, of course, knew nothing about the reported burglary at Ponte's house, in which Swire and Rochelle were said to have stolen Kenny Ponte's pistol.

Again, Pina did little to clear up the confusion; after all, the police knew for sure from Detective Dextradeur that the last time anyone had seen Rochelle, she was with *Frankie Pina* on April 27, 1988, not Ponte, or even Swire, and that was more than two weeks *after* Rochelle supposedly apologized to the man she was then still accusing of raping her.

Despite all the inconsistencies, Boyle apparently concluded that with Swire she was on to a good thing. The following day, Boyle published another tale from Swire. In a story headlined, "Ponte Seen With Three Highway Killing Victims, Witness Says," Boyle quoted Swire as saying he had seen Ponte with two other victims of the Highway Killer, but didn't name them.

Swire now added that he had seen Rochelle with Kenny "four to six times a day." Boyle failed to ask Swire, however, just why it was that he saw so much of Rochelle and Kenny; nor did it occur to Boyle to ask Swire how *he* knew three of the victims, a circumstance that at least superficially made him as much of a suspect as Ponte, to say nothing of Frankie Pina.

But by this point, the bloodhounds of the news media were in full cry, and within a few short days, Kenny Ponte was most thoroughly spitted and roasted.

Despite the omnipresent term *news media*, so often used as a catchall to roundly condemn, news gatherers/disseminators are hardly alike. Different readerships, viewerships, listening audiences, coupled with different formats and deadlines, create a multiplicity of presentations—and conflicts. But one thing news organizations have in common is their intense competition to get new facts, and eastern Massachusetts was a major news media center where this competition was fervent indeed.

In addition to the *Standard-Times* in New Bedford, the city was also covered by the *Herald*, *The Globe*, and the Providence *Journal*, network television affiliates in both Providence and Boston, as well as a plethora of radio stations and weekly newspapers.

The concentration of news outlets that generated such tremendous competition among the news organizations drove reporters to stick to Pina and the investigators as if they were presidential candidates. Indeed, the investigation began to have more and more of the earmarks of a political campaign—nowhere more than in the way Pina used spin control to direct the news coverage in his favor.

As the man in charge of what was becoming such an intensely watched effort, Ron Pina had the duty of deciding what information should be released publicly, and what should be withheld.

For police officials, there is always a fine balance to such decisions: say too much and run the risk of damaging an investigation; say too little and potential sources of information might never realize that what they know is valuable, and therefore not come forward.

In Pina's case, in the winter of 1988–89, the balance was affected by his natural political instincts. In effect, Pina wanted to say as much as he could to keep the news media happy and favorable toward him, but without getting caught. Thus, a charade of sorts unfolded, in which the reporters played a sort of 20 questions game with Pina, and Pina encouraged the reporters in the directions he wanted them to go by oblique suggestions, broad hints, and refusing to deny certain leaks that emanated from others in his office.

But what was inexcusable was Pina's use of the investigation's inherent secrecy to *withhold* potentially exculpatory information that might have saved at least a part of

Kenny Ponte's reputation. Pina had facts that were contrary to the story being spread by Swire: Rochelle Clifford had hardly last been seen by Kenny Ponte on April 3, 1988, but rather, by Frankie Pina and Detective John Dextradeur, on April 27, 1988.

Pina's failure to make clear *who* last saw Rochelle—and when—served to put the spotlight squarely on Kenny, and helped feed a growing popular belief that the lawyer was a possible serial killer. Holding the critical date back allowed Pina to keep the reporters focused on Ponte, and prevented them from asking more troubling questions.

At the same time, Pina also withheld another vital fact relating to Kenny Ponte. While confirming that the police dog searching Kenny's office had alerted to a spot on the carpet, Pina failed to explain about the ammonia, or to provide the rest of the story: the dog, a Massachusetts State Police German shepherd named "Syros," had been previously trained as a drug-sniffing dog. As it happened, dogs alerting to drugs gave exactly the same sort of excited signals when they smelled ammonia, or corpses.

Syros's new corpse-smelling assignment was recent, and his effectiveness in sniffing them out was doubtful. Throughout much of December, in fact, Syros searched both sides of Highway 140, and had found nothing—erroneously, as we will see.

Thus, when Syros alerted at Kenny Ponte's old office, it wasn't possible to tell for sure whether the well-intentioned Syros had sniffed corpse smell—ammonia—or drug smell. But Pina said nothing of this uncertainty, leaving the distinct public impression that Ponte was a possible murderer, or at least a conniver in murder.

As the first month of the year unfolded, an informal leak hierarchy developed in Pina's office. For the most part, Pina handled the interactions with reporters for *The Globe*, while the Saint made use of his prior relationships with several reporters, including Levin from the *Herald*. In another move, Pina drew upon his wife Sheila's longtime relationship with the Providence TV station WJAR to hire a news producer there, Jim Martin, to act as his official spokesman. Martin's previous experience in the news business in Providence and southeastern Massachusetts qualified him to handle reporters from the Providence media and from the *Standard-Times*.

With all of these sources operating on "background," it wasn't long before most of Kenny's past was revealed, and in particularly lurid terms.

First came Kenny's honorary deputy sheriff connection. "Lawyer Did Nothing As Deputy Sheriff," the *Standard-Times* headlined.

The newspaper reported that Kenny's appointment might have been a reward for his political support of the elected sheriff, David Nelson. Nelson quickly announced that an internal investigation into Kenny's activities was underway. The subtext of the story, however, was Kenny's possession of a deputy sheriff's badge. That dovetailed nicely with earlier reports that a man posing as a policeman had been terrorizing women in the Weld Square area the previous summer.

The next day, Kenny was indicted by a grand jury and charged with assaulting Roger Swire by menacing him with a gun.

With a formal charge filed and a plethora of leaks making the link between Kenny and the murders, media restraint began to evaporate. A bench warrant was issued for Kenny's arrest if he failed to return voluntarily to Massachusetts for arraignment on the assault charge.

The following day, the Boston papers gave the full lowdown on Kenny's prior drug history.

"Serial Probe Targets 'Ex-Junkie,'" the *Herald* reported. Kenny, it appeared, had been arrested numerous times in the late 1960s and early 1970s for drug violations.

Burrowing into Kenny's records with the state's Board of Pardons, the story claimed Kenny had been nabbed for using heroin, prescription pills, and marijuana, that he had been twice convicted of conspiracy to possess drugs, and that he had served three months in jail in 1971. He had been granted a pardon in 1975 by former Governor Francis Sargent after the intercession of a New Bedford-area state senator.

Infuriated again, Kenny called New Bedford and this time demanded to speak with Pina. As usual, St. Jean came on the line. According to Kenny, the Saint was laughing again.

"Boy, they sure did their homework on *you*," the Saint told Kenny, at least in Kenny's version. Kenny told the Saint he was sure that St. Jean had led the *Herald* by the nose. "Oh, we wouldn't do that," the Saint supposedly said. "We'd *never* do that."

Within the next 24 hours, all the other media had much the same story as each tried to outdo the others in finding new dirt on Ponte. In vain, several of Kenny's friends and acquaintances protested.

"He's disappointed, surprised, outraged," Thomas Hunt, a New Bedford lawyer, told the *Standard-Times*'s Boyle. "He can't understand it, and frankly, neither can I. I am disappointed that a man who has not been indicted and has not been charged . . . in a series of heinous crimes . . . could have his personal life depicted in your paper."

And the state senator who had sponsored Kenny's pardon in 1975 similarly complained, saying that the news media had assassinated Kenny's character with innuendo, and that Kenny should instead be seen a shining example of rehabilitation, having served his time, recovered from his drug addiction, and gone on to become a practicing lawyer. Kenny's former landlord joined in, saying that the move to Florida had hardly been "abrupt," that in fact Kenny had been planning the move for months.

But the protests had little effect, and Kenny was quickly perceived as a central figure in the unfolding drama of the Highway Murders.

Almost unnoticed in the commotion was the apparently coincidental arrest of Roger Swire—the man Kenny Ponte had allegedly assaulted the previous April. Even as the entire town was talking about Kenny, Swire was being arrested and accused of breaking into an apartment and threatening a 20-year-old woman with a knife. Just what Swire wanted with the woman was never made clear.

In Florida, Kenny was growing ever more horrified and frightened about this sudden cascading of events. His mother and sister back in New Bedford had been besieged by reporters seeking comments on Kenny's possible involvement with the murders. They, too, were shocked and frightened. To Kenny, the whole affair was beginning to smell like a lynch mob in the making.

As he searched his mind, trying to identify just what he had done to deserve this treatment, it did not take long for Kenny to decide that Pina was out to get him for personal reasons. But why? Kenny couldn't understand it. Hadn't he supported Pina in each of his reelection efforts? What had he ever done to Pina?

As he ruminated on his past relationship with the district attorney, Kenny zeroed in on an old case he had handled—a case in which Pina's office had failed to secure a prison term for an accused child rapist, whose wife was defended by Ponte. That had to be it, Kenny decided; he'd made Pina look bad in public, and now Pina was getting even. Pina, of course, denied any such motivation, and said he barely knew Kenny Ponte.

Kenny and his family weren't the only ones undergoing a news media siege. The families of the victims were also put under the microscope. Squads of reporters and photographers camped out in front of people's houses, waiting for them to emerge to make statements. Judy DeSantos, for one, quickly grew to hate the newspeople. On one occasion she slammed a door in a reporter's face almost as soon as the reporter identified himself.

"I was tired of it," she recalled. "They're bombarding you, you're thrown into a world that you never had to deal with before. And I was confused. I hated people being near me, and I didn't want to have to deal with that. You know, there are some real rude reporters. I had someone follow me into the house, carrying my groceries . . . I put my groceries on the sidewalk and he followed me in the house, carrying my groceries. I never knew he was behind me until he started talking." Judy adopted evasive maneuvers to keep away from the reporters, going in neighbors' front doors and exiting out the rear to throw the newspeople off the scent.

To Judy, the intense pain of trying to accept Nancy's death was made far worse by the public nature of the event. It was as if all these shallow people, the reporters, were trying to crowd in on top of her grief, to use Nancy for crass commercial purposes. Judy detested it, just as she hated being watched, observed, made to react by rude reporters for the benefit of the evening news. Eventually Judy bought a telephone answering machine to screen all of her calls; if it wasn't someone she knew, Judy wouldn't answer.

At home, the pressures intensified. After learning that Nancy had been murdered, Judy's 12-year-old son's first reaction was to declare his intention to buy a gun and kill the murderer. Her daughter began having trouble in school, and woke up one night crying uncontrollably. When Judy asked what was wrong, her daughter explained that she'd had a vision of Nancy, who had appeared to urge Judy to fight for her. Judy herself was still so angry at Frankie Pina that when her daughter gave her a small key chain with a plastic figure attached to it—telling her to just squeeze the plastic figure every time she got mad at Frankie—Judy squeezed the stuffing out of it almost immediately.

What bothered Judy most was the seeming indifference of most people to the fate of the dead.

"Nobody cared," Judy said later, speaking of the town as a whole. "And they don't care because these women weren't Chamber of Commerce material. I've always contended that if Nancy or any one of them, if they had been little college coeds, we might have had a different reaction from the public."

Slowly, as the anger in Judy built, she began to change. The shyness and diffidence of the old, deferential Judy fell away, and a new Judy emerged—someone who was increasingly assertive, verbal, and occasionally, even caustic. Her children marveled at her transformation.

"Well, I think Auntie Nancy jumped in my body and said, 'Girl, you just better get going here . . . if you're going to fight for Nancy, you can't keep your mouth shut,' " Judy said. "I always worried they would perceive me as being the bitch—'Uh-oh, here she comes again.' Then I said, Hey, they work for me. They may say that Nancy belongs to the state now, that it's a crime against the state.

"But it was a crime against her family. Now, you have, and not only Nancy, but all of them, you have motherless children; they're all growing up without the parent. And most of them were single parents."

So Judy began to channel her anger toward the police and the prosecutors, prodding, pushing, demanding action for her sister. "When they drew that chalk outline, she could not stand up for her rights anymore, so I'm going to have to do it," Judy decided. By June 1989, Judy would actually take driving lessons, and then obtain her license. One reason: Judy wanted to be able to drive out to the place on I-195 where Nancy's skeleton had been found. Judy would never be exactly sure why she wanted to do this; but it was as if being there somehow put her in contact with Nancy, giving her the strength and the power to keep on pushing.

But all the publicity had at least some positive aspects. Soon several other people in New Bedford had called the police to report their loved ones missing. By mid-January, in fact, the list of missing and possibly dead had risen to five, including Mary Rose Santos, Sandra Botelho, and Robin Rhodes, who had been reported during the summer and fall, in addition to six known dead.

The new missings included Marilyn Cardoza Roberts, 36. Marilyn was also a drug addict, but there was no evidence she had ever been involved in prostitution. The daughter of a retired New Bedford police officer, she'd first been reported missing in April 1988, then was said to have been seen in the city in June. But because no one had seen her after that date, the investigators decided to include her on the possible Highway Murder list.

The case of a second missing person was particularly suggestive. Christine Monteiro, 19, also had a drug addiction, along with an arrest record for prostitution. She had last been seen in late May 1988. But what grabbed the investigators' attention was Monteiro's address: she had lived next door to Sandy Botelho, also missing, and certainly knew Sandy very well.

What were the odds of two women who lived next door to one another both being killed, possibly two months apart, by a *random* killer? To some, it seemed far more likely that the killer had to be someone who knew both women—and likely, the others as well. That scenario, of course, promised to derail the theory that the murders were the work of a typical serial killer, as the state troopers continued to believe.

Troopers like Gonsalves knew that it was almost unheard-of for a serial killer to prey upon people he knew, rather than selecting victims entirely at random. Gonsalves and the others were intrigued by the connections between the victims, but thought the connections showed more about the social group the killer had preyed upon than anything else.

But Pina and the Saint thought differently. To them, the connections between the victims suggested strongly that something more than typical serial murder was going on in New Bedford; indeed, that was one reason why Pina refused to use "the magic words" about a serial killer with *Globe* reporter John Ellement. Essentially, Pina did not believe that the person responsible for the murders was a true serial killer. There had to be another motive for the killings, Pina concluded.

But what? What was the connection between the victims and the killer, if it wasn't a random encounter during the act of prostitution? Was there anything going on that tied the victims and the killer together in some sort of hidden way? Pina was sure there was, and he intended to find out.

— 26 —
A Reasonable Hunch

While most of the public attention was centered on Kenny Ponte in January of 1989, the investigators of the Massachusetts State Police were busy sorting through the Weld Square subculture in search of facts. For this, the troopers went to prison.

Massachusetts Correctional Institutes at Framingham and Lancaster housed a large number of women who had spent time in New Bedford. While many were serving terms for drug violations, many also had backgrounds in prostitution, and were familiar with the Weld Square subculture. Troopers from Pina's office began interviewing these women.

Interviewing witnesses who are in jail is a fine art. The largest difficulty is separating demonstrable facts from rumor and speculation. The problem of sifting the real from the fantastic is compounded by the closed society inside prison walls. In a confined setting, stories circulate like hothouse viruses; one prisoner may borrow details known originally by another to augment her own veracity.

This is particularly true when witnesses have strong motives to cooperate with the authorities. Repeated psychological studies have shown that prisoners frequently identify with the goals and objectives of their captors as their captivity lengthens.

Psychologists call this phenomenon the Stockholm syndrome, after a lengthy hostage situation in that city. Moreover, in interviewing women under sentence for drug and prostitution violations, the state troopers were already dealing with a population that was predisposed, by their own inherent lowered self-esteem, to cooperate with those holding power.

Such prisoners are often quite suggestible, and under most circumstances, great care must be taken by the interviewer not to inadvertently supply the witness with the information being sought. Finally, incarcerated witnesses often seek—and gain—favors from law enforcement in return for cooperation, even if the cooperation is based on perjury. For all of these reasons, the credibility of jailhouse informants is usually suspect.

On the other hand, the state troopers conducting the investigation felt they had nowhere else to go if they hoped to understand what was happening in the Highway Murders.

If the five known victims of the killer weren't exactly like the women in Framingham or Lancaster, the prisoners were close enough in lifestyle and the places where the victims lived and worked to have possibly been victims themselves if they hadn't been in jail. The troopers' task was to find out from the imprisoned women what they knew about the victims, and learn what they had observed about men who frequented the Weld Square area.

But by the time the troopers got to both prisons, rumors and speculation about the murders had spread so widely through the inmate populations that there were real questions as to the validity of any information that might be learned.

Many of the news media reports about Neil Anderson and Kenny Ponte had been read, viewed, and discussed among the inmates. It is therefore not surprising the troopers quickly began to hear unsubstantiated stories, some of them wild beyond belief, about the murders, and about Ponte, Anderson—and several others—as January of 1989 came to a close.

On Wednesday, January 18, 1989, Kenny Ponte returned from Florida to appear in court on the indictment charging him with the assault of Roger Swire. If anyone at that point thought that real reason for Kenny's appearance had anything to do with threatening Roger Swire with a gun, they had probably just dropped in from the moon. There was little doubt that Pina and the police were using the indictment to force Kenny to return to the state.

A huge crowd of reporters and camera people camped out in the hallway outside the judge's chambers, waiting for both sides to emerge from the closed hearing. At one point the noise was so loud the judge had to order a court officer into the hall to clear the corridor.

Pina's first assistant, Ray Veary, had already filed a motion to compel Kenny to turn over samples of hair and saliva, as well as pose for photographs. Kenny at first agreed to turn over the hair and the saliva, but when the investigators wanted him to remove his clothes so they could take pictures, Kenny refused.

Pina and Veary could hardly contend that the hair, saliva, and photographs were necessary to identify Kenny as the person who allegedly assaulted Swire; after all, it wasn't as if Kenny had spit on Swire or had showered him with clumps of his hair!

Actually, the hair and saliva samples were to be used by a forensic laboratory to compare with similar samples found with some of the murder victims, as everyone including Ponte himself well knew. Just why Kenny was willing to cooperate until it came time for the photographs was known only to Kenny and Harrington, his lawyer, but his reticence about posing for the police cameras later gave rise to all manner of guessing, little of it favorable to Ponte. Kenny contended that the police wanted him to remove all of his clothes, which was an indignity he simply refused to submit to. Not so, said the police; they only wanted Kenny to roll up his sleeve so they could photograph a tattoo they believed was on his arm.

In any event, at that point, Ponte's lawyer, Joe Harrington, asked that the hair and saliva samples be impounded because Kenny had withdrawn his consent. And a judge agreed with Harrington: Kenny had been charged with assault on Swire, not on the murder victims. There was no legal basis to collect the samples from Kenny if the district attorney only intended to charge Kenny with the assault on Swire. To get the samples from Ponte, the judge said, the district attorney had to show there was some reason to believe—even a "reasonable hunch," as the judge put it—that Ponte was involved in the murders.

Veary said the investigators were still working, but as far as a connection was concerned, they'd already been able to establish that one victim had lived with Kenny shortly before she disappeared. The victim: Rochelle Clifford.

At this point, for whatever reason, Veary and Pina provided what now appears to be false information to the judge to justify their taking of the samples.

"We can only trace her back to about the time of this very encounter on April 3, 1988," Veary told the judge. "We have no reliable information placing her anywhere at any time beyond that—or at least much beyond that . . . I think it's fair to say, based on our investigation, that Miss Clifford became a missing person to all who were concerned about her welfare on or about the time of this assault (on Swire), making Mr. Ponte, at the very least, one of the last persons to see her alive . . . We're not saying he was the last one, but certainly was one of the last ones."

Veary's remarks were directly contradicted by Detective Dextradeur's information that he had seen Rochelle with Frankie Pina on April 27, 1988—more than three weeks later—but either Veary was unaware of this information or he simply chose to ignore it as unreliable. But then Pina himself added the kicker:

"Our office," Pina now told the judge, "also has information from Miss Clifford's mother . . . Her indication to the state police and the district attorney's office was that, when in fact she tried to contact her daughter here in New Bedford, her daughter gave her Mr. Ponte's home as the location where she was staying and Mr. Ponte's personal phone number as to how her mother could reach her, and that was where she was living . . ."

Actually, investigators had found Kenny's phone number on dental records for Rochelle Clifford, and the date on the charts indicated that Rochelle had provided that

number to the dentist about the time she was seen with
Kenny. But providing a number where someone can leave
messages is not the same as living with someone. Later,
Rochelle's mother was to deny that she had ever told the
police that Rochelle was living at Ponte's house.

The judge did not seem convinced by Veary and Pina's
arguments, but agreed to impound the hair and saliva
while he thought the matter over. He said he'd rule on
the issue later. The judge also ordered that all the motions
and transcripts of the closed hearing be impounded, or
withheld from the public.

Meanwhile, Kenny pleaded innocent to the assault
charge, and was released on his own recognizance into a
storm of questions from reporters. He declined all
comment.

But Pina lost little time in putting the popular onus
back on Ponte.

"He refused to help us," Pina told the assembled reporters after the hearing, which was held behind closed
doors. "He had nothing to say. We were hopeful we would
be talking with him today."

Asked if it were really true that Ponte knew one of the
victims, Pina responded, "It's not just one. It's not just
two. It's not just three. It could be four." And, said Pina,
the relationship between Ponte and the victims was personal, not a lawyer-client relationship. "He's important,
without a doubt," said Pina, who added that Kenny might
have vital information about the crimes.

"I don't give up," Pina continued. "I can do a lot of
things." To Ponte, that sounded like a threat, and he was
right. The following day, January 19, 1989, Pina's spokesman, Jim Martin, suggested that a grand jury might take
another look at Kenny Ponte in connection with still other
charges—but *not*, said Martin, in connection with the murders. That, of course, was difficult for anyone to believe,
even if it later turned out to be absolutely accurate.

On the following Monday, January 23, 1989, State
Trooper Kevin Butler and city detective Gardner Greany
were working way down the list of New Bedford women
at MCI Framingham. That afternoon, the two officer's

met with a 30-year-old woman named Heidi Caton, who claimed to know some of the Highway victims. Heidi also said she knew Kenny Ponte. Kenny, Heidi told the investigators, was a user of cocaine. Heidi claimed Kenny liked to have Heidi inject him with the drug.

This was not the first time the troopers had heard that Kenny Ponte was a drug user. That was one reason the troopers had asked him to show them his arms. As early as January 7, 1989—two days after Kenny's name had first surfaced publicly—a self-admitted drug dealer named Stephen Bobola told Trooper Butler and Detective Greany that he'd sold cocaine to Kenny for four years prior to 1988. Still others in the drug community said the same.

But how true was any of this? The stories about Kenny's heroin-using past had been reported in all the newspapers and on television; meanwhile, almost all of the people being interviewed by detectives were quite familiar with drugs, and a lot of them were anxious to get on the good side of the Bristol County district attorney and his police. How far of a reach would it be for them to *say* that Kenny was a drug user, too, even if he wasn't?

And once one person told the tale—and was taken seriously—the word would spread quickly that tales of Kenny and drugs were exactly what the cops wanted to hear.

Heidi, like many of the others, was pretty specific, however. She said she'd known Kenny for about six years. When Kenny used cocaine, Heidi said, he tended to become very paranoid, which usually made Heidi afraid of him. When she was over at his house, Kenny liked to get high and watch pornographic movies, Heidi added.

The pornography claim was also interesting to the troopers. While it was difficult to say where the story had originated, a theory about the murders was beginning to gain some credibility—at least among the inmates of MCI Framingham. That was the belief that the murders were in some way connected with the pornography business. Naturally, from that guess it was only a small jump to conclude that the murders had to do with so-called snuff films.

Snuff films are something of an urban myth—something akin to tales about pet alligators loose in the sewers of New York. A snuff film is defined as pornography that ends with one of the actors actually being murdered on camera. Those who claim such films exist—including some police officers—point to other, equally bizarre behavior throughout society as proof of the films' possibility.

Yet, few claim to have actually seen such a film, or are able to authoritatively point to the existence of any such thing. There have been some rare cases in which murderers have videotaped their crimes, but the idea of such films being made for commercial distribution is ludicrous.

For one thing, such a film would be powerful evidence of murder—obviously dangerous to make and to possess. For another, such a film would be exceedingly difficult to distribute for profit. Put into cold business terms, how could enough buyers be found to assure a worthwhile return on investment, without also having the film wind up in the hands of police, sooner or later? Those who subscribe to the snuff-film belief contend that the buyers are rich men in Mexico or South America, or some other such place, conveniently far away, willing to pay huge sums for this sort of thing.

That, of course, doesn't explain why such an unusual, almost unique-in-number pervert would bother to come all the way to the United States for victims when his own country already had plenty of people to choose from, to say nothing of less efficient police.

Still, the rumors and speculation about the so-called snuff films circulated widely through the prison, and the troopers were bound to ask. Heidi said she had once been asked to participate in a pornographic film, but she wasn't interested; she threw the man's business card away, she told the troopers. In any event, it certainly wasn't Kenny Ponte who had asked her to make any movies, contrary to rumors that were to begin much later, when all of these stories began to get garbled together on the prison grapevine.

Now Heidi told the troopers a few other interesting things: she identified photographs of Debbie Medeiros, Christine Monteiro, Robin Rhodes, and Mary Santos. And she claimed that all of them knew Ponte, and that Kenny knew them.

What about Neil Anderson? "(Heidi) recognized a photo of Neil Anderson," Butler wrote three weeks later in his report, "and stated that she used to go on (motorcycle) runs with Anderson, and knew him well. She stated Anderson never hurt her, and she would be surprised if he murdered these girls."

Then Heidi pointed the troopers in an entirely new direction.

"(Heidi) suggested we check out another male who drives a red or black pickup truck, and owns a business in Fairhaven. (She) stated the male is an ex-boxer who has raped several girls in the past ... She described the male as 25 or 30, with short brown hair, a flat nose which had been broken in the past. ..."

She'd once gone out with Flat Nose during the daytime, Heidi told the detectives, and on that occasion the man had not assaulted her, but had paid her $40. It was another time, some months later, that the man, seeming drunk, had attacked her, punched her, and tried to choke her while threatening her with a knife. She had seen the man driving around Weld Square several other times after that, she added.

But now she remembered the man's name, because on the first date Flat Nose had gone to a bank to cash a check to get the $40. She'd seen the check, Heidi said, and the name at the top was spelled Degracia ... or something like that.

Flat Nose finally had a name.

27

Group Therapy

If Pina was being successful in orchestrating news media coverage of the investigation into the murders, a far different situation was developing inside of his own office. By early February 1989, in fact, communications between Pina's staff, the local police, and the state police were already breaking down.

Detective Alves, from Freetown, was one of the first who noticed that the state police and the district attorney did not always seem to be on the same page. Moreover, Alves also noticed that the state police seemed less than forthcoming with just about everyone else.

Pina, of course, had already announced that the city and township police departments would be part of a joint state-local task force to investigate the murders. But Alves noticed that when he attended meetings of the task force, very little was accomplished or decided. Later, Pina's spokesman Jim Martin would refer to the meetings as "group therapy sessions."

A large part of the wheel-spinning had to do with the conflicting lines of authority between Pina, the state police, and the local police departments, like Alves's. Pina had envisioned some sort of cooperative effort between all the agencies; the state police saw things quite differently. The troopers were glad to have the assistance of local detectives, who often were the people best suited to locating witnesses and filling in their background. But the troopers were sometimes far less forthcoming in providing their own information to the locals, which naturally bred resentment. Pina tried to work through the jurisdictional obstacles by convening the all-agency meetings every Tuesday, but candid exchanges became the exception rather than the rule.

"I think two things happened," Pina later recalled. "I think that some of them, I don't know if they didn't like me, (but) ... I like to get results, I'm a bottom-line guy and I can probably drive you nuts, but I don't like bullshit. I hate to sit in a meeting and spend a whole afternoon, someone starts to tell you a story ... okay, I've heard the story once, okay, let's move on and let's get down to basics.

"And I think that part of the problem I had is that because of the (troopers') lack of training and background, you get people with all kinds of theories and hypotheticals that didn't deal with the evidence. And I'm a trained lawyer and my background is, click, click, click, now let's either go this way or this way or this way. Don't start fudging the line. And I can be abrasive, I'm sure. When someone's in a room and you cut 'em off and you say, look, can we keep going down this road, I really don't want to hear the history of this thing. And I say history, I really mean bullshit."

As a result of Pina's impatience, the long-simmering, incipient problems between the district attorney and the state police began bubbling to the surface. The troopers resented Pina's arrogance and his constant pushing. Some troopers began to grumble privately that Pina intended to use the murders to get more publicity for himself—how else could all of the leaks be explained? For his part, Pina, never very trusting of the state police to begin with, suspected that the troopers were out to sabotage him by dragging their heels.

A major bone of contention was the troopers' overtime. As Boyle had noted, some of the troopers had been working nonstop on the case for nearly two months. As a result, the CPAC overtime fund of $170,000 was almost exhausted. Most of the overtime had gone to Jose Gonsalves and Maryann Dill; much of it was rung up when Gonsalves

and Dill worked late at night trying to locate and interview
Weld Square habitués. Gonsalves and Dill were working
as much as 90 hours a week.

Well, thought Pina, *if the troopers need to talk to people
who stay up all night, why didn't they come in and work a
night shift at regular pay?* The way things were, Gonsalves
and Dill came in for their regular morning shift (that was
one of the perks of being in the CPAC) and stayed late
on overtime to interview people.

Pina went to Gale Stevens, the sergeant in charge of
the CPAC unit and asked him about that. Stevens, a hale
and hearty fellow with a disconcerting conversational habit
of blinking his eyes—his nickname was "Blinky" although
he kept telling everyone to "Call me Pat"—could only
shrug. It was the regulations, Stevens told Pina. It was in
the union contract. There would be a grievance, a lot of
paperwork, people would get mad.

Well, that's fine, said Pina, but we're running out of
money here. Do you have any suggestions? Stevens
shrugged again.

Pina went back to his own office and sorted through
his account books. Eventually he took $25,000 from the
office's seized drug money account and used it to pay the
overtime bill. That put a crimp in drug enforcement, but
it was necessary, Pina reasoned. In the meantime, Pina
decided to pull a few political strings. He called Governor
Michael Dukakis, then finishing the last two years of his
second term, and prevailed upon his old friend to somehow find the money to pay for the investigation's overtime.

Meanwhile, Alves and two detectives from neighboring
Dartmouth were beginning to sour on Pina and the investigation. While their respective chiefs had authorized them
to participate in Pina's task force, to the three township
detectives, it seemed like it was all take and no give. Alves
was asked to go down to Weld Square, but wasn't given
any instructions on what to look for. Alves began to suspect that the troopers—or Pina—weren't really interested
in his assistance.

Alves had his own ideas about the murders. Because he
was familiar with satanism, Alves still wondered whether
the crimes were connected with devil worship. A man once

called Alves to suggest that every place that skeletons were found, a wooden cross was to be found nearby. Alves went out to see for himself, and it appeared to him that the man was right—although sometimes the crosses were some distance away from where the victims were discovered.

Alves tried to interest the other investigators in his theory, but everyone rolled their eyes as if to say, well, that's Alan, he sees Satan everywhere. Alves denied being the source of the newspaper story suggesting that the Highway Murders were somehow connected to satanism, but few believed him.

Then, when the leak to the *Herald* about Ponte surfaced, suspicion fell for a time on Alves. Alves recalled that Pina called up Alves's chief and accused the Freetown detective of having been the source of the information. Alves indignantly denied it.

"I didn't even know what he was talking about," Alves said. According to Alves, Pina said he wanted Alves off the task force. That was it, as far as Alves was concerned. He didn't want any part of Pina after that. He quit attending the meetings. Later, Alves conjectured that the reason Pina did not want him on the task force was that Alves did not believe that Kenny Ponte was in any way involved in the murders, and that Pina was concerned that Alves would go public with his doubts. That seems a little unlikely, but there is no question that Pina and Alves did not see eye-to-eye. "We had a lot of trouble with Alan Alves," Pina's spokesman Jim Martin said later.

In any event, by the end of January, the three detectives from Freetown and Dartmouth were out of the investigating pool. Detectives from New Bedford, however, remained in place, except for John Dextradeur, who by this time had retired.

The city detectives—Richard Ferreira, Victor Morgado, Gary Baron, and Gardner Greany—were actually ideal for the investigation. All four men, because of their long experience in the city, were intimately familiar with the criminal class in New Bedford—who lived where, who knew whom, who had what sort of problems. The four city detectives were also known to the Weld Square people, and therefore were able to introduce the troopers to the witnesses and establish trust that probably would never have been reached if the troopers had acted by themselves.

By the first two weeks in February, in fact, the teams of city-state detectives had contacted a great number of people, in prison, on the street, and in court, and had begun to zero in on two major suspects—Kenny Ponte, and the man called Flat Nose, who was almost instantly identified by Alan Alves, among others, as Tony DeGrazia.

28

My Girl

By late winter 1989, Tony was in bad shape. He kept trying to forget Kathy, but it wasn't any use. In October, right after the breakup, he'd gone scallop fishing with a friend, and talked about Kathy the whole time. He was miserable. He blamed himself. The breakup only proved what Tony had always suspected: that he just wasn't good enough for "my girl," as he kept referring to her.

When he thought about it, which was quite often lately, Tony couldn't help but feel his whole life had been one problem after another. At five feet seven inches, weighing around 160 pounds, Tony was a strong, powerfully built man who kept himself in good shape with a lot of physical labor. But Tony was particularly self-conscious of his appearance. It was the nose, he knew. People stared at him and asked him what had happened. Tony's nose lay flat against his face, as if it had once been crushed by some tremendous force. The truth was far different.

Sometimes Tony told people that he was a boxer, and that his nose had been damaged in the combat of athletic competition. And Tony's left arm was slightly impaired. Those disabilities had marked Tony deeply; every time he looked in the mirror he was reminded of how different he was. And Tony hated it when people asked him about his nose, because it only reminded him of that hole in his soul, the one thing he craved but would never believe he had, at least on this earth: his own mother's love. So, in his misery and to blot out the searing pain of rejection, Tony took refuge in the bottle.

The truth was, Tony had long had a drinking problem, and the departure of his dream girl made the drinking much worse. Night after night Tony made the rounds of the bars and taverns north of New Bedford—a roadhouse on Route 18, the Eagles Club in Lakeview, the VFW in Freetown. Usually Tony drank beer, but when he was depressed—which was much of the time now—Tony escalated to Jack Daniels and Coke. On Jack and Coke Tony tended to get obnoxious and mean, as well as grabby with women. If he drank a lot, Tony tended to have blackouts; the following morning he rarely had a complete recollection of what he had done the night before.

As January turned into February, Tony continued struggling with his life. He missed Kathy terribly; it was particularly bad when he ran into her from time to time with her new boyfriend. The pressures kept mounting, and Tony kept on drinking. There was something inside of him that made him do bad things, Tony realized, but he couldn't get control of it, and it seemed to be getting bigger and bigger.

---- **29** ----

Hear, Consider, and Report

In the third week of January, legal action on the gun charge against Kenny Ponte was delayed for the foreseeable future when Kenny's lawyer, Joe Harrington, filed a motion for an indefinite continuance. The publicity against Ponte was so massive, so pervasive, that it was unlikely Kenny could get a fair trial anytime soon, Harrington argued.

The judge refused to rule on that request, but did allow a continuance for another reason: after thinking it over as promised, the judge ruled that Pina had no legal right to take any hair, saliva, or blood samples from Ponte, and could only take photographs that would allow Pina to prove whether Ponte was the person who had threatened Swire with a gun; the continuance would be granted to allow Pina to appeal that decision to a higher court. The judge also ordered the public release of the transcripts and motions from the closed-door hearing.

Thus, for the first time the public learned that one of the victims, Rochelle Clifford, was allegedly living with Kenny Ponte at the time of her disappearance, even though, as we have seen, that simply wasn't true. No one outside of Pina and the police, however, had access to any information to the contrary.

Undaunted by these developments, Pina considered a new strategy. By late January, the investigators had talked to enough people who said that Kenny was a drug user himself that it seemed possible to get a new charge against Kenny, one involving drug use or possession. Of course, all of this information was coming from people who used or sold drugs themselves, so it wasn't necessarily true.

But now Pina came up with a new twist: he would use a special grand jury to investigate the homicides. That way, he reasoned, he could work around Kenny's refusal to cooperate. And if he could get an indictment for a lesser charge, who knew—maybe that might persuade Kenny to come in for that little talk St. Jean wanted to have.

In Massachusetts there are two types of grand juries. A regular grand jury is empaneled every six months; it meets to vote on indictments requested by prosecutors as part of the normal course of business, as when Kenny Ponte had been indicted in early January in connection with the gun incident.

A second type of grand jury, however, is far more powerful because it may be called to focus on one specific area of inquiry; its job is to "hear, consider, and report." Such a jury is also more powerful because its term may be extended as needed. The special grand jury may thus sit continuously, and in effect, act as an investigative body—under the control, to some extent, of the district attorney.

The use of a special grand jury was, along with the leak of Kenny Ponte's name to the news media, one of the critical developments in the investigation of the Highway Murders. Years later, many who investigated the case agreed that using a special jury might have been a bad mistake. At the time, Pina's chief deputy, Ray Veary, tried to dissuade Pina from using a special jury to investigate the murders.

"Personally speaking, I would have preferred to see it done without a grand jury," Veary later recalled. "It had always been an issue between Ron and me, among other matters, about using the grand jury." Using a special grand jury frequently had a political significance, in part because of the intense publicity it always attracted. That's one reason Veary didn't like using them, he said.

Pina had asked a special grand jury to investigate the Big Dan's case; the secret deliberations of the jury on the sensational pool table rape case had cranked up the public attention in a way no ordinary indictment would have done, which Veary thought was bad. Years later he still shuddered at the recollection of the hatred let loose in the city because of the highly publicized nature of the Big Dan's investigation and indictments.

But Veary also acknowledged that Pina's use of the special grand jury in the Big Dan's case was extraordinarily effective.

"That was one case where he was right and I was wrong," Veary said. "Ron Pina's most significant contribution to the Big Dan's case was in going right to a grand jury. Without that grand jury testimony, we could not have successfully prosecuted that case. Because, in the period of time between the indictment and the trial, there was tremendous backtracking on the part of witnesses. Had we not had their testimony under oath in front of a grand jury, we would never have been able to bring those people back to admitting what they said during the course of the investigation."

In effect, by bringing witnesses before the special grand jury, Pina could use the threat of perjury to sort through all the wild stories about the murders, the victims, the suspects, the drugs, the snuff films, all of it—and come up with some sort of theory of the case that would fit the facts. Or vice versa, as some of the detectives grumbled.

The downside, however, was that a special grand jury, sitting for months to investigate a complex, sensational story like the Highway Murders, would instantly become a magnet for every news organization in two states. In the frenzied climate that already existed, it was hardly likely that pulling in witnesses to testify in secret was going to go unnoticed. The whole case thus had the potential of mushrooming into a huge circus, and that's exactly what happened.

Pina's decision to call for a special grand jury was made in the second week of February 1989. While some of the state troopers sourly noted that the special jury would once again tend to put Pina in the publicity spotlight, there was another dimension to the maneuver.

Now, for the first time, he could tell the investigators who he wanted them to talk to, and when, and the troopers had to comply. All Pina had to do to effectively control the direction of the investigation was issue subpoenas. That would circumvent the state police bosses in Boston. If he was going to rise or fall on the outcome of the Highway Murder case, Pina decided, at least he'd be able to do it his way.

30

Linkages

On February 10, Pina and his media spokesman, Jim Martin, dropped in on Martin's old employer, WJAR-TV in Providence, and agreed to be interviewed. The other reporters were allowed in to watch the show.

The news: the list of suspects had been narrowed to three or four people, one of whom might be in jail. That, of course, included by inference Neil Anderson, who was still in jail awaiting trial on the rape allegations from December. Pina refused to name anyone a suspect, telling the world that the list was down to "three or four," which hardly helped make Kenny Ponte look innocent.

Then Pina added some interesting things: the victims, he said, were probably lured to their deaths by the promise of drugs. This was a seemingly slight but actually significant adjustment in the theory of the case.

Previously, the idea had been that the murders were connected with the practice of prostitution: that the killer was a john who enticed women with money.

But the supposition that the inducement was drugs instead of money reflected the work that had been done on the five identified victims as well as the missing. While some of the victims had no known links with prostitution, *all* had drug habits.

And, Pina added, the method of killing appeared to be the same in all six cases. "In every situation they are identical, as far as I'm concerned," he said. The positions of the bodies as discovered, he added, led him to believe "that some type of activity (such) as sexual assault may have occurred."

Years later, this question of whether some or all of the victims were sexually assaulted at the locations where the skeletons were recovered was to be one of the murkiest secrets of the Highway Murders.

Alves, for example, remained convinced that the way Debra Medeiros's skeleton was left by the side of Route 140 showed that she was sexually assaulted at that location. Pina believed the same about several other victims, as well. Years later, Jim Martin—who wasn't an investigator but who had seen the photographs of the scenes—was certain that many of the victims had been raped on the spot.

The chief reason for this belief was that several of the skeletons were recovered in fetal-like positions that appeared to indicate that the killer or killers had attacked the victims while they were in a vulnerable position. Additionally, investigators were able to recover articles of clothing showing the presence of semen. That was one reason investigators wanted to collect the hair, blood, and saliva of suspects—in order to see whether it might match the deposits found with the victims.

But the truth was, determining whether a skeletonized victim had been sexually assaulted on the spot was far more difficult than merely observing the position of the skeleton. If some of the victims were found in folded or fetal-like condition, it was possible that they had been placed in their locations while already in that condition.

It is known, for example, that some serial killers take particular pleasure in leaving the bodies of their victims in such vulnerable positions. This so-called staging often indicates, at least to the FBI's Behavioral Sciences Laboratory, a killer (or killers) desperate to demonstrate his total control of the victim, even after death.

Another possible explanation for the position of the bodies, however, is far simpler. The folded or fetal condition of the skeletons may have been due to the phenomenon of rigor mortis, the postmortem condition that begins about six hours after death and continues for up to 72 hours, depending on the air temperature.

If related to rigor mortis, what the fetal condition may have meant was that the killer or killers, immediately after the murder, may have placed the murder victim in an enclosed space—like a tool chest or an automobile trunk. There the body may have rested, folded in the fetal position for some hours after the murder. Later, because of rigor mortis, the victim would have remained in the folded position when the killer or killers removed the body from the trunk to be placed at the discovery location.

And because investigators had recovered some critical pieces of trace evidence—mainly tiny nylon fibers, that appeared to come from an indoor carpet, as well as others from a vehicular carpet—it seemed to many that the murders had most likely taken place somewhere indoors, with the transporting of the body occurring later.

Finally, while the locations where the skeletons were recovered were not as heavily trafficked as a major metropolitan expressway, there *were* cars passing by every few minutes, even late at night. It seemed unlikely that a killer or killers would drive a live victim five or ten miles out of town, pull her out of the car on the side of a major roadway, drag her away from the pavement, then rape and strangle her only a few feet from the traffic lanes.

There were, in fact, literally thousands of much quieter, less risky places off the beaten track to do that sort of thing. On balance, it appeared that the victim locations were selected for one reason, and one reason only—to get rid of the victim and make a fast getaway.

But on the other hand, roadside rape is exactly what Neil Anderson had been accused of only a few months before.

On the last day of February 1989, the Smithsonian's Ubelaker was finally able to make a positive identification of the sixth victim—the skeleton whose discovery along Route 140 in early December had so incensed Ron Pina.

Deborah McConnell, 25, was originally from Rhode Island, and was the mother of a ten-year-old daughter. While there didn't seem to be any evidence that Debroh, as she was known to her friends, had ever been arrested for prostitution, at least in New Bedford, investigators determined that she was well-known among people who frequented Weld Square. Like all the other victims, Debroh suffered from a drug addiction.

With Debroh's identification, more possible connections began falling into place, at least in the mind of Ron Pina.

For one thing, it appeared that Debroh was friends with Nancy Paiva and probably Dawn Mendes, who were dead, and Mary Rose Santos, who was still missing. In 1985, in fact, Debroh had worked at the Town Tavern in New Bedford's north end with Nancy, and later had frequented the Homeward Bound tavern on the edge of Weld Square, along with Dawn and Mary Rose. Both taverns were owned by the same person, Faith Alameida—who also owned the Quarterdeck Lounge, where Mary Rose had last been seen on July 14, 1988.

And detectives also discovered that Debroh was friendly with Robin Rhodes, who was also still missing. Rhodes, it appeared, had once worked with Mary Rose and her husband Donald Santos in a fish-processing plant. Robin Rhodes in turn was friends with Nancy Paiva, and Sandy Botelho, who had lived next door to Christine Monteiro.

But were all these interrelationships meaningful? After all, New Bedford was a small city, and the victims were all part of a distinct subculture—people who used drugs. It didn't have to be an unusual coincidence for the victims to have known one another.

For the state troopers, the additional fact that some of the victims—Dawn Mendes, Deborah DeMello, Debbie Medeiros, and the missing Christine Monteiro and Sandy Botelho—had arrest records for prostitution was a powerful suggestion that the killer was a prostitution customer who had merely happened to unwittingly select victims known to each other. Just because the victims had known each other didn't mean the killer knew *them*.

Serial murder experts agreed with the troopers: serial killers almost always selected people they didn't know as victims. That was part of the thrill of the game, for the murderer, the experts pointed out. And, the troopers argued, there was no way to know for sure that the other victims hadn't occasionally practiced prostitution when

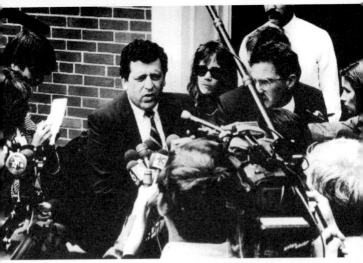

New Bedford lawyer Kenneth Ponte (*left*) and his attorney, Kevin Reddington (*right*, behind light boom), following Ponte's arraignment on one count of murder. (Hank Seaman, New Bedford *Standard-Times*)

Tony DeGrazia (*left*) conferring with attorney Ed Harrington in court in May 1989, just after his arrest on charges of raping and assaulting prostitutes in 1988 and 1989. DeGrazia was one of four potential suspects in the Highway Murders. (Hank Seaman, New Bedford *Standard-Times*)

Paul Walsh declaring his candidacy for Bristol County District Attorney in Weld Square, March 1990. Walsh was critical of Ron Pina for his actions during the Highway Murders investigation. (Mike Valeri, New Bedford *Standard-Times*)

Bristol County District Attorney Ron Pina reaches his car, August 17, 1990, just before a special grand jury voted to indict New Bedford lawyer Kenneth Ponte in connection with the Highway Murders. (Dana Smith, New Bedford *Standard-Times*)

Chandra Greenlaw, daughter of murder victim Deborah DeMello, speaking angrily about Kenneth Ponte from the window of a special bus arranged by Pina, following Ponte's arraignment on one count of murder, August 19, 1990. (Hank Seaman, New Bedford *Standard-Times*)

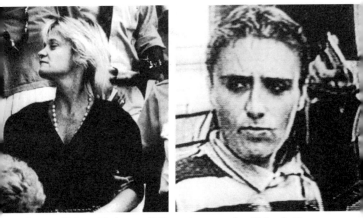

Witness Diane Doherty (*left*) arrives at the Bristol County Courthouse to testify about Kenneth Ponte just before his indictment, August 17, 1990. A grand juror called her "a fruitloop." (Dana Smith, New Bedford *Standard-Times*)

Admitted prostitute Margaret "Peggy" Medeiros (*right*) on television as she told reporters that police believed Tony DeGrazia was the Highway Murderer. (Richard Lodge, New Bedford *Standard-Times*)

State Trooper Kevin Butler emerges from brush with cut twigs as Massachusetts State Police process the scene where the remains of Robin Rhodes were discovered on March 28, 1989. (Jack Iddon, New Bedford *Standard-Times*)

(*above*) State Trooper Ken Candeias (*left*) with divers searching a water-filled ditch for possible evidence near the place where the skeleton of Sandra Botelho was discovered in Marion, Massachusetts. (Ron Rolo, New Bedford *Standard-Times*)

Connecticut State Trooper Andrew Rebmann, (*right*) an expert in the training and use of search dogs, was called by Massachusetts authorities to search for remains. (Ron Rolo, New Bedford *Standard-Times*)

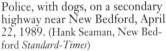

Police, with dogs, on a secondary highway near New Bedford, April 22, 1989. (Hank Seaman, New Bedford *Standard-Times*)

A grim-faced Ron Pina (*right*) and chief deputy Ray Veary (*left*) watch as troopers examine the place where Robin Rhodes's remains were discovered. (Jack Iddon, New Bedford *Standard-Times*)

Officials removing the remains of Sandra Botelho near Marion, Massachusetts. The discovery of Sandra's skeleton in a different county complicated the politics of the Highway Murders investigation. (Jack Iddon, New Bedford *Standard-Times*)

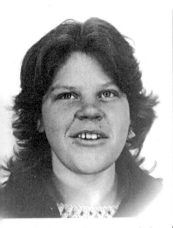

Clockwise, from upper left, the victims in the approximate order of disappearance: Marilyn Cardozo Roberts, Robin "Bobbie" Rhodes, Deborah McConnell, Debra Ann Medeiros, Christina Monteiro, Nancy Paiva, Debra Greenlaw Perry DeMello, Mary Rose Santos, Sandra Botelho, and Dawn Mendes. Not pictured: Rochelle Clifford.

Candlelight march for victims of the Highway Murderer, held in downtown New Bedford, December 28, 1988. In the first month of the Highway Murders investigation, New Bedford women's groups criticized police for not acting sooner to stop the murders. (Ron Rolo, New Bedford *Standard-Times*)

JURORS
USE
SIDE DOOR

Kenneth Ponte gesturing at a photographer at the New Bedford Courthouse. Ponte often complained that the news media was unfair to him. (Jack Iddon, New Bedford *Standard-Times*)

money was tight, and so thereby subject themselves to the killer.

But because Nancy Paiva, Mary Rose Santos, Robin Rhodes, Marilyn Roberts, and Debroh were not known, at least officially, to practice prostitution, something else might be afoot, at least in Pina's mind.

Throughout February, in intense discussions, the state police continued to press the prostitution customer idea. But Pina, doubting the competency as well as the loyalty of the state police, was almost sure that the close connections among the victims and their consistent involvement in the drug use meant something far different—something, in fact, that Pina was increasingly convinced had to do with Kenny Ponte, who seemed to be one of the people known to most of the victims, prostitutes or not.

Then, in late February, even before Debroh McConnell's skeleton was identified, Pina's theory of the murders was given a boost by what initially appeared to be an unrelated matter. Two New Bedford detectives assigned to Pina's controversial Bristol County Drug Task Force made a major cocaine-dealing arrest in the city's south end.

The proprietor of the Whispers Pub was taken into custody by Detectives Paul Boudreau and Bruce Machado, and charged with running a cocaine ring that allegedly did nearly $5.2 million a year in sales. It was another striking coincidence: Nancy Paiva, Robin Rhodes, and Sandy Botelho were frequent patrons of Whispers. Indeed, it had been just after leaving Whispers that Nancy had last been seen on the afternoon of her disappearance the previous July. Was this the cocaine connection that tied the victims together?

Moreover, Mary Rose, now known to be a cocaine user, lived only a few short blocks from the establishment, as did Dawn Mendes, also a known cocaine user.

All of these possible links gave Pina a working hypothesis: that the women were all known to one another, and that they had come into contact with the killer or killers in one of four places: Whispers, the Quarterdeck, the Homeward Bound, or the Town Tavern. Although it appeared, according to Faith Almeida, that the Town Tavern

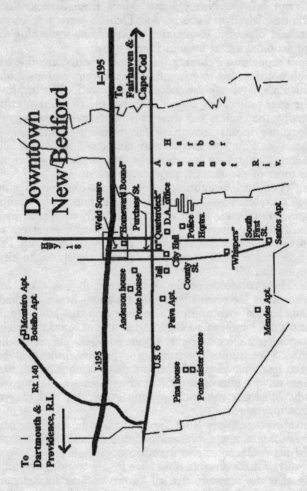

Downtown New Bedford

To Fairhaven & Cape Cod

I-195

Acushnet River

Weld Square

"Homeward Bound"

Purchase St.

"Quarterdeck"

D.A. office

Hwy 18

City Hall

Police Hqtrs.

"Whispers"

County St.

South First St.

Santos Apt.

Anderson house

Ponte house

Jail

Paiva Apt.

Monteiro Apt.

Botelho Apt.

I-195

U.S. 6

Pina house

Mendes Apt.

Ponte sister house

To Dartmouth & Providence, R.I.

Rt 140

and the Homeward Bound had been closed from March to September of 1988—that was yet *another* coincidence: that was, of course, the exact period the murders were taking place. Was the killer somehow part of the tavern milieu? And—was Kenny Ponte known to frequent Whispers or the Quarterdeck?

On the surface, it didn't look that way; Kenny wasn't much of a drinker. But one of Kenny's friends *was* familiar with the four taverns and their clientele, and that was enough for Pina.

In any event, as Pina prepared to convene the special grand jury to look into the murders, he and his investigators were already working along diametrically different paths. The troopers thought Pina was about to go off on a wild-goose chase, in a fruitless search for some rational motive for the murders; meanwhile Pina was growing more and more frustrated by what he saw as a lack of cooperation from the troopers in investigating matters *he* thought were most important.

To head Pina off, the troopers conceived of a plan to heal the breach between Kenny Ponte and the D.A., an effort to put Ponte behind them, once and for all.

Indeed, as February drew to a close, the state police were deeply involved in negotiations with Kenny's lawyers as part of an effort to convince him to cooperate with the district attorney. Everyone except Pina and the Saint agreed that Ponte had been badly handled, especially with the leak that had made Ponte's name so public. The troopers believed that if only Kenny would agree to tell Pina what he knew about the victims, then Pina would agree that Kenny was a dry hole, and agree to move on to more promising suspects.

In the troopers' view, a deal was possible: if Pina would agree to drop the indictment against Kenny relating to the Roger Swire assault charge, Kenny would in return agree to testify in front of the special jury about the Highway Murder victims he knew. It seemed simple, but it wasn't. Kenny wanted more than just a dismissal of the gun charge. He wanted Pina to agree not to prosecute him for anything, short of murder.

Apparently some in the state police thought Pina had agreed to that, which would get Kenny off the hook for any drug allegations that might be brought against him, and allow the investigation to move forward.

But the negotiations foundered at the eleventh hour, and a lawyer negotiating for Kenny wound up tape-recording state police detective Jose Gonsalves in a conversation that made Pina look deceitful. The tape survived the next 18 months, and was ultimately broadcast in New Bedford at a critical time in Ron Pina's life.

The negotiations were conducted by Ponte's lawyer Joe Harrington and Pina, with the assistance of Norman McCarthy (the New Bedford lawyer who had earlier bought Kenny's house) and Gonsalves. Gonsalves and McCarthy thought Pina had agreed to the deal, but for some reason Pina had rebuffed Harrington. This was news to Gonsalves, which shows that communications between Pina and the state police were already at low ebb.

"Boy, I'll tell you," McCarthy told Gonsalves, "I'm just amazed. There is really a breakdown in communication here or there's a lot of deception going throughout your office, Jose. And I don't mean to cast any aspersions at you, I don't know what is going on. Absolutely not. Joe (Harrington) talked to him (Pina). 'Absolutely no deal. Never has been, never will be.'"

"Never will be?" Gonsalves asked, disbelieving.

"Right," said McCarthy. "Well, not 'never will be.' I won't . . ."

McCarthy didn't want to slam the door completely.

"Well," Gonsalves said, "he (Pina) definitely wants something face to face . . . but did he (Pina) indicate to him (Harrington) what he was going to agree to?"

"What happened was, according to what Joe told me, he talked to (Pina) . . . and Ron knows this, and it's just terrible that, you know, it's almost like a license to deceive people. You know, I'm trying to help everybody . . ."

"Yeah . . ."

". . . and people are putting me . . . and trying to make me look like a fool. According to what Joe had to say, is that he talked about the gun charge, he mentioned that.

He also mentioned the . . . this thing about no prosecution for anything . . . and Ron Pina says, 'Absolutely not, no one's ever talked to me . . . no one ever . . .' "

"No one ever what?"

" 'No one's ever even approached me about that.' "

"That's what Ron said?"

"That's what Ron said to Joe."

"Well, that's not true," Gonsalves told McCarthy. "I mean, there were enough people here when I asked (Pina) about it. The Sergeant (Gale Stevens) was here, and Mary Ann (Dill) was here, when I made that representation to (Pina)."

"I don't know what type of games are going on here," McCarthy said, "but I don't like them. I'll be honest with you—"

"Well," Gonsalves interrupted, "I'll go talk to him . . . well, I won't be here in the morning to speak to . . . I wish I knew this this morning because we just had a meeting early this afternoon. I would have brought it up in front of about eight people." Gonsalves was referring to one of the so-called group therapy sessions.

"Nothing," McCarthy said. "Nothing at all."

"So, that's what Joe said that Ron said?" Gonsalves still didn't believe it. "Or did he say, 'that can't be finalized until he is up here in person'?"

"No."

"That isn't what he is saying?"

"No."

McCarthy went on to say that he believed Harrington was telling the truth, and that Pina had made a complete turnaround on a deal to get Ponte's testimony.

"And then he mentioned your name," McCarthy added. "Joe mentioned your name. (He said) 'Well, Mr. Gonsalves sort of worked this out behind the scenes, subject to my clearance and your clearance, this deal.' (And Pina's response was) 'Absolutely not, I've never talked to Mr. Gonsalves about it *at all*.' "

Gonsalves was now dumbfounded. "Oh, wow," Gonsalves said. "That's totally untrue. I mean, I have enough people who are here who . . . Maryann, Sergeant Stevens,

I think St. Jean was here in the doorway when I mentioned it . . . Well, I'm very surprised."

"So am I," McCarthy said.

Pina had decided that Ponte would be his target, no matter what the troopers believed.

31

Present No Man

The special grand jury that convened on March 2, 1989, was comprised of 23 people, drawn from all the communities of Bristol County. The law required Pina to ask the state attorney general to authorize the special jury.

Once the presiding judge signed an authorizing certificate, the court's clerk obtained the names of 45 people, placed them in a box, and then drew the names of 23 at random. It turned out that only seven people from New Bedford were chosen for the jury. All the rest were from outlying townships or smaller cities like Fall River or Taunton. Nine of the 23 were women.

Late in February, as they were sworn in, the special jurors took an oath to "diligently inquire . . . (and) present no man for envy, hatred or malice . . . but . . . present things truly, as they come to your knowledge, according to the best of your understanding, so help you God." Every member of the jury was legally obligated to keep the proceedings secret. That was a stricture that did *not* apply, however, to either Pina or the police, according to several legal cases that had already made their way through the Massachusetts courts in previous years.

On March 2, 1989, the 23 special jurors assembled behind closed doors in the ancient, two-story, red-brick Bristol County Courthouse—the former high school—and readied themselves to hear the first of 21 witnesses who had been subpoenaed by Pina to testify. The jurors did not know it then, but the session was to be only the first in a series that would occupy their lives for almost 18 months. That things didn't quite turn out the way Pina hoped was in part due to the testimony that was presented, and also due to Kenny Ponte's own maneuvers.

While it isn't possible to know precisely what was said by the witnesses in the four days of what Pina subsequently referred to as "phase one" of the jury's investigation—the records remain sealed—enough leaked out either then or later to approximate the subjects covered in the sworn testimony.

Essentially, Pina wanted to present enough information about Weld Square and its subculture to give the grand jurors some idea of what was to come.

By this time, Pina and his investigators had narrowed their focus to "three, possibly four" area men, as Pina and Martin readily admitted. No one knew for sure which of the three or four men might be responsible for the crimes, if any indeed were involved; as a result, Pina, the Saint, and Sergeant Stevens decided to place their bets across the board by assigning different investigating teams to each man.

One suspect, naturally, was Tony DeGrazia, and as February unfolded, State Troopers Kevin Butler and Lorraine Forrest interviewed a steady progression of women who claimed that a man with a flat nose who drove a pickup truck had beaten and raped them. As Butler and Forrest displayed photographs of Tony, victims told them over and over again, "That's him, that's him."

Meanwhile, Jose Gonsalves and Maryann Dill concentrated on a third suspect, a man Weld Square people had identified as a Tiverton, Rhode Island, diesel mechanic named James Baker. According to the Weld Square women, Baker was a frequent visitor to Weld Square, and was said to have had some contact with the victims. Some said Baker was a nice, pleasant man who was friendly and helpful to women in trouble, while others told of having been choked or harassed by him. Several said that Baker liked to preach to women about their drug habits; he would get angry at women who wouldn't listen, they said.

One woman even claimed she had seen identification papers for two of the victims at Baker's house.

Other troopers, backed up by the Saint and information from the city police assigned to Pina's Bristol County Drug Task Force, concentrated on Kenny Ponte. In contrast to some of the troopers, Pina and the Saint remained convinced that the murders were the work of someone who had a personal relationship with the victims. That meant Ponte and his friends, as far as they were concerned. Pina and the Saint were also swayed by Kenny's emotionally volatile behavior, and his steadfast refusal to cooperate with them.

With all of these possibilities in mind, Pina wanted to bring enough witnesses before the jury to begin to sort through the lies and evasions that were making the investigation so difficult. By using the threat of perjury, Pina hoped to sift through the conflicting stories so that some clear direction might emerge, just as he had done years earlier in the Big Dan's case.

The witnesses called before the jury during this first session in March 1989 thus represented something of a grab bag: detectives to set the scenes of the murders, and the sort of evidence recovered there, followed by a variety of people familiar with Weld Square and some of the victims.

A man who owned a restaurant called Pal's on Acushnet Avenue in the north end identified several pictures of the victims, along with a photo of Kenny. He'd seen Kenny talking to women in the restaurant—including Robin Rhodes—and Kenny had once written a check to another person who owed the restaurant money, but the check bounced, he said.

Several women who frequented Weld Square also testified, along with a man who operated a magazine store in Weld Square used as a hangout by some of the Square's habitués. Donald Santos, the husband of Mary Rose, testified, telling the jury that he and his wife had hired Kenny Ponte to represent them on an accident claim.

When Mary Rose disappeared, Donald Santos added, Kenny Ponte had photocopied flyers showing Mary Rose and helped distribute them at Faith Alameida's taverns.

Alameida also testified, saying she'd employed Nancy Paiva in 1986, and Debroh McConnell in 1987, but that she'd fired them because their boyfriends were abusive to other customers.

Several women were shown pictures of a few men who were believed to have frequented the Weld Square area, including Kenny, and at least one told of being assaulted by a man who was identified as Tony DeGrazia. A photo of Neil Anderson was similarly identified. Significantly, however, the bail for Anderson was reduced just before the jury began taking testimony, which appeared to be a sign that Anderson had been cleared of involvement in the murders.

The news from the most important witnesses, however, did not leak. By now, investigators had talked to a woman named Violet Farland, and Stephen Bobola, the self-admitted former drug dealer who claimed to have sold cocaine to Kenny Ponte.

Farland contended that she had consumed cocaine with Kenny. Kenny had given her money to buy the drug, she said, and then had told her to inject him with the substance in hard to reach places such as his neck, behind his knee, or directly behind his scrotum.

But Farland's testimony seemed suspect: she asserted that Kenny had picked her up near Weld Square in December 1988. Of course, during that month, Kenny had already moved to Florida, and it seemed unlikely that he would return to New Bedford just to consume drugs even while St. Jean was conversing with him by telephone about the murders and trying to coax him into coming back.

A taxi driver, Arthur Goldblatt, was similarly accused of furnishing cocaine to Kenny and the women. Before going in to testify, Goldblatt told reporters he would refuse to answer any questions. Pina was just on a fishing expedition, Goldblatt said, and the whole thing was a waste of time. He offered the opinion that the murders weren't even connected.

"It's not the same pattern," he said. "Some of the girls are being killed because they're ratting on the drug dealers, some of the others because there's some nut on the street." The following day, however, Goldblatt spent 30 minutes in front of the jury, and then was issued a subpoena to come back later. "I just want to go home," he said when he emerged, clearly unhappy.

What wasn't immediately apparent to the grand jury or the newspeople, however, was that Pina had already embarked on a program that would inexorably range ever closer to Kenny Ponte. It may have been that in March 1989, not even Pina or the Saint knew how this investigation was going to come out, but it is evident from the witnesses who were called that even at that early stage Kenny was definitely a target.

Indeed, the testimony from Bobola and the women were the first planks in a case that Pina hoped to eventually build against Ponte.

Pina, in fact, had gradually begun to form an idea about the crimes.

Sitting up late at night at home, thinking about the murders, making notes to himself on a legal pad, Pina kept coming back to the fact that all of the victims seemed to be connected. The killer, he had already reasoned, had to be someone who knew or who had contact with the interconnected victims. In Pina's mind, the name that kept coming up was Kenny Ponte. But why?

Slowly, Pina came to believe that Ponte—the former heroin addict who had received a pardon—was so paranoid about the prospect of being revealed as a drug user once again that he would do *anything*, even murder, to keep his latest addiction secret.

After all, Pina reasoned, being unmasked as a drug addict would probably cost Kenny his law license, and his very livelihood. Even more, Pina believed, the revelation of Kenny's return to drug addiction would destroy his public image, and that was something Kenny, for emotional and psychological reasons, simply could not allow. So Kenny was driven to murder the women with whom he had shared illegal drugs.

In the cold light of reality, however, Pina's idea hardly seems like a viable motive for murder.

Every day, somewhere in America, lawyers are referred for treatment of drug or alcohol dependency by their own bar associations, or even more frequently, by their own families. Most, after treatment, are returned to practice in good standing. Almost certainly similar treatment would have been available to Kenny Ponte, even if he did have a drug addiction, which was far short of being proved.

Moreover—even if *all* of the dead women had once or more times sold cocaine to Kenny, and thereby provided Kenny with a murder motive to keep them quiet, how would one explain why Kenny hadn't murdered Violet Farland, or any of the several other women who would later testify that *they* too obtained drugs for Kenny? Why wasn't Bobola dead, for that matter, or Goldblatt, or any of several other men who supposedly knew the secret?

This was the major flaw in Pina's theory of the murders: as a motive for killing, it simply didn't stand up. As a result, over the next 18 months, a hybrid motive of sorts emerged, at least among those (like Pina) who believed that Kenny Ponte was responsible for the murders: that Kenny was the killer, and that he had first killed Rochelle Clifford to keep her quiet about the drug use. This murder supposedly became necessary when Detective Dextradeur insisted on interviewing Rochelle about her activities with Kenny (an interview Pina believed Kenny was desperate to prevent), followed by a more traditional psychosexual murder series in which Kenny, having once killed, discovered how enjoyable it really was, and so began working down the list of the other victims, one by one over the next five months, perhaps in concert with one or two others.

To that end, Pina became particularly interested in tales about Kenny's alleged sexual perversity. And, as the investigation unfolded, there seemed to be a large supply of imprisoned women who were eager to supply Pina with such lurid details.

But Pina had poisoned this well. To begin with, he assured everyone who agreed to provide testimony that his office would not prosecute if the witness admitted illegal activity. And, for some, special favors were granted: a dropping or delay of other charges, or help getting into drug treatment programs or halfway houses. These arrangements, while effective in getting cooperation of reluctant witnesses, also served to undermine the witnesses' credibility. It was like bribing a witness to provide information that the witness knew full well was exactly what the district attorney wanted to hear.

Pina's only useful cudgel for keeping the witnesses honest was his power to charge them with perjury. But for many women, being safe in prison on a perjury charge was infinitely preferable to the perils of drugs and beatings on the street, and it was hardly an effective deterrent to giving false testimony.

On the first day of the session, Kenny waited in the courthouse for his turn, trying to keep out of sight of the reporters. It proved to be impossible, especially at the end of the day when the jury adjourned without calling him. A swarm of newspeople descended on Kenny, pushing microphones in his face and shouting questions at him.

"Just get away from me, just get away," Kenny told the reporters, his hostility apparent. When that didn't work, Kenny turned to a friend who had accompanied him, Daniel Branco. "Let's get away from these maggots," Kenny said angrily, as he and Branco began walking rapidly toward their parked car, followed by reporters and camera crews. When a few got in his way Kenny elbowed them aside. As a public relations man, Kenny was a disaster. It was a media mob scene that was repeated twice more during the first week of testimony.

Finally, on March 7, the final day of the grand jury's "phase one," as Pina called it, Kenny was called to testify. Once he was seated in front of the jury, according to legal papers filed later, Pina asked him whether he knew any of the six victims, showed him some photographs, and asked whether Kenny was familiar with any of the names on a list of witnesses, some of whom had already testified. Kenny refused to answer any questions, citing his privilege against self-incrimination.

Kenny's decision to take the Fifth was not a surprise to Pina, nor did it surprise anyone else in the courthouse. Previously, in fact, Pina had been asked by reporters what he might do if a witness took the Fifth. Answering obliquely, Pina said that a Fifth Amendment privilege could be countered by a grant of immunity. Would he grant Kenny immunity? Again, Pina declined to answer. But then he told reporters that if they saw him emerge from the jury room and go into the judge's lobby, reporters would probably not be wrong if they concluded he was seeking immunity for a witness. As to whether that meant a witness had claimed the Fifth Amendment, Pina left that to the reporters to conclude for themselves.

Ten minutes after Kenny went before the jury, Pina emerged to go into the judge's lobby, accompanied by Kenny's lawyer, Joe Harrington. Behind closed doors, Pina argued that because he wasn't asking Kenny whether he had killed the women, only whether he knew them (not a crime) Kenny had no right to claim the Fifth. Harrington said Pina's argument was poppycock. *Any* answers Kenny might make that would "furnish a link in the chain of evidence needed to prosecute" was covered by the Fifth, Harrington said. The judge agreed with Harrington. Pina did not ask that Ponte be granted immunity.

The consequences of this maneuvering, however, were fourfold:

First, Ponte's claim of the Fifth gave Pina new grounds to be suspicious of Kenny.

Second, in deciding *not* to immunize Ponte, Pina essentially deprived the jury of whatever information Ponte might have actually had about the victims, whether worthwhile or not.

Third, the jury was allowed to believe that Ponte *did* know something of value, and was made suspicious by his refusal to provide it, whatever it was.

And fourth, by his public behavior suggesting that Kenny had in fact taken the Fifth, Pina in effect told the whole world that Kenny had something to hide.

That in turn made Kenny look guilty, at least in the public eye, which in turn further fueled Ponte's determination not to cooperate with Pina.

The day after Ponte's appearance, Pina drove this latter point home even further by telling reporters that the investigation was "targeting"—Pina's word—two suspects. "We're closer than we were before," he said. "There are two suspects in particular that need a lot of work . . .

"It doesn't look like a stranger may have grabbed some-body," he added, an obvious reference to Ponte's supposed relationship with the victims. The *Standard-Times*'s Boyle followed up that remark with the observation that Ponte knew three of the victims, connections that were also pointed out by every other news outlet, and indeed had already been made clear by Pina himself. Pina also made statements that implied Kenny Ponte was a user of illegal drugs—just like the victims. Thus, by the end of winter 1988–89, Kenny Ponte had been publicly identified as a suspect in the most notorious serial murder case in Massa-chusetts since the time of the Boston Strangler.

SPRING 1989

"Human madness is oftentimes a cunning and most feline thing. When you think it fled, it may have but become transfigured into still some subtler form . . ."
—HERMAN MELVILLE, *Moby Dick*

32

A Letter

With the coming of warmer weather, the grim search for more skeletons resumed. Josie the German shepherd from the Connecticut State Police returned. Soon she and Syros were out sniffing along the highways. The police refused to say where the searches were being conducted to keep the media away.

Almost immediately, however, Josie alerted at a spot along Route 140, this one heading southbound toward New Bedford, about midway between the two earlier victims found on the opposite side of the highway. The new skeleton was lodged inside the trees about 25 feet from the shoulder of the road. Syros had searched the area during the winter but had found nothing. Pina now had to admit that Syros had originally been trained to sniff drugs, but guessed that the reason Syros had missed finding the skeleton earlier was because of the cold weather. The skeleton was intact, and a full complement of teeth was recovered.

The next day, the teeth told the tale: the victim was identified as Robin Rhodes.

Hadn't the New Bedford restaurant owner testified that Ponte had been seen with Rhodes? And wasn't Rhodes friendly with Mary Rose and Donald Santos? And hadn't Ponte represented the Santos couple? Pina declined comment, but Ponte's name and his refusal to cooperate with Pina were reiterated in all the news media.

Two days later, two children playing along the side of Route 88, an arterial highway in the southwestern part of the county, discovered an eighth skeleton. The new remains were miles away from either I-195 or Route 140, the places where the first seven victims had been found. But like the previous seven, the latest skeleton was found in brush some 20 or 25 feet off the side of the road. No clothing was recovered, and it certainly appeared that the newest discovery was related to the others.

Pina was electrified by the news. Two weeks earlier he had received an anonymous letter suggesting that the police search the sides of Route 88. The letter writer said she had seen something unusual along that road in the summer of 1988, and believed that a body might be found there. The letter writer added that a copy of her letter was being kept between the pages of a family Bible to prove her authenticity.

This, indeed, was good news: a possible eyewitness to one of the crimes. Pina immediately went public with the existence of the letter, while withholding its details, and asked that the writer come forward to be interviewed.

It appeared that the letter writer *had* seen something suspicious. During the summer of 1988, she had been driving north late at night on Route 88, the writer told Pina and the investigators. As her vehicle accelerated up a long hill, she saw a white pickup truck stopped on the opposite side of the road. A man appeared to be struggling with a woman near the truck. The writer sped past, and as she approached the junction with Highway 6 a few miles north, she saw headlights in the rearview mirror. It looked liked the truck was coming after her.

Near the junction, the pickup overtook the writer; as he drew even on the left, the driver stared hard at her as he passed. The writer stared straight ahead, pretending not to notice the man staring at her. She was frightened, she said later; she didn't want him to know she had seen anything. After a few seconds, the white pickup truck pulled ahead, and the letter writer soon lost sight of it.

The letter, Pina said, was "right on the money." The place where the writer had seen the man and woman struggling was almost exactly where the latest skeleton had been found. But the bad news was, the letter writer never looked directly at the face of the driver, and thus was unable to provide a good description. Nor could she recall a license plate. Even more frustrating, the letter writer was unable to recall what the struggling woman looked like.

But two days later, the skeleton found by the side of Route 88 was identified as that of Mary Rose Santos.

Pina was meanwhile preparing for a new round of witnesses before the grand jury. He took time out to reflect on the identification of Mary Rose, and its possible significance. "This is getting to be a morbid ritual," he said, as he opened a press conference to announce Mary Rose's identification.

On reflection, Pina added, it now appeared that with Mary Rose the killer had shifted his pattern. The first three victims—Robin Rhodes, Debroh McConnell, and Debbie Medeiros—had been placed along Route 140 north toward Freetown, Taunton, and Boston, Pina said.

Then, after Debbie Medeiros had been found on July 2 along Route 140, the killer shifted west to I-195 with Nancy Paiva, Deborah DeMello, Mary Rose on Route 88, and then Dawn Mendes back on I-195. Police, said Pina, were checking news reports to see whether Debbie Medeiros's discovery had been publicized anywhere outside of the New Bedford vicinity. If only New Bedford residents had been made aware of the discovery of Debbie Medeiros, that might be inferential evidence that the killer had to be a local reader of the *Standard-Times*.

It was a good try, but it didn't stand up to scrutiny. For one thing, the first victim was, according to Pina's theory, probably Rochelle Clifford, and *her* skeleton had been found not only west of Route 140 and New Bedford via I-195, but down two lonely roads as well.

That, of course, meant the killer had already shifted his "pattern," even before any of the victims were discovered. And why would the killer have returned to I-195 with Dawn Mendes's body in early September 1988 after Nancy's Paiva's skeleton was discovered on July 30, if he

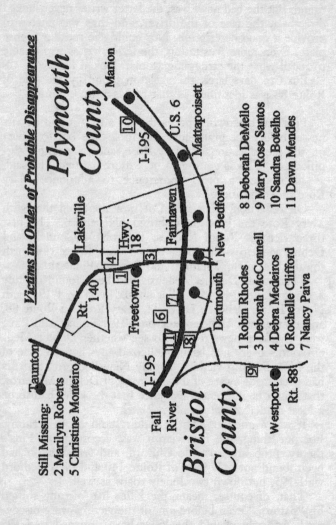

Victims in Order of Probable Disappearance

Plymouth County

Bristol County

Still Missing:
2 Marilyn Roberts
5 Christine Monteiro

1 Robin Rhodes
3 Deborah McConnell
4 Debra Medeiros
6 Rochelle Clifford
7 Nancy Paiva

8 Deborah DeMello
9 Mary Rose Santos
10 Sandra Botelho
11 Dawn Mendes

Taunton

Lakeville

Marion

Rt. 140

Hwy. 18

I-195

U.S. 6

Freetown

Fairhaven

Mattapoisett

Dartmouth

New Bedford

I-195

Fall River

Westport

Rt. 88

was so concerned about the possibility of detection of his "pattern"?

But Pina's reference to a local reader only lent support to his previously expressed opinion that the killer was a local person—someone like Kenny Ponte, for example.

33

Dealing Days

As Pina and his investigators prepped for the next session of the grand jury, a steady stream of female convicts paraded out of MCIs Framingham and Lancaster on the pilgrimage to the Bristol district attorney's office. The word spread throughout the prison dormitories that the Bristol D.A.'s shop window was open for business, and soon the authorities were bombarded with tales of drugs, sex, perversion, and violence, at least some of it true.

Among the most popular targets in the hit parade was Tony DeGrazia. By late March, nearly everyone in the two prisons and many of the people on the street had heard of the police interest in Tony, also known as the guy with the Flat Nose. The word spread quickly that if you wanted to make a deal with the district attorney, all you had to do was give a little. Flat Nose was a safe bet; after all, when the cops asked who had attacked you, all you had to do is look for the picture of the guy with the smashed-in nose, and you won the prize. It helped when Tony's picture was the only person in the photo spread with a flat nose.

In truth, while it isn't possible at this point to say with accuracy just how many people Flat Nose had attacked during the years 1986 through 1989, what *was* striking was how similar all the attacks seemed.

In almost every case, the man with the Flat Nose had been driving a dark pickup truck, had been drinking, and

172

came around late at night. After getting a woman into his truck, he asked for fellatio. The woman almost always demanded money first, at which point Flat Nose usually went berserk, screaming, swearing, choking, hitting, threatening with his knife as he proceeded on to vaginal rape. In a few cases Flat Nose cut women with his knife, and in one case knocked out several of his victim's teeth.

Also noticeable was that the level of violence by Flat Nose seemed in direct proportion to the amount of resistance offered by the victim. Those women who were quickly terrorized suffered less than those who struggled. And finally, part of Flat Nose's m.o. (detective talk for *modus operandi*) seemed to include a frantic haste to get away as soon as the rape was over. "Get out of the truck, bitch!" Flat Nose would shout, and then open the door and literally give his victims the boot before zooming off.

But were these stories real? Or were they shared lore, passed from prisoner to prisoner for use by all, once the word circulated that the Bristol D.A. was willing to deal? The very similarities made some of the stories suspect. Worse, from a legal point of view, only two of the attacks had been reported contemporaneously with the events, and in no case was any physical evidence taken—no samples of semen, fingernail scrapings, or blood, for example. In most cases, the physical injuries reported had long healed by the time the victims reported the attacks to the city detectives and the troopers.

The cases thus all hinged on eyewitness identification in darkened locations—by victims who were often tired, under the influence of drugs, and who had rather impeachable credibility to begin with. Despite the sheer volume of cases, any charges against Tony DeGrazia as Flat Nose would be difficult to prove.

But as women rode the circuit between MCIs Framingham and Lancaster, and New Bedford, the stories that circulated grew ever more wild. It wasn't long before some prisoners with nothing to sell but their own desire to make a deal began working their way in on the action.

One of these was a 36-year-old blond woman named Diane Doherty. Years later, trying to piece Diane Doherty's story together remains an exercise in frustration—simply because Diane said so many different things to so many different people, and then had trouble remembering what she'd said, and where and when and to whom, that it's virtually impossible to make all the parts fit together coherently. In literal truth, Diane Doherty was a dizzy blonde.

For one thing, Diane claimed she suffered from narcolepsy, the nervous ailment that literally puts its sufferers to sleep when least expected. For another, Diane claimed—at times—to be the recipient of dreams and visions. For a third, Diane couldn't tell the truth about the Highway Murders because she wasn't anywhere near New Bedford when they were taking place, and she knew nothing about either the victims or the suspects.

Diane and her daughter spent most of 1988 in Arizona along the banks of the Colorado River. On their return to Massachusetts in late 1988, the Highway Murders were just beginning to gain publicity. In early 1989, Diane was sent to jail for some sort of minor offense; she once claimed it was parking tickets, but it appears she was involved in collecting rent on property she did not own.

In any event, by February or so of 1989, Diane was securely lodged in MCI Framingham, listening goggle-eyed as women returned from New Bedford and the relay teams of cops and lawyers talking about murder most foul. Gradually, as February turned into March, some of what the other prisoners were saying about the murders and the police began to seep into Diane's consciousness. The other prisoners were talking about somebody with a flat nose, and about a lawyer—somebody named Kenny Ponte.

Initially, at least, Diane envisioned Kenny Ponte as some sort of blond mastodon, standing over his pathetically if romantically broken victims; it was like a scene from a gothic romance, even if it was about murder. The handsome blond figure of her imagination fascinated Diane, and it wasn't until much later that Diane realized the real Kenny Ponte was neither exceptionally tall, nor blond, nor handsome, but *was* a real person. But by then it was too late, at least for Kenny.

In mid-March, Diane was released from Framingham, and that's when her part of the Highway Murder story really begins, although it was a part that would shift constantly throughout the next year and a half as other events intervened.

34

Triggers

On April 4, a second gaggle of witnesses was flushed before the grand jury, and as before, Pina tried to apply coverage across the board on his three remaining suspects.

Seven witnesses who knew Kenny Ponte were called, including the dentist who had treated Rochelle Clifford. The taxi driver Goldblatt was recalled. Four women who claimed to know Kenny or who had been assaulted by the man with the Flat Nose were brought before the jury as well. Two of the women, in fact, claimed to know *both* Kenny and Flat Nose; like others before them, they swore that they had consumed cocaine with Kenny, and that on entirely separate occasions, Flat Nose had raped them.

One of these women was Adele Leeks, who was one of the few women who knew both Kenny Ponte and Tony DeGrazia.

What the jurors weren't told was that Adele had been located at MCI Framingham, and that within a week after telling investigators about her relationship with Kenny, she was in a halfway house. Later, at the end of the summer, when investigators returned to Adele to get more information, Adele's memory suddenly went south. Troopers were convinced that Adele, having finished her time at the halfway house, recovered from her drug addiction and about to be released, had simply lost interest in cooperating with the investigators.

Whether that was true or not isn't certain; what is true,

however, is that when Pina finally decided to indict Kenny for conspiring to possess drugs, in the spring of 1990, he also indicted Adele, along with Jeanne Kaloshis and Goldblatt.

Among the other witnesses were three friends of Kenny. One, John Rebello, testified that he had once sold cocaine to Kenny. Two others said they saw no evidence of hard drug use on Kenny's part, although one of the pair, Daniel Branco, was himself a convicted drug dealer who had once been represented by Ponte.

Branco, in fact, provided what amounted to comic relief as the second day of testimony concluded. As Branco completed his testimony and rose to exit the jury room, a juror thought he heard a clicking sound coming from Branco's pocket.

"Frisk him," Pina ordered a trooper as Branco left. "Make sure he doesn't have a tape recorder. One of the jurors heard something clicking as he went by."

"This is ridiculous," Branco said as he was led away by officers for a check of his pockets. No recorder was found. "Clicking Witness Frisked," the *Standard-Times* reported. Just as Branco said, it all seemed a little ridiculous.

Outside the jury room, late at night or in the early morning hours, Flat Nose was still marauding the streets. While by day grand jurors heard of his depredations, by night Flat Nose remained unencumbered. Two days before the jury took testimony, Flat Nose attacked two women less than an hour apart. A week later, Flat Nose got yet another woman.

State Troopers Kevin Butler and Lorraine Forrest felt that Flat Nose was in some sort of rape frenzy. To them, Flat Nose appeared to be a very viable suspect in the Highway Murders. After all, he'd threatened numerous women with death; one had told the troopers that Flat Nose had a pair of handcuffs, while another said that Flat Nose had reached for a black rope after he'd attacked her.

Some serial killers, both troopers knew, began taking larger and larger risks just before being caught, as Flat Nose appeared to be doing. Similarly, some serial killers nearing the end of their depredations occasionally descended into a frenzy of increasing violence; judging from the more recent attacks, Flat Nose's violence appeared to be getting worse.

Both troopers believed that Flat Nose had to be Tony DeGrazia. There were simply too many consistencies between the facts of Tony's life as the detectives had developed them, and the string of rapes. Besides, witness after witness had identified Tony from his photograph as the man who had attacked them. The big question was whether Tony was the Highway Murderer, and as the troopers considered that possibility, they were well aware of aspects about Tony's life that seemed to eminently qualify him as the long-sought killer. Forrest was particularly convinced.

In mid-April of 1989, Tony was stopped while driving drunk in Raynham, a small town northwest of New Bedford. He took a poke at the cop and ran off, leaving his truck behind. The truck's registration yielded Tony's name and address. The Raynham police ran his name through the computer and discovered that Tony had three times been arrested in the early 1980s on sexual assault charges—once in 1982 when he was accused of picking up two female hitchhikers in downtown New Bedford and raping one of them in the Freetown forest. At his arraignment that year the mother of one of the girls rushed across the courtroom and slugged Tony in the face—in the nose, of all places. Six months later Tony was acquitted of the rape charge when Kathy Scanlon testified that he had been with her just before the attack.

On the drunk driving night in April 1989, the police brought a search dog to the area, and several hours later Tony was found hiding in the woods nearby. The Raynham police told Tony that with his track record, he looked like he'd be a good candidate as the Highway Murderer, which by then had received massive publicity. The Raynham police were unaware of the information that had already been collected on Tony by the state troopers and their assisting detectives in New Bedford.

Tony denied any knowledge of prostitutes or the Highway Murders, and the following day bailed out of jail on the drunk driving and assault charges. But the talk with the police stuck with Tony. A few days later, Tony was

visiting with his mother, who had taken possession of his
truck to prevent Tony from driving drunk again.

"You know, Mom," Tony said, "they're looking at me
as a suspect in the Highway murders."

"Come on, Tony," said his mother. She thought Tony
was being melodramatic. He wasn't.

In investigating Tony, the two state troopers learned
what had long been common knowledge in Freetown,
where Tony lived. Tony, it appeared, had told his closest
friends that as a child he had been physically abused by
his mother. His mother hated him, for some reason, Tony
told the Scanlons and others. While still a toddler, she
habitually reached into Tony's crib to grab him painfully
by the nose. That was one reason why Tony's nose was
so disfigured. Tony also said that his mother often reached
into the crib to pull his arm, twisting it so badly that its
development was arrested. When he wet the bed, his
mother hung the bedsheet out the window, thus advertising Tony's embarrassment to the world at large. Tony's
mother and father had divorced over issues of sexual fidel-
ity, and a nasty court case ensued in which Tony's father
accused Tony's mother of vicious abuse of Tony.

From the outside, then, it appeared to the troopers that
Tony might have had deep-seated psychological reasons
for killing women. From others in Freetown, namely at
the bars and taverns Tony frequented, it appeared that
Tony had occasionally expressed hostility toward
prostitutes.

As Butler and Forrest assembled more and more information about Tony's recent history, still other potential
homicidal triggers popped up: Tony had apparently been
fired from a job in April 1988, when the murders first
began; Kathy Scanlon had first been introduced to her new
boyfriend in that same month; Tony's birthday was in late
May, just about the time that victims Christine Monteiro
and Debbie Medeiros had last been seen; Tony had become engaged to Kathy on July 3 (Kathy's birthday) just
four days before Nancy Paiva was last seen; Tony had
allegedly started using cocaine in late July or August of
1988; Kathy spent every other weekend that summer

working at a nearby hospital; Tony broke up with Kathy just about the time that Dawn Mendes had disappeared. And hadn't one woman told detectives that the last time she'd seen Dawn, she was getting into a pickup truck? Hadn't Tony owned a succession of pickup trucks? And finally, the detectives knew that Tony had written a check to Sandra Botelho. That clearly put Tony in contact with Sandy, who was still missing.

There was only one thing to do, the detectives decided: Tony had to be confronted. Plans were made to search Tony's house and trucks for evidence that might tie him to the crimes. Meanwhile, Tony would be brought in for questioning.

On the afternoon of April 19, 1989, Butler and Forrest drove to Tony's small house on Long Pond in Freetown and asked him to accompany them to the district attorney's office to answer questions about the Highway Murders. Tony agreed to go voluntarily. He had nothing to hide, he claimed. On the way into the office, Tony insisted that he had never picked up a prostitute.

35
Admissions

Shortly after 6 P.M., while Trooper Kenneth Martin was collecting most of Tony's clothes and samples from his carpets, Tony began answering questions from Forrest and Butler.

This interview was extraordinary in that it apparently was not tape-recorded—virtually a requirement for suspects in serial murders, according to experts. It appears that Butler took extensive notes, however, notes that contain lengthy verbatim statements attributed to Tony. Later, however, Tony was to deny that he had said some of the things Butler claimed he said, which is one of the reasons why it's advisable to record such statements.

After agreeing to waive his rights to a lawyer, Tony was asked again whether he had ever picked up a prostitute. Now Tony backtracked: he had picked one up once, he said, a long time ago.

But after Butler and Forrest told him that they'd received information from at least 17 women that Tony had assaulted them while they were working as prostitutes, Tony backtracked a bit further and admitted that he had picked up several women more than a year earlier. Sometimes women in Weld Square told him he looked familiar, and accused him of assaulting them in the past, Tony said, but it was a case of mistaken identity. When Butler and Forrest suggested that Tony sometimes suffered blackouts while drinking, Tony denied it.

Now the two detectives began dealing photographs in Tony's direction. Tony looked at the first three pictures and said the women didn't look familiar to him. He seemed defensive about being accused of consorting with prostitutes.

"I know nothing about these whores on the street," Tony said, according to Butler's report. "I don't want to have anything to do with these girls. These girls have come up to me and said, 'You're the guy, you're the guy,' and I have to physically put them out of the truck." Then Tony put the blame on the police.

"Why don't the police get these girls off the streets?" he asked. "They are hurting people. Now everyone thinks I killed them and I didn't. These girls are the scum of the earth. I go out with other girls all the time and they don't accuse me of things. I'm never in New Bedford. I'm never in Weld Square."

Tony did not explain why "everyone" thought he had killed the Highway Murder victims, and Butler didn't ask. Instead Butler wanted to know, if Tony never went to Weld Square, why did so many women there keep identifying him? It was, Tony again insisted, because someone else who looked like him was often in Weld Square.

Butler kept dealing Tony photographs. As he looked at each one, Tony retreated a bit on his story. "I could have picked them up, but I don't remember them," he said. "I have picked up girls I don't remember. These girls are such scumbags that I don't want anything to do with them." When several of the rape allegations were read to Tony, he remarked that "it seems like the same story over and over again."

After more discussion, Tony admitted picking up prostitutes and taking them to parking lots and other places. But Tony tried to explain: sometimes he felt the urge to pick up a woman, but after looking more closely at her, thought better of it. Then Tony wanted them to leave his truck, but the woman wanted money for her time. Tony refused to pay, and a fight ensued. Or, he admitted, on some occasions, the women took his money and bolted from the truck; thus Tony felt that not paying others but having sex with them was fair play. Usually he had been drinking when he picked up women, Tony admitted.

Still more pictures were produced, and Tony backtracked even more. "I've seen her before," he said, when shown a picture of a woman who was friends with Dawn Mendes. "I may have picked her up." But he had certainly never pulled a knife on anyone, he insisted. He claimed he didn't even have any knives, except for kitchen knives.

When the detectives showed him a picture of Adele Leeks, Tony seemed to be getting tired of the game.

"I could have picked up any of these girls," he said, "and not remembered them. The way I feel about them, I don't know why they are there in the first place with the laws we have. I don't remember them because I don't respect them. They are not people I want to be associated with.

"You have a couple of drinks, you get horny, sometimes it happens. You just stop, get a blow job, and leave. Then I forget about them. As time goes on, I put them out of my mind. I don't want to be associated with the scum of the earth. I know plenty of nice girls. I don't want to get sick over doing something sick. It's immoral. It's not right. I'm disgusted I picked them up."

Late in the interview, Tony was asked whether he had been abused as a child.

According to Butler, Tony became very emotional. "How do you think I got this?" he asked, pointing to his left arm. Butler followed this up.

"When asked if he has any hate for women as a result of his abuse," Butler wrote, "DeGrazia stated that he has talked to a priest about his feelings, and the priest told him he has 'pent up' problems.

"When asked if he hated his mother, DeGrazia said he would rather not think about it because she is the only mother he has."

Tony started crying. Finally he burst out, "Why don't you guys just get rid of these people? I don't want them near me. I always ask to be forgiven for doing something so low (as picking up prostitutes, Butler noted parenthetically). I think I've scared some of these girls when I've been drinking, but I didn't rape them."

More pictures followed, and Tony acknowledged that some of the women seemed familiar, and said that with one, he'd got into a fight with her in his truck.

Now Butler and Forrest moved in. Tony was shown pictures of each of the murder victims, but the detectives didn't tell him the new photos were of women who were dead. They wanted to gauge his reactions to the photos. Asked if he'd ever picked up Dawn Mendes, Tony said, "I can't say no, I can't say yes." Tony admitted it was possible, but couldn't remember when.

Tony also thought that Debbie Medeiros looked familiar. Asked if it was true he had once chased Debbie De-Mello down the street, Tony denied it. He'd never seen Mary Rose Santos, he said. The same was true with Rochelle Clifford, Nancy Paiva, and Robin Rhodes. He couldn't remember Christine Monteiro, and said he didn't think he would have picked up Debroh McConnell. "She would scare me," he said. Sandy Botelho looked familiar, Tony said, but he didn't know whether he'd ever picked her up.

Now the detectives told Tony that each of the last ten photos were of women who were dead. Tony insisted he had never killed anyone, but admitted that he might have assaulted some women, but only to get them out of his truck.

Well, said the detectives, wasn't it possible that he had accidently killed someone during one of these fights? And wasn't it possible that Tony had blacked out, and that's why he couldn't remember?

Tony now became concerned about being arrested and prosecuted. "Please don't send me to court," he said. "I'll get help." When Tony was asked what sort of help he needed, he got confused. "They're the ones that need help," he said, referring to the prostitutes. "I'm sorry. I know I've screwed up, but I didn't go dragging anyone off into the woods."

The detectives returned to Tony's childhood abuse, but Tony was reluctant to talk about it. He explained that when he was little "his mother used to twist his nose, and twist his arm because he wet the bed," Butler wrote. "He was reluctant to discuss the abuse in detail, and was more concerned about who might have told us that his mother abused him than with the abuse itself. He was extremely worried about who might know that he was abused by his mother."

Tony again denied killing anyone. "If I killed one person," he said, "the next person would be me. My guilt feelings would kill me."

When he was asked why anyone might kill the women, Tony offered a suggestion: maybe, he said, someone had gotten AIDS from a prostitute. "He assured us," Butler wrote, "that he did not have AIDS."

"I have nothing to do with the girls who have been found dead," Tony added. "I'm not a madman. I get scared. I get nervous. These girls are full of diseases and needle marks. They look good until you see them up close."

Tony now agreed to take a lie detector test about the murders, but refused one on the rapes. An appointment was set for the following Monday.

Around 11 that night, Jose Gonsalves returned to the office from Tony's mother's house in Taunton, where he and Maryann Dill had gone to retrieve Tony's truck. The truck was seen as a potential repository of trace evidence, and the troopers hoped that any hairs, fibers, or bloodstains found in the truck might link Tony to the murders. But first Gonsalves wanted to ask Tony some questions.

Gonsalves asked Tony about the check he'd written to Sandy Botelho. At first Tony said he'd given the money to Sandy because she'd been crying about her children. Then Tony admitted he'd given her the money for oral sex.

Now Gonsalves asked whether the police would find any blood in Tony's truck. Tony assured them they would not. Although he said nothing to Tony, Gonsalves was already pretty sure that wasn't true. It appeared that there was a large bloodstain on the passenger seat of Tony's truck, and spatters in several other places as well.

At quarter to one in the morning, Tony finally asked to be allowed to go home. Forrest and Butler drove him back to his house, and then explained to Tony that his truck and much of his clothing had been seized for examination. Then the detectives said they wanted the clothing that Tony was *wearing*, too. Tony literally gave the detectives the shirt off his back. Butler and Forrest told Tony they'd see him again the following Monday for the lie detector test.

But when Monday rolled around, Tony didn't show. Instead, he'd hired a lawyer: Eddie Harrington, the former mayor of New Bedford, and Joe Harrington's brother. But that was the same day another public works crew, clearing brush and trash along the north side of I-195 some eight miles *east* of New Bedford, discovered the remains of a ninth presumed victim of the Highway Murderer.

── 36 ──

Spies Like Us

Like several of the earlier victims, the latest discovery was of a female skeleton without clothes. The remains appeared to have been folded in the fetal position. The discovery seemed identical to the earlier eight, at least in the assessment of Gonsalves, Dill, and forensic expert Kenneth Martin. But there was one difference: the newest remains had been found in another county, Plymouth County, and that meant there would be another district attorney, not Ron Pina, in charge of the investigation.

Three days after the discovery, the remains were identified as those of Sandy Botelho. Sandy's family was devastated by the news. Soon the news media was camped on the Botelho doorstep. Sandy's father, Joseph Botelho, said he intended to leave New Bedford. "New Bedford," he told the *Standard-Times*'s Boyle, "is one of those cities that hurts everybody. It's a city of hurt."

Now began a rather strange dance between the offices of Ron Pina and Plymouth County District Attorney William O'Malley. Legally, Botelho's murder was the responsibility of O'Malley. But Pina and his people had done virtually all of the work investigating the earlier eight homicides. It was only logical to allow them to continue with the latest case, since it appeared that the same person or persons were responsible for all nine. But the law wasn't always logical.

187

A second jurisdictional complication developed because Botelho's remains had been found inside the boundary line of the township of Marion. Marion was about as far away from New Bedford as Beverly Hills is from Brooklyn, culturally and economically speaking. Marion, in fact, is one of the wealthiest cities in the entire state of Massachusetts. What on earth was the killer doing in Marion? That was what Marion Detective John Torres wanted to know, and because the remains had been found on his turf, he had every legal right to try to find out. And with Plymouth County D.A. O'Malley sensitive to the interests of one of his wealthiest constituencies, it wasn't going to be easy for Pina and his people to keep Torres and O'Malley out of the investigation—at least, that's what Torres thought. He hadn't counted on Pina's intense interest in the case.

Later, Detective Torres recalled that he quickly began having real trouble getting information about the murders from the Bristol County people.

"Well," he said, "there was never a problem with sharing *our* information, it was the problem of obtaining *their* information." Part of this bottleneck occurred because two different counties were now involved in the investigation, along with two different district attorneys, and two different CPAC units. When CPAC investigators from Plymouth County tried to find out what had been done in the investigation so far, they were rebuffed by their counterparts in Bristol County.

According to Torres and former Plymouth CPAC Sergeant Nelson Ostiguy, the Plymouth contingent was told that the Bristol troopers couldn't give them certain kinds of information without Pina's prior approval. That in turn created embarrassment and some friction among the state police of both counties, who worked for the same organization.

This was an eye-opener for Torres, who was working on his very first homicide investigation. Murder, of course, was a rarity in a place like Marion.

"I could not believe that guys on the same job were doing this to one another, you know what I mean?" Torres said later. "They work on the same job ... But I think that the politics of it all screwed it up, and had the politics not been involved, had the cops been allowed to work and to do what they get paid to do, I think that there's a good possibility the investigation would have gone further than it did."

The facts unearthed by the investigation became a sort of currency in a subterranean competition between the investigators and their nominal bosses, the district attorneys, Torres concluded. "It was almost like, 'you can't have my marbles, because I have more marbles than you and I wanna win the game,'" he said.

Eventually Ostiguy, Torres, and others in the Plymouth CPAC group found themselves acting like spies—conducting secret rendezvous in parking lots with the Bristol County people, who slipped them information but begged them not to say where it came from. But the flow of information was haphazard and interruptible at any time. After several weeks, Torres and Ostiguy went to O'Malley to complain. O'Malley said he'd see what he could do.

On the first of May, another round of witnesses was brought before the special grand jury. Most of them were people who had worked at three taverns in New Bedford, including the Quarterdeck Lounge and the Town Tavern. Somewhat surprisingly, little of this testimony was subsequently leaked, although it may contain some of the most significant information developed by the jury, because of the frequent presence in the taverns by many of the victims. Still, the leakage of other information from the closed-door hearings continued to be remarkable.

Pina's spokesman Jim Martin, in fact, was increasingly upset by the leaks. It was part of Martin's job to keep track of virtually everything published or said about the investigation, and the burgeoning leaks were driving him to distraction. The news media always knew when the grand jury was in session, and planted themselves right outside the jury's door. As soon as a witness emerged, they would be bombarded with questions.

"How many courthouses have you gone into where the press can stand right outside of the judge's lobby?" Martin asked, later. "I mean, the judge can't even go into the courtroom without walking by the reporters. It's absurd to have that."

And Veary, too, was upset with the situation.

"There were a lot of people," Pina's chief deputy recalled, "who, for whatever reason, perhaps this was their moment in the sun, came in and talked, and gave press conferences moments later, despite all our efforts to try to respect the secrecy that's supposed to surround grand jury proceedings.

"We had people conducting press conferences and occasionally talking about everything that they said; occasionally talking about things they didn't say; occasionally embellishing their stories; occasionally, just coming up with something from Mars and then, of course, pontificating or giving their own opinions as to who the real culprit was. It was an amazing situation."

Veary remonstrated with Pina about the problem, but Pina didn't seem that concerned. Although Pina advised witnesses not to talk to the news media, he also made it clear that nothing would happen to them if they did. Indeed, the law gave Pina no power to keep the witnesses quiet.

Thus, on the afternoon of May 2, Margaret "Peggy" Medeiros emerged onto the courthouse steps after testifying, and in front of a national television audience, accused Tony DeGrazia of being the Highway Murderer.

This may in fact have been Peggy's moment in the sun, as Veary would have put it. Peggy told the astonished reporters that the investigators had told *her* that Tony was the killer, when in fact, Peggy had just told the investigators that *she* thought Tony had committed the murders. Peggy added some details:

"He told me, 'I'm going to do to you what I did to the other bitches,'" Peggy said. Pina had showed her Tony's picture in the grand jury, she added. "You don't forget that face when someone tries to kill you."

Reporters for the *Standard-Times* rushed back to their office and dug into their files, unearthing old stories about Tony's previous arrests, including the three for sexual assault in the early 1980s. Whether because Peggy lacked

Pina's credibility, or because of growing doubts about the
propriety of naming names, the paper at first withheld
Tony's identity.

That lasted for just a day, however; on May 4, 1989, a
warrant for Tony's arrest was issued, and the search war-
rants against Tony's house and truck were released. Now
Tony's name, as well as his alleged crimes, were known
to everyone. The investigators, reporters noted, had recovered samples of blood from the truck, and one victim had
told police she had seen a black rope under the seat. The
detectives had been watching Tony for two weeks, the
papers reported.

In East Freetown, Tony first heard of all this when a
horde of reporters began banging on his front door. He
was astonished to find himself at the center of their frantic interest.

"I didn't do anything," he said. "I'm guilty until I've
proved myself innocent." He claimed the police were rail-
roading him. "I've been advised by my lawyer not to talk
to the media. I don't want my name in the paper, people
believe what they read in the paper. I'm confused, I don't
know what to do." Then he shut himself inside and called
his mother.

In Dartmouth and in Taunton, Tony's family rallied
around him. "Tony has been through hell," said his father,
a Dartmouth dairy farmer. He added that police had offered Tony a lie detector test but that Eddie Harrington
had advised him against it. At the time, that was probably
the wrong thing to say.

37

Video Fun

Tony turned himself in on the following day and immediately pleaded innocent to any of the rapes and assaults. Based on several of Tony's statements made the night they interviewed him, some troopers thought that Tony was a prospective suicide. As a result, a psychiatrist was appointed to assess Tony's mental state. The doctor concluded that Tony was extremely depressed, that he seemed to exhibit signs of at least two personalities, that he suffered from flashbacks of childhood abuse, and that he was a danger to himself, or possibly others.

Now all the stories about Tony and his mother were spread across the front page and on television. Tony was held under a suicide watch at the county jail, with bail set at $75,000. Trooper Martin wanted to take samples of Tony's hair and saliva. Tony had no objection, but his lawyer did. A new hearing was set to determine whether Pina had grounds to take the samples.

While Tony waited in jail for this hearing, two other odd events unfolded. A team of ten drug detectives smashed in the front door of the apartment occupied by Donald Santos, the grieving husband of Mary Rose, and there arrested four women and seized a thousand dollars' worth of cocaine. Santos wasn't present at the time, but a warrant was issued for his arrest.

Two days after that, the city of New Bedford was named as an All-American City, a prestigious designation sought by municipalities all over the country. While the mayor was inviting the whole city to attend a parade and celebration, Donald Santos appeared in court to claim innocence of charges of cocaine possession with intent to distribute it. Santos also told reporters that he thought police no longer believed his story about the night he'd left Mary Rose at the Quarterdeck. He'd had no idea his apartment was being used to distribute coke, Santos said.

In mid-May, the simmering rivalry between Pina and Plymouth County District Attorney William O'Malley suddenly lurched into public view. Where Pina had long been quoted as saying there were "three or four" suspects in the murders, now O'Malley's office was saying there might be as many as a dozen. That clearly implied that Pina and his investigation had overlooked some possible suspects—about nine, to be exact.

Talk also circulated widely that Pina's investigators refused to share information with the Plymouth people, or even to invite them to coordination meetings. As a result, the Plymouth County detectives had been sneaking into New Bedford to investigate on their own. Obviously, it appeared, communications between the two offices had severely broken down.

Pina tried to defuse the embarrassment. He told reporters he intended to visit O'Malley at his home, where the Plymouth district attorney was recuperating from a severe hip injury, to iron out any differences. For his part, O'Malley acknowledged that there were some bitter feelings between the two offices, but seemed to put the blame more on the troopers in each CPAC, rather than on Pina himself.

"They're all very capable investigators," O'Malley said, "and they don't all like each other. There's not much you can do about it." Part of the problem, O'Malley intimated, had to do with lingering bitterness from the 1982 election. Some of the troopers Pina had evicted from his office in that year had later wound up working for the Plymouth County CPAC—among them Nelson Ostiguy—and bad blood remained.

Then Jim Martin, Pina's spokesman, muddied the waters further by telling reporters that some of the Bristol County people distrusted the Plymouth County people because they were prone to leak to the press. Some reporters thought this claim, made with a straight face, had to be the howler of the year, given the leaks that had already gushed from Pina's own office in the preceding months.

Pressed for examples, Martin said he was referring to a Marion detective—Torres was the only detective Marion had—who had made an offhand remark to a reporter about the position of the last skeleton. That was confidential information, Martin said sternly, and shouldn't have been discussed.

Asked to comment on Martin's inference that he was not to be trusted, Torres ignited and demanded a public statement from Martin clearing him of any wrongdoing. A correction followed in both papers within a day or so. Martin apologized to Torres personally, but Torres was still furious.

In the midst of this flap, a new uproar unfolded when the ever-eager search dog Syros, working the sides of I-195 with Torres and a state trooper, alerted one day at a possible new body site.

The trooper put the report of Syros's reaction on the troopers' radio network, where it was picked up by the news media, who immediately flocked to the scene. One television editor broke into regular programming to report that a new body had been found. But Syros had struck out again: instead, on further investigation, it appeared that all Syros had sniffed out was an abandoned cache of ammonia-containing dirty diapers.

As May turned into June, Pina found himself increasingly frustrated. The overtime budget had run out again, and this time the troopers had publicly announced they wouldn't work any overtime without getting overtime pay. While Pina gave political cover to the troopers, noting that most of the people the investigators needed to talk to could only be found in the wee hours, inwardly he fumed.

It seemed to him that the troopers were repeatedly getting bogged down; and, he noticed, it was becoming harder and harder to get them to do what *he* wanted them to do. It wasn't that they overtly refused, he thought, it was just that certain tasks never seemed to be accomplished, no matter how much he asked that they be done.

Tony DeGrazia had been sent to a secure mental hospital for an extended examination. Tony's blood, hair, and saliva, along with a massive amount of clothing, dirt, hairs, and fibers found in his truck and his house, had been dispatched to the FBI's forensic laboratory in Washington, where it was slated to be compared with similar samples recovered from the skeletal sites, as well as with control samples taken from Tony's alleged victims.

But this examination was a painstaking, time-consuming process. First, the samples had to be collected from the questioned items—like Tony's clothes—and then they had to be microscopically compared with the known samples, including the materials taken from the skeletal sites. Although the FBI gave top priority to the Bristol County samples, it would be several months before anything could be definitively established.

Meanwhile, the stories purveyed by the MCI prisoners continued to roll in. Gonsalves and Dill continued to assemble information about James Baker, the Rhode Island mechanic. Baker appeared to be a mixed bag, with some women insisting that he was not a violent person at all, but with others swearing that he was both mean and dangerous. Some said he once stalked Sandra Botelho, and others said he had picked up a young woman in 1987 who had been found dead two days later. The tale about the identification papers of two victims being seen at Baker's house was reprised, although by now Gonsalves and Dill were certain that was bogus information dreamed up on the prison grapevine.

At the end of May, the troopers searched Baker's car, with his permission, and vacuumed the interior for any hairs and fibers. Those samples were shipped to the FBI, along with the usual complement of Baker's own hair, saliva, and blood.

And although the bail for Neil Anderson had been sharply reduced—indicating he probably wasn't a viable suspect in the crimes—information about the former fish

cutter continued to come in. A motorist told Torres and
the Plymouth County CPAC people that she'd seen a man
driving a pickup truck pull off I-195, get out of the truck,
and carry what looked like a rug into the woods. The
motorist had noted the description of the vehicle and a
part of the license plate, and when Torres checked, the
information seemed to match Anderson. Although Anderson had not been tied to the crimes by forensic evidence,
here was a new possible link, so investigators decided to
see if any more information could be developed.

In mid-June, Pina reconvened the grand jury for more
testimony. This time about a dozen witnesses were called,
and almost all of them were then reinterviewed by reporters after they left the jury room. A taxi driver told how
he'd once taken Tony DeGrazia to Weld Square in the
early morning hours, an excursion Tony later told the
driver never to conduct for him again, even if Tony offered him $1,000. A New Bedford furniture store owner
testified that he hired Kenny Ponte to collect on bad debts,
and that his store owned a white pickup truck.

On the second day, James Baker himself testified for
just over four hours. One Weld Square woman was
brought into the jury room in handcuffs, took one look at
Baker, and said, "That's him, get me out of here."

But was any of this testimony pertinent, or even truth-
ful? While the grand jury process might have worked in
the Big Dan's case—when a known crime occurred on a
specific date at a specific location, with identifiable witnesses—it wasn't necessarily effective or reliable in a case
where no one could say for sure when a victim was last
seen, or where, or by whom.

The wobbly nature of the testimony was never more
obvious than the offhand remark by one witness, a woman
familiar with Weld Square, that she knew of a pornographic videotape featuring eight of the victims, and star-
ring dogs and a pig. The tape, said the woman, had been
directed by Kenny Ponte.

Where was the tape? The woman told the jury that
she'd buried the tape in her mother's backyard.

Pina was nearly overcome with excitement. He rounded

up several troopers and rushed over to the address. He
was thinking, *This is it! In half an hour, it's going to be all
over* ... Soon the troopers were digging up the backyard
at the place where the woman said she'd buried the tape.
There was no tape.

Investigators rushed back to the jail to interview the
woman again. What side of the yard did you dig on? the
woman asked. Oh, she said, that's your problem, you dug
up the wrong side of the yard.

Back to the address, and more digging. Now the opposite side of the yard was attacked with shovels. Still no
video. The woman's mother kept shaking her head. I told
you, she said; I told you my daughter is an accomplished
liar ...

The sweaty troopers looked at each other and rolled
their eyes. Pina's excitement now gave way to frustration.
He didn't want to let go of the videotape story. He talked
to the woman once more, and this time the woman suggested that a second woman had stolen the tape in order
to blackmail Kenny Ponte!

Attracted by all the activity, reporters asked Pina what
was going on. The investigation, Pina told them, could be
over very soon if only the troopers and the city detectives
could confirm some new information. And in a front page
story published the following day, the *Standard-Times*'s
Boyle reported: "The district attorney hopes to indict the
highway killer in about a month if information given to
the grand jury probing the slayings pans out."

"If it pans out," Pina said, "then I think we're very
close to a situation where we can be in an indictment
stage. People have said some things to us that I hope are
true. If they (aren't true), we're back to the grinder.

"We've gotten some very good information, if it's for
real," he continued. "I'm encouraged by that, more so
than I have been in the past." Did Pina still want to talk
to Kenny Ponte? "Absolutely, at some point in life."

Later, Pina looked back on the videotape episode as
one of the worst moments of the whole experience.

"It was all kinds of crazy," he recalled. "You're dealing
with people who dealt with the drug world, who dealt with
the prostitution worlds, so you were into everything. I

mean, the space cadets were here too, you might as well check that out.

"What got me going (on the videotape) is, they said, 'If you go to the place *right now*, you'll get it,' so we went. I can't believe it . . ."

But Pina wasn't done with wild stories—not by a long shot.

38

"I Took Them"

By the end of June, the troubles between the district attorney and his state police contingent were worse than ever. The videotape fiasco had embarrassed everyone, especially when the woman who had supposedly stolen the tape swore she didn't know what the first woman was talking about, and then told reporters that everyone knew the woman who had first told the story was a wild fabricator.

Pina's frustration with the troopers had grown to nearly unmanageable proportions. The troopers still refused to work overtime without overtime pay, and that meant witnesses who could not be interviewed. Worse, Pina felt absolutely in the dark about what the troopers had so far discovered. His only source of information was the Tuesday "group therapy sessions"—the meetings that Pina thought were aimless and meandering. Suspects, victims, and witnesses would be discussed, and Pina would ask how someone knew something that had been asserted as a fact or a possibility.

"Someone would say," he recalled, " 'Well, it's in this report,' and I'd say, 'What report?' " The troopers' reports were not routed to Pina, but to the state police bureaucracy in Boston.

"They go to the colonel in Boston," Pina said. "The sergeant gets a copy. But Colonel Wonderful, it's directed to him from Trooper So-and-So. It goes into space. It's beamed off to Boston somewhere . . . how the hell it gets there, don't ask me. The sergeant gets a copy of it, okay, but I don't get one, and somewhere, I guess, the sergeant's got 'em in boxes. (But as for what's) in Boston, I never see what's up there. I would love to see where all those reports go, because I'm sure they don't read them."

Pina began asking to see all the reports.

"And I know they collect reams of data and they had, and probably still do, files and files of reports. I'd say they're down there and they'd say, 'Oh yeah, we got 'em in that drawer.' What are they doing there—can I see them? 'Oh, we haven't had a chance to get to them.' This is from the beginning of the investigation."

In late June, Pina boiled over. "They'd had reams of interviews they had done. They'd forgotten all those interviews, right after the first one. They couldn't remember if they'd met this woman, or that.

"They'd say, 'I think we did an interview with that person.' And they'd look at each other, and one would say, 'Yeah, I think so.' It was just two people talking to each other . . . and they had it all, it was right there in that filing cabinet. And I'd say, 'Where do I find it, let me look, I wanna read it myself,' I'm that way. And frankly, in all fairness to them, they didn't *know* what was in those boxes and what was in those filing cabinets."

So Pina took the files. "I physically went out and took them," he said. He went down to the troopers' floor in his office, picked up the file cabinets, and carried them out. The troopers were not happy.

As the summer of 1989 wore on, Pina decided it was absolutely critical to get control of the information that had been collected so far. He decided to computerize the files he'd take from the troopers. He turned to a Raynham police captain, Louie Pacheco, who was a computer buff, and also one of the prime movers in the Bristol County Drug Task Force. Pacheco looked around and found some text-based software that ran on a microcomputer. Now the problem was getting the information loaded into the computer.

As it happened, Pina's office had a number of summer interns—law students, mostly, who worked for low wages to gain experience. Pina decided to put the interns to work on the murder case.

"I had these summer interns," Pina said later, "and I said, 'What are we doing for the summer? Instead of doing legal research, you're going to be going into those files, you're gonna read 'em, you're gonna put 'em on that terminal.' Louie (Pacheco) was helping them put them on the terminal."

The troopers didn't like this at all, according to Pina. They started chiding Pacheco and the interns for wasting time. Relations deteriorated even further. "And they were bullshitting," Pina said. "They were bullshitting Louie, they were bullshitting the summer interns, because we violated their space. (But) what I wanted to do was get that information into a usable form. Now, if I have to ask questions, maybe there's somebody's name on there that might have the answer."

But the computer, of course, was only as good as the information that was put into it. And in the end, the answers it gave were a product of the questions that were asked; no one has yet designed a computer that can think, a point that the troopers made among themselves.

SUMMER AND FALL 1989

"Nor did wild rumors of all sorts fail to exaggerate, and still the more horrify the true histories of these deadly encounters. For not only do fabulous rumors naturally grow out of the very body of all surprising terrible events, but . . ."

—HERMAN MELVILLE, *Moby Dick*

39

Positive Thoughts

As the summer following the murders wore on, the relations between Pina and the troopers grew even worse.

"At that time," Pina said later, "there was some dissension going on in the office. And part of the dissension was that I had pretty much, more or less, taken it away from Jose (Gonsalves) and Mary Ann (Dill).

"They were burnt out, as far as I was concerned. I wasn't getting information, I was asking for things to be done that weren't getting done, I was not pleased with their production or their lack of production. And it was spinning my wheels. I felt like, 'What are you doing?' and I couldn't get any answer.

"So there was a real gap there at that point. They weren't exactly the people I was relying on. I was relying more on Lou Pacheco and the drug guys to get a fresh view of this thing.

"Not that I was replacing them, they were all coming in, but I wasn't getting a fresh view, and so as this thing developed, as the information came in, Jose and Maryann had their noses really bent out of shape, and I could see them dragging their feet.

"When I'd ask them to just check on another witness, it didn't happen. Or they couldn't find her. And somebody would say, 'Oh, I saw her last night.' A local police officer would say, 'She's standing on a Weld Square street corner, (if) you go over there around two o'clock, you'll see her.'

"(But) They couldn't find her; it was that kind of foolishness that was going on. Why? They were resenting the other guys getting involved, I think.

"But in any case, I wasn't getting cooperation at that point. I was getting foot-dragging. So I did shift over to St. Jean, and Paul Boudreau was seeing more of it than Jose and Maryann ..." In fact, Gonsalves and Dill were returned to the office's on-call board, which meant they would be assigned any new, unrelated cases for the first time in nearly a year.

But if Pina and the troopers were feuding, that didn't stop the stories from rolling out of the prisons and the House of Corrections. Late in June, a man who had known Neil Anderson contacted investigators and told them he'd once been riding around out on I-195 with Anderson, and Anderson had acted "odd."

The informant, like many others who had contacted the investigators, had spent time in jail. He said sometime during the summer or fall of 1988, he'd ridden with Anderson out to a rest stop near the Sippican River on I-195 near Wareham, on the road to Cape Cod. At that point, Anderson had walked off into the nearby woods by himself for about 15 minutes.

Nothing was said, according to Anderson's companion; but then Anderson had returned to the truck, left again by himself for five minutes, and came back once more. Anderson got back into his pickup truck—so did the companion—and together the pair drove south to Route 6, then east to the Weweantic River.

There Anderson once more got out of his truck and looked under the Route 6 bridge crossing the Weweantic River. Then, without a word from Anderson, both men left the area, according to the companion.

Because the Sippican River empties into the Weweantic, which forms the border between Marion and Wareham, some investigators speculated that this behavior showed Anderson first checking for a body in the Sippican near the rest stop, then, failing to find one, driving to the bridge over the Weweantic; the idea was that Anderson might have been checking to see if a body might have floated downstream.

As a result, on June 27, 1989, the troopers put four divers into the Weweantic near the Route 6 bridge. But nothing was found.

Later, Anderson learned of his former companion's tale, and rejected it utterly.

In a conversation in July with *Globe* reporter Ellement, Anderson not only denied acting oddly while at the two rivers, denied murdering anyone, but also denied raping or assaulting anyone. At the time, he was still facing trial on three rape charges. But then Anderson went on to criticize Pina's conduct of the murder investigation. The main problem, he said, was that Pina and the police were relying far too heavily on the credibility of unreliable witnesses.

"He's got all these people here (in jail) who are junkies," Anderson told Ellement, "(and) there's a whole bunch of people who, instead of spending time in jail, (will) do a deal with the D.A."

That was exactly what transpired a few weeks later, when a man named Ronald Ray Griffith, a 38-year-old Missouri man, confessed to committing one of the murders, and claimed to have information about several others. Griffith was in jail in Missouri. It appeared he had been in the New Bedford area during the summer of 1988 with his former wife. He was hauled back to New Bedford and grilled. Griffith claimed he could lead investigators to more bodies, but it turned out Griffith knew nothing. He had, it appeared, fabricated his entire story by weaving together news accounts and prison gossip.

"It all appeared to be very valid information that you had to take seriously," Jim Martin told Ellement afterward. "All the information turned out to be false. He has, at least at this time, been eliminated as a suspect."

Later, it turned out Griffith made his false confession to induce the authorities to bring him back to Massachusetts so he could see his former wife.

It went unreported at the time, but in early September, the FBI sent Pina's office the results of their tests on all the hairs, fibers, saliva, and bloodstains found in Tony DeGrazia's house and truck. Considering that the lab had received the materials in April, and that there was such a voluminous number of items to compare, the FBI's turn-around time was amazing.

There was bad news and good news, Pina was informed: the bad news was, *none* of the samples had been matched to any of the materials found in connection with the nine murder victims. The good news: several hairs found in Tony's truck matched those taken from some of the women who claimed Tony had raped or beaten them. That meant the prosecutors had physical evidence that could tie Tony to the rapes of the Weld Square women.

The absence of matches to the items found at the murder sites was not dispositive—in other words, Tony could not be completely eliminated as a murder suspect. But the likelihood was greatly reduced. One victim not having any hairs or fibers linked to those found with Tony could be a coincidence; but nine without a single link almost certainly meant, statistically speaking, that Tony wasn't the killer.

Later, analysis of Tony's blood and saliva, compared with similar samples found at the murder sites, seemed to confirm this assessment. Exactly why Pina did not announce this to the world is unclear, but as Pina later indicated, he had a general policy of refusing all comment on trace evidence, even when it tended to acquit.

Yet it did appear that Tony was responsible for at least some of the alleged rapes and assaults attributed to him, if not all of them. Pina resolved to bring Tony to trial on those charges, although he knew they might be hard to prove. After all, the best evidence against Tony was from the eyewitnesses, and their credibility was eminently assailable.

Meanwhile, Tony's lawyer Ed Harrington, had similarly realized two things: if Tony came to trial too soon— say, before the murders were solved—he would be hard-pressed to gain an acquittal for Tony, even if the witnesses *were* wobbly, simply because of the urgent desire on the part of the public to find someone, anyone, to punish for the murders, even if that wasn't what Tony was actually being tried for. And Harrington also realized that the longer the time between the crime and the courtroom, the more likely it was that the victim/witnesses would move away, forget what happened, or get caught up in other

unrelated troubles. Time, Harrington knew, was on
Tony's side, so he was in no hurry to get to court.

Tony, of course, didn't see things that way at all. As
he kept protesting to his sister, his mother, the Scanlons,
and his priest, he hadn't raped anyone, and he certainly
hadn't murdered anyone. He wanted to have his trial as
soon as possible, get it over with, and return to normalcy.
He didn't understand why Harrington wasn't in the
same rush.

On his return from the mental hospital, Tony was declared competent to stand trial. He was put back into the
House of Corrections, in isolation, to prevent one or more
of the other prisoners from trying to kill him. The isolation cell was a hellhole. Covered with urine stains and
feces, with vomit on the walls, the normally fastidious
Tony was nauseated and disgusted. When he asked that
the cell be cleaned, he was told to clean it himself.

Later, Tony learned that some of his personal posses-
sions had been stolen by someone in the jail while he had
been at the hospital, including the earphones required of
prisoners to watch television in their cells—a big loss for
a man in solitary. But Tony at least had occasional visitors:
Father Bob Harrison, his mother, the Scanlons, and occasionally, Kathy herself. As the summer turned into the
fall, Tony settled into the jail routine and tried to think
positive thoughts.

40

"He'll Make It Up"

Pina's decision to rely more and more on Louie Pacheco
and the officers of the drug task force slipped by most of
the news media in the summer of 1989, but what did not
escape their attention was the impression that the investigation had reached a brick wall.

After the videotape embarrassment was followed by the
fruitless search of the Weweantic River and Griffith's false
confession, Pina had to admit that his earlier optimism
was unfounded. In early July, in a story headlined "Hope
Wanes for Quick Indictment," the *Standard-Times*'s Boyle
reported that the district attorney was subdued. The information he had believed would solve the case had turned
out to be groundless, he admitted.

Pina refused to discuss the videotape, but Boyle was
able to learn some of the supposed details, and made the
immediate link to the earlier rumors about the so-called
snuff films. Thus, like a virus making the rounds to rein-
fect its original host, the yarns about videotapes, pornography, and on-camera murder were backhandedly validated,
and reintroduced with the legitimacy of publicity to the
prison population that by now believed them. That, of
course, made it extraordinarily difficult for investigators to
distinguish fact from fantasy. The rumor mill was further
fueled when Jim Martin admitted that investigators were
looking into the local pornography business to see if there
were any links to the murders.

But there matters seemed to rest. No new information appeared to be forthcoming, and Pina made no moves to reconvene the special grand jury. Late in September, Boyle and others reported that the trail of the killer had gone completely cold. In October, Pina announced that the search dogs would return to work along the highways; there were still two missing women, he noted.

But after a week of searching by the dogs, including Josie from Connecticut, no new skeletons were discovered.

Relatives of the dead, however, weren't about to give up. Judy DeSantos, for one, wasn't about to let up on the pressure on Pina and the police.

Ever since Pina had convened the grand jury, Judy had been one of its most faithful observers. Each time the jury convened, there was Judy, waiting on a bench outside the jury room, scrutinizing the witnesses as they went in to testify. When rumors about the supposed snuff movie circulated, a reporter for the Providence newspaper approached her and asked what she thought.

Judy didn't even know what a snuff film was. Before she could say anything, the reporter told her that some people had never heard the term.

"Now, I'm not going to admit that *I* don't know what it is, so I stand there, nodding, 'oh yeah, uh-huh, yeah ...' " as if she knew all about it. The reporter filled in the particulars, adding that the victims were supposed to have been made to have sex with pigs and chickens before being murdered on camera. Judy gripped the table in front of her hard to maintain her composure. She thought for a minute that she was going to pass out as images of her sister Nancy with pigs and other animals passed before her eyes.

Was it possible? Would Nancy have participated in a pornographic film, never realizing she might be going to her death? When Judy thought about it, she realized that it *was* possible, given Nancy's addiction. Judy briefly considered going to the local video store to rent some pornographic videos on the chance she might recognize her sister, and that the video might lead to Nancy's killer. But Judy also realized that this was desperation on her part.

In the aftermath of the video episode, Judy decided that she needed to have some contact with the families of the other ten victims. There would be strength in numbers, she realized; and besides, Judy was tired of dealing with her feelings alone. With the help of Pina's victim assistance office, Judy convened a meeting of the victim families at a church in Fairhaven, just across the river from New Bedford.

As the families shared their stories with each other, one name seemed to pop out: Kenny Ponte. Nearly everyone had some anecdote about Kenny—he'd represented the Santos couple, for example; or Sandy Botelho's boyfriend; he'd even gone to high school with Deborah Greenlaw DeMello's former husband. The stories shared by the victims' families reached a critical mass, and soon, many family members were convinced that either Kenny had killed their loved ones, or at the very least, knew far more about the crimes than he was willing to tell.

To the families, most galling of all was Kenny's steadfast refusal to cooperate with Pina and the police. Kenny had to be hiding something, they decided; why else wouldn't he testify along with everyone else? To them, it seemed as though Kenny was denying any personal connection with any of the victims. But their hearts told them otherwise.

As the summer rolled on and the publicity receded, the families decided to redirect public attention at the murders. They allowed Maureen Boyle to attend one of their meetings, and eventually, the mother of Deborah DeMello went on television and pleaded for anyone with new information to come forward.

"Every night is a nightmare," said Madeline Perry, "because I lie in my bed and wonder who did this and why. He's still out there."

In the vacuum of new information, Pina's erstwhile allies in the news media began, for the first time, to turn on their benefactor. As long as Pina could endeavor to feed the machine, delivering new sensation upon sensation, the media was willing to stand back and allow Pina and his forces to set the pace.

But once the grand jury stopped meeting; once the leads seemed to peter out; once the information ceased to leak, the newspeople turned their attention to Pina himself, and his conduct of the investigation.

In mid-November, a Boston television station suggested, for the first time, that Pina had been manipulating both the news media and the investigation for political purposes. In a six-part series, the broadcasters from WCVB reviewed the Highway Murder events from beginning to end, and threw a roundhouse punch at Pina with the implication that Pina had leaked selective information about the investigation to make himself look good. The station used Tony DeGrazia as Exhibit A.

"Mr. Pina basically is involved in something that has turned from criminal to political," Tony told the broadcasters from inside the jail. "There's a difference between prosecution and persecution and I've been persecuted because of those murders I didn't have anything to do with."

Tony's assertions were sloughed off by Pina's office. "We do not comment on media reports," Jim Martin said, which had hardly been the case in previous months.

Tony went on to castigate Pina for allowing his name to be made public by Peggy Medeiros on the steps of the courthouse.

"I had nothing to do with it," he said. "You know? I wasn't even given the benefit of the doubt. All of a sudden, just like that, I'm a serial killer." Using clips of Tony in jail interspersed with Peggy's comments on the courthouse steps, the station showed how Tony had been portrayed to the public as a serial murderer. Eddie Harrington was then shown saying that there was no doubt in *his* mind that Tony's high bail was the direct result of the statements made by Peggy.

The station interviewed Pina:

"I'm not going to talk about Tony DeGrazia or anybody else," Pina told the station. "I'm not saying he's a suspect—"

The interviewer cut in: "Your people have, though."

Pina stammered, "Uh, you know, if they have, then I, shame on them. I don't think they have. One of the things I've found here is that a little bit of information to the media—it's a competitive industry, so if one reporter has a little piece of information and he doesn't have the rest, then he goes back to his editor (with that part of) the story, and he'll make it up."

The television reporter then came to the point:

"The fact is, it didn't happen that way. Despite Pina's efforts to maintain secrecy, information *was* given out. Secret grand jury witnesses *were* talking, and some of Pina's investigators *would* give information to reporters. They desperately wanted to convince the public that they were out there working, (that) they were making progress. And often, we in the media played right along.

"Four different men would take their turns as suspects in the murders. Attorney Ken Ponte knew several of the dead women. He now lives and works in Florida. New Bedford handyman Neil Anderson is facing unrelated assault charges; he's out on bail. Mechanic James Baker, who told investigators he tried to help some of the victims kick drugs, lives and works in Fall River. And, finally, Tony DeGrazia. Each man would be labeled a suspect in the mysterious murder of nine women over ten months.

"Whether Ron Pina knew it or liked it, suspects' names *were* getting out."

In early December, Harrington was finally able to get Tony's bail lowered; for the first time in almost seven months, Tony had hope of getting out of jail. Harrington argued that Tony's original $100,000 bail was solely the result of hysteria from the murders and all the publicity. There was no connection between DeGrazia and the murders, Harrington argued. By this time, Harrington had been given the results of the FBI's testing, and officials of Pina's office had acknowledged that they had no physical proof that Tony was involved in the murders.

Tony's television counterattack wasn't his only effort against the district attorney. In early December, Tony wrote to the Massachusetts bar's disciplinary arm, complaining that Pina had violated professional ethics by causing Tony's name to be publicly circulated as a suspect in the murders. Pina responded that he had nothing to do with Tony's name having been made public, and pointed out that Tony was still awaiting trial on a number of felony rape counts. The bar group declined to investigate any further.

A few days after Tony made his complaint, the *Standard-Times* headlined, "Anthony DeGrazia Not Highway Murderer," and went on to report that, according to Harrington, the FBI's testing had shown that Tony was not the culprit. But Pina still refused to discuss any evidence tending to clear any of the four named suspects.

But if the reporters thought Pina was beaten, they had seriously misjudged him. Because, on December 6, 1989, a key witness was released from prison for the first time in more than a year. Jeanne Kaloshis was out, and she was now ready to tell everything she knew—or imagined she knew—about Kenny Ponte.

41

Two-Headed Machine

Jeanne had been in jail since late September 1988—since, in fact, just about the time that Kenny had left New Bedford for his Florida retirement. And while the police records seemed to put her with Kenny in June 1988—after all, she'd been arrested with him then—and while investigators had heard Jeanne say she had been doing drugs with Kenny, it wasn't until the fall of 1989 that the various pieces of Jeanne's version of events began to fall into anything approaching a theory for murder.

Jeanne's tale, when it was finally told, was the most hair-raising yet about Kenny Ponte. But the juxtaposition of her story with her release from prison has to cast doubt on her complete veracity.

That Jeanne's tale was taken seriously at all was mostly the doing of New Bedford Police detective Paul Boudreau—the drug task force member who had earlier in 1989 busted the drug ring at Whispers Pub, which was the same place that four or five of the victims had been known to frequent, including Nancy Paiva.

Boudreau was a native of New Bedford, and as such, was quite familiar with Kenny Ponte. Both men had grown up in the same town at the same time in the late 1960s. But where Kenny had migrated into the drug culture, Boudreau wound up with an appointment to the police department.

During the 1970s, when Kenny was going to jail, then recovering from his drug addiction, Boudreau was working his way up the ranks of the New Bedford Police Department. After Pina became district attorney, Boudreau was one of the first police officers invited to join the new drug task force. By that time Kenny had been pardoned, and had opened his practice as a lawyer. Occasionally Boudreau and Kenny crossed paths, particularly in cases in which Boudreau was the cop and Kenny the lawyer. But the two men had minimal contact until about January 1984, when Ponte called Boudreau to report that he'd seen something very strange on television.

By this time, Boudreau had developed an interest in video technology, and in fact, was about to open his own business as a renter of video movies. The way Boudreau recalled it later, Kenny called him to say that a video he had rented was filled with images of mutilations, impalings, torture, and bondage.

"It was very bizarre, to say the least," Boudreau recounted. "He was seeing things into the tape, such as mutilation, raping, killing, torturing, heads cut off, you know, very descriptive things done with babies and women hanging upside down by a clothesline and cutting all their heads off and impaling children through their rectum, I mean, this guy was really off the wall with what he was telling me ... but he was so sincere."

Boudreau filled out a report, then went over to Ponte's house to see for himself. But first he collected several witnesses from Pina's office.

"So we put the movie on and we're all sitting there in anticipation of these gross scenes and he said, well, 'What I have to do to get into the movie is, I have to put it into slow motion.'

"He had a two-headed machine, so when you put it into slow motion, it sort of distorted the picture and as he did that ... he actually sat there in front of the—he had a wide-screen TV—he sat there on the floor and looked at it and started describing things that he'd told me before about. 'Look at the little babies, they're getting chopped up,' and we're all sitting there looking at each other, going, you know, he's lost it, the man's absolutely lost it.'"

Neither Boudreau nor anyone else could see what Kenny was talking about. But Boudreau wanted to be sure. He took the videotape and ran it on his own machine in slow motion. "It took me hours and hours, just in case there was some kind of a glitch there or somebody maybe taped something into it and spliced it," Boudreau said. "I didn't know. So, I did, I looked it over." He couldn't find anything wrong with the tape. Eventually Boudreau decided Kenny had gone around the bend.

In the next year or so, however, Boudreau recalled, he began to hear from informants—many of them prostitutes—that Kenny had fallen back into drug use. It wasn't that Kenny was selling the stuff, at least as far as Boudreau knew; it was just that different street people kept contending that Kenny had hired them to buy drugs for him; or, in some stories, Kenny had traded legal services for drugs. Boudreau filed these stories away at the time, since even if they were true, they only seemed to involve small amounts of drugs.

At one point, however, Boudreau arrested a man who lived across the street from Kenny, and that man led Boudreau to a major cocaine ring involving a man from Brownsville, Texas. There was no evidence that Kenny was at all involved with the Brownsville group, but Brownsville was a location well known as a major border crossing for drugs such as cocaine and marijuana; and in later years, Kenny *would* be connected to another man— Paul Ryley—who *did* spend time in Brownsville.

In any event, it was sometime during the summer or fall of 1989 when the drug task force's Pacheco asked Boudreau to take a look at Kenny Ponte's possible involvement with drugs as part of the Highway Murder investigation.

By the time Boudreau got involved, most of the police reports had been loaded into Pacheco's computer system. Boudreau started playing with the data, and was immediately struck by how many of the reports mentioned drugs, Ponte, the victims, and Ryley, he said later.

"The thing with Kenny Ponte's really deep," Boudreau said years later, "because there's so many players involved, so many people from the New Bedford area in this drug

world and prostitution and so forth, prostitutes, you know
... a lot of these prostitutes were informants of mine, see?
And I had a good rapport with them." By the fall of 1989,
Boudreau had assembled the stories of a variety of people
who claimed they had sold drugs to Kenny, or who
claimed they had injected him with cocaine. But Boudreau
wasn't satisfied; he was particularly puzzled by the relationship between Kenny and Ryley.

In retrospect, what is almost equally as striking as the
frequency of Ponte's name popping up on Pacheco's computer is the parallels between the lives of Boudreau's suspects—Ponte and Ryley—and Boudreau's *own* background.

For one thing, in addition to growing up with Kenny,
Boudreau was also a longtime friend of Ryley. Ponte was
said to have contact with women in Weld Square; so did
Boudreau, who frequently used them as informants. In
fact, Boudreau later claimed that he'd also used *Ryley* as
an informant. Ponte and Ryley were said to like to rent
videos; Boudreau owned a video store. Ponte and Ryley
moved to Port Richey, Florida; the adjacent city of New
Port Richey was the home of Boudreau's father, and Boudreau often went there. Ponte, at least, was said to be
involved with drugs; Boudreau was a narcotics detective.
And, Boudreau later contended, Ryley had once offered
him a $100,000-a-year job as a private detective—during
the summer of 1988, when the murders were going on.

Thus, it seems entirely possible that, in his suspicions,
Boudreau focused only on the issues that were most familiar to him, in an effort to make the facts of the murders
fit circumstances he himself knew the most about. In turn,
there might have been facts or circumstances about the
murders that Boudreau unconsciously discounted because
of his belief in his own theory.

Whatever his predilections, as Boudreau began assembling the information on Kenny and began to unearth the
name of Ryley over and over again, he became curious
about his old friend, Paul Ryley.

"Again, there's a guy that I'd known very very well for
many many years and their names kept coming up together," Boudreau said later, "and it just didn't seem right
that these guys would be together. Because Kenny Ponte

was just a strange character allegedly using drugs, hanging around with known prostitutes.

"Paul Ryley actually was a friend of mine at the time ... he was a businessman, a family man, now all of a sudden he's involved with Ponte. And he's not only involved with him—I find out he's living with him in Port Richey in Florida, and he's getting himself involved (with) all these people. So that got me even more interested, and I started working diligently on that whole thing because of Paul Ryley."

42

"She Did Die"

Ryley *was* a curious figure—just the sort of person someone like Diane Doherty might have fantasized about. Handsome—blond, in fact—well-dressed, polite, seemingly suave, Ryley also seemed to be rich. He'd been a former prison guard, but had left that work in the early 1980s; he'd left his job when he'd begun to take care of his great aunt, Margaret Sundelin, in the middle of 1984, and had obtained her power of attorney, with its access to Mrs. Sundelin's $620,000. By early 1985, Ryley was involved with Ponte in the videotaping of Mrs. Sundelin's last will—the one that was disputed by Ryley's cousins.

"So it was an incredible entanglement of all these people," Boudreau recalled, "and then Paul Ryley steps in. Paul Ryley, again, I've known him for 20 years. My parents lived right across the street from him in New Bedford. His kids played Little League baseball with mine, we were very good friends. I knew his wife very well, I'd been to his home.

"But I didn't see him for about three or four years, he just sort of disappeared. All of a sudden he came up to my video store one day with a Lamborghini, money, diamonds, gold. I said, 'What're you doing?' He said, 'Oh well, I just bought a string of theaters last week, I just invested in a gold company in Acapulco.' It just didn't make sense to me. He said, 'Well, I inherited some money.' I still didn't think much of it. A few months later he comes back again to see me, he offered me a job as a private investigator, with an incredible salary and benefits and so forth."

All of this made him suspicious of Ryley, Boudreau later said. He began poking around in Ryley's affairs, and learned that Ryley traveled frequently to Puerto Rico, the Cayman Islands, Texas, Florida, Mexico—all sorts of exotic places. And when Boudreau tried to confirm all of these supposed investments, none of them turned out to be real, according to Boudreau.

"Now I'm starting to get a little suspicious of the whole thing, so I start doing a background on him and I find out that a lot of the things that he's told me and told other people were not legitimate, they were not, they were not even real, they were just figments of his imagination, I suspect. Although he was at the time spending tremendous amounts of money—where he was getting it, I don't know. He was traveling constantly to Puerto Rico, up and down the East Coast, he was in New Bedford a lot, he was on the West Coast, he was in Mexico a lot, and I find out he's with Kenny Ponte. And I couldn't figure out why."

What Boudreau didn't know about Ryley was something Ponte *did* know, or at least believed: that Ryley was involved with selling guns abroad.

As his interest in Ryley deepened, Boudreau decided he needed some local eyes and ears in Florida to keep tabs on the comings and goings of Ponte and Ryley. He made an arrangement with a local police officer in Port Richey to keep both men under a covert watch. Pulling some other strings, Boudreau was able to get copies of Ponte's telephone bills, and business papers that seemed to connect Ponte to Ryley. Soon he learned from the Port Richey police that Ryley had a house in Spring Hill, Florida, but that he often stayed for days at a time at Ponte's house in Port Richey.

Boudreau also learned that some of Ryley's relatives were unhappy with the way he'd handled a family trust in Massachusetts, and that a lawsuit had been filed accusing Ryley of fraud.

As a result, in December 1989, as Boudreau was trying

to sort through all his suspicions about Ponte and Ryley, a request was made to the Port Richey police to arrest Ryley and hold him for extradition to Massachusetts on criminal charges of theft and forgery.

From the Pasco County Jail in Florida, Ryley called Boudreau to ask him why he'd been arrested. Boudreau told Ryley he didn't know anything about the charges, but two days after Christmas in 1989, Boudreau and the Saint flew to Florida to interview Ryley about Ponte.

At first, according to Boudreau, Ryley denied having contact with Kenny, but then Boudreau told him that the Port Richey police had seen him visit Ponte on numerous occasions. And Boudreau pointed out that Ryley's Florida driver's license had Ponte's address on it. Why? Ryley told Boudreau he was "hiding out," Boudreau said later.

Why was he giving money to Kenny? Well, said Ryley, Kenny didn't have any money. In fact, Ryley suggested that a friend of his, Elsa Johnson, move into the other side of the duplex to help Kenny pay the bills. Elsa did move there, and Ryley sometimes visited her. Boudreau knew that Elsa, also from New Bedford, was a drug addict and a severe alcoholic.

Had Ryley ever seen Kenny use drugs? Never, he said. What about watching pornographic movies? Never, Ryley repeated. He didn't remember watching a movie at Ponte's house with a woman named Jeanne? No.

"Well," persisted Boudreau, "do you remember watching a movie with Jeanne with Kenny Ponte? Jeanne was sitting next to you watching an adult movie of a woman being raped by several men and then strangled to death?"

Ryley got mad, but Boudreau continued. "Do you remember her asking you whether the woman *did* die in the film, and you answered, 'Yes, she did die on the film. These movies cost a lot of money.' You said, 'You can get $100,000 for these movies. We use women who are homeless or terminally ill, and they get killed on the film. We get big bucks for it.' "

That was ridiculous, Ryley retorted. Where was Boudreau getting all this?

The answer, of course, was: from Jeanne Kaloshis.

43

Making It Run

At first, earlier in the fall, as they had begun their work with the computer, Boudreau and Pacheco weren't exactly sure what sort of case theory they were going to come up with. They had begun with a drug conspiracy involving Kenny Ponte and several of the victims, namely, Rochelle Clifford, Nancy Paiva, and perhaps several others. They were sure they could show that Kenny had been consuming cocaine.

But the idea of Kenny killing all of the women over an extended period—six months—seemed to rule out the notion that Kenny had killed the women to silence them about his supposed drug use. Clearly, there were other women who had the same knowledge who weren't dead, so Boudreau and Pacheco scratched their heads and thought some more.

Maybe, Boudreau told Pacheco, it had to do with Ryley. Why was Ryley hanging around with Ponte, anyway? Hadn't Kenny helped Ryley with the will involving Ryley's aged aunt, who had then so conveniently died and left Ryley with all the money? How's this: Ryley wanted the aunt's money, so he hired Kenny Ponte as the lawyer to make the will; Kenny performed some legal sleight of hand to make sure Ryley got the dough, then together, Ryley and Kenny conspired to do in the old lady with poison. Boudreau liked that one; he'd discovered that Ryley's friend Elsa Johnson had worked as a maid for the aged aunt shortly before the untimely death. But how did it relate to the Highway Murders?

Well, okay, said Boudreau, let's try this: suppose, after the aunt died and Ryley collected the money and gave a share to Kenny, the lawyer, in one of his cocaine-induced frenzies, had inadvertently told Rochelle Clifford about the poisoning of the aunt. Then, when Rochelle tried to blackmail Kenny, Kenny had had to kill her.

Okay, but that didn't explain why all of the other women were also dead. Did that mean the babbling Kenny had told *ten* other women the same thing he told Rochelle? And even if that were true—and the victims died because they knew the Secret of the Will—why did it take Kenny so long to kill all of them? Wouldn't they have told someone else, if only to protect themselves? As each victim disappeared, wouldn't the remaining women have grown suspicious?

Well, maybe Kenny only killed Rochelle, then. But what about the trace evidence that seemed to link Rochelle's site to several of the other victims?

It was all a tangle. Try as they might to find some way to link all the information together, loose ends kept popping out. Every time a new explanation came forward, more inconvenient facts emerged to make it break down. It was like trying to tune a balky engine; it would turn over a few times, but then sputter to a stop. Boudreau and Pacheco decided they'd left some parts out.

Back to the computer. What else tied all of these people together? How about videos?

Well, yes: Ponte was a videophile, everyone knew that. Hadn't Kenny once called Boudreau himself to complain about the movies with all the mutilations that never were? Ryley liked video movies, too, Boudreau noted: in fact, he'd rented them to Ryley himself from his own video store, and the records showed Ryley was a consumer of X-rated videos.

What else was there about videos? Well, hadn't Nancy Paiva, who knew Kenny Ponte and who had actually once worked in his office, hadn't she also worked in a video rental store? The computer said she had.

And what about Elsa Johnson? Hadn't she once lived

with Paul Ryley at a Dartmouth address that was only a short skip-and-a-jump away from a video production company that police believed produced pornographic videos? Right, said the computer.

And hadn't Ponte and Ryley videotaped the will of Ryley's great aunt, Mrs. Sundelin—the one who'd died and left all the money? Right again, the computer answered.

And hadn't several women from Weld Square said that Kenny liked to pick them up and watch dirty movies? You are so smart, said the computer, and Boudreau and Pacheco decided they might get their engine to run, after all. What they still needed, however, was better fuel—like evidence.

That was where Jeanne Kaloshis came in.

WINTER
1989–1990

"All that most maddens and torments; all that stirs up the lees of things; all truth with malice in it; all that cracks the sinews and cakes the brain; all the subtle demonisms of life and thought; all evil, to crazy Ahab, were visibly personified, and made practically assailable in Moby Dick."

—HERMAN MELVILLE, *Moby Dick*

44

Screen Test

While Pina wasn't entirely sure he agreed with the ideas of his task force investigators, at least they were giving him something to work with. Best of all, he thought, Boudreau and Pacheco were *aggressive*, not like the troopers. And Pina believed that he had the appropriate tool to open the can of worms: the grand jury. Just as with Big Dan's, Pina would get all the players under the strobe lights and find out, once and for all, what was going on.

In early January 1990, Pina announced that the special grand jury investigating the murders would reconvene. Subpoenas were issued, and on January 25, 1990, the hunt for the Highway Murderer resumed. The first witness was Boudreau himself.

Answering questions, Boudreau sketched in most of his work for the past few months: his interest in Ryley, his prior experiences with Kenny Ponte, the connections between Ponte and Ryley, Ryley's interest in guns, the alleged New Bedford pornography business, the fact that Ryley lived not far from that business, and the incident in which a woman named Jeanne claimed that she had once seen a possible "snuff" video with Ryley and Ponte, and Ryley's reaction to this allegation.

But the jury wouldn't have to take Boudreau's word for it, because Jeanne herself was now about to testify.

* * *

Essentially, Jeanne told the grand jury, Kenny was one strange person. And it was through her that Kenny had first come to know Rochelle Clifford, who was, as Jeanne put it, her getting-high partner.

She'd met Kenny for the first time in April 1988, Jeanne said, when she had been visiting her husband at the House of Corrections. Kenny had seen her arrange to smuggle drugs to her jailed husband. He threatened to expose her if she didn't cooperate with him, Jeanne contended.

"He asked me if I wanted to get high," she said. "I told him I did. He said he wanted to do some coke. I told him I didn't want to do coke, that I wanted to do heroin. And he said, 'I'll buy you heroin.' And we went to his house."

At that point, Pina attempted to pin Jeanne down as to the time frame of this supposed first encounter with Ponte.

"Okay," said Pina. "Let me get a time on this. When was your husband in jail?"

"He was in jail in April."

"Of '88?"

"Of '88."

"So would that be around the time you met Ponte?"

"Right."

"So after that, you're going to—Rochelle gets to meet Ponte, right?"

Right, said Jeanne. "Must have been around the end of April when Rochelle met him. Maybe the beginning of May."

While Pina then complimented Jeanne on the quality of her memory, this exchange has to stand as possible evidence that Jeanne was fabricating her story. After all, the police *knew for sure* that Rochelle had been seen with Kenny on April 3, 1988—apparently weeks before Jeanne supposedly introduced them. Jeanne could not therefore have been right about introducing Rochelle to Kenny, if indeed it took place in late April or May.

Later, Jeanne went on to claim that Kenny asked her to inject him with cocaine.

"In his neck," Jeanne agreed.

"And then what happened? You said he freaks out."

"He pulls his clothes off, and he freaks out. Sweats. Just a nightmare."

"So that happened once? Or did you do it again?"

"Many times."

Jeanne went on to claim that she or Rochelle had injected Kenny with cocaine on many different occasions. Usually, she said, Kenny would become heavily paranoid, and worried that the police had surrounded the house.

"Did he ever get violent with you?"

"Just—no. He never got violent with me. He never got violent with me to the point that I couldn't handle it. You know."

"What do you mean by that?"

"I'd tell him, 'Let's do some more drugs, Kenny.' You know. And I kind of played him out until he needed another shot."

Eventually, Jeanne told Pina, she met a man at Kenny's who claimed to be a multimillionaire. "Preppie. Good-looking. Very clean cut. Nice eyes. Piercing eyes. Square jaw. Very well dressed. Well-manicured nails. Looks like he walked out of a yacht club and told me he was a multimillionaire." The man Jeanne described fit the description of Paul Ryley.

Jeanne went on to say that during the summer of 1988 she'd spent a considerable amount of time doing drugs with Kenny. Once, she said, they'd been stopped on South First Street by the police. That was when the New Bedford cops found Kenny with a gun, in June 1988. Near the end of the summer, she met the man who looked like Ryley at Kenny's law office. The man told her he had $40,000 in cash. He also had a gun. Kenny took some of the money and bought drugs with it after the man left, Jeanne said.

Early in September 1988, Jeanne continued, Kenny called her again and asked her to come over to his house.

"It was like midnight," she said. "I came back to his house and the man (who looked like Ryley) was there."

"Do you remember talking to the man? Do you remember anything that happened that night?"

"We were getting high. He didn't like—he didn't get high."

"The man didn't use drugs, right?"

"No. Like he was drinking. I don't know if he was drinking soda or alcohol."

As the night wore on, Jeanne continued, a videotape was put into the VCR.

"There was the tape that was put in; and they were like, 'Watch this.' They were asking me if—will you play this with Kenny? And I was like, well, let's get high. Let's keep getting high. And I saw a tape with them that was really bizarre."

"They asked what?" Pina demanded. "Would you play with Kenny the role in the movie? Or would you play some game with him, or what?"

"Yeah. It was like into S and M (sadomasochism) and stuff like that. They wanted me to dress up in, you know, studs. They were talking about, you know, like S and M type of stuff."

"I really don't know," said Pina. "If you could help us out. I'm trying to get you—I don't want to embarrass you."

"I *am* embarrassed."

"What were they asking you to do? I mean that's—"

"The other—the—"

"Take your time."

"The man who I don't know his name wanted to watch me and Kenny play games. And then when the movie came on, I was—after I saw the movie, I got scared."

"Okay. But you said something about the movie, play games like the movie."

"First one I saw, I don't know if it was a tape or not. It was S and M, hitting, tying up; stuff like that."

"And they wanted you to play those games with Kenny?" Pina persisted.

"And I was like, no way," Jeanne said. "I don't do that. I don't play those games. And the other one, they were like, 'Watch this.' And Kenny was flying around really high, really off the wall. Sweating. Took his clothes off. He runs around the house without his clothes on. And I saw a film. And it scared me."

"Do you remember what was in the film?"

"I just remember it was a rape. And it was strange. And it was—it looked like a dead stare."

"I'm sorry?"

"A dead stare," Jeanne said. "A dead stare. Like when the hands were put around her throat."

"Was it a violent scene? Was the girl getting raped?"

"She was being raped. And she was—" Here Jeanne put her own hands around her throat and bugged her eyes out to indicate strangulation.

"And then what happened? How did the movie end?"

"The girl got—it was really bizarre. Her eyes looked like they were dead. And I said, 'That's not just a movie. That's not just acting.' The man was telling me movies like that cost a lot of money, but this isn't a real one. And he was telling me the prices of how much people pay for snuff films. And he said that wasn't a snuff film, because nobody—they're too expensive. And you have to buy them or something. I went in the bathroom. You have to buy them from certain people. I never even heard of somebody like that."

The man who looked like Ryley tried to convince her, Jeanne said, to go into the pornography business as a model. That's why they wanted her to act out some of the scenes from the tape—a sort of screen test.

"Act out some of the S and M scenes," Jeanne added. "Not from the rape. Not from the videotape. I just—I really got scared. I went into the bathroom. I did that to myself to see if your eyes look—" Jeanne bugged her eyes out again to show what she would look like if she were being strangled.

"I put my hands on my neck. And I tried to look in the mirror. Just, I'll never forget it. It was—it was so real. It didn't seem like it was—you know how those—I don't know if you've ever seen a porn movie. And they just seem so much like acting. They seem so fake."

"And this movie didn't seem that way?"

"No," said Jeanne.

Later that night, Jeanne continued, Kenny and the man who looked like Ryley decided that she was flipping out, acting bizarre. Jeanne wanted to leave, but the door was locked, she said.

"Did you ever get out of the house that night?"

Jeanne said she had. "I fought with him (Kenny)," she added. "And he ripped my shirt. And I said, 'I'll get you another girl.' Because I just wanted to leave. I was just in pending fear of doom." Jeanne said she called another woman, who came over. Jeanne said she left and never spent any time with Kenny again. She went to prison in late September of 1988, just about the time Kenny moved to Florida.

——— 45 ———
Memories

Now the jury had heard from a witness who testified under oath that she had seen Kenny and, presumably Ryley, together; and that she had seen both men watch a video that appeared to contain a violent rape scene in which a woman was supposedly strangled. Even more significant, the jury now had testimony that the man who looked like Ryley was allegedly familiar with such films, and knew how they could be marketed, and for how much.

But a close inspection of Jeanne's story—and Pina's attempt to interrogate her about it—reveals several important problems. The first problem was that Pina never showed Jeanne any photographs of the man who looked like Ryley. Therefore, one is forced to conclude that Pina wasn't sure that Jeanne could positively identify him.

Second, nowhere did Jeanne tell the grand jury what Boudreau had just said she *would* she say: namely, that Ponte and the Ryley look-alike had claimed to her that they actually made videos with real murders in them, using "homeless and terminally ill women."

Indeed, Jeanne's information to the jury clearly indicated that the Ryley look-alike had assured her that the choking scene she supposedly saw was *not* real. The only discussion about snuff films came when Ryley assured her that such films existed, not that he was in any way involved with them. That was Jeanne's sworn testimony, not Boudreau's description of it.

A final problem with Jeanne's story arose when Pina told her he did not plan on prosecuting her for anything she might say. Yet, four months later, Jeanne was in fact indicted by the district attorney for conspiring to possession of drugs with Kenny Ponte.

Later, Pina would say, in defending the use of the grand jury, that very few people had repudiated their testimony—not more than two or three, he said. That raises the question of whether Jeanne told Boudreau things that she declined to repeat later in front of the grand jury under penalty of perjury, which naturally raises questions about her earlier veracity with Boudreau.

But those questions might be resolved another way—Ryley himself could be called to testify. And that's exactly what Pina did.

That afternoon, Ryley went into the jury room, accompanied by his lawyer, Joe Macy of Fall River. Under Massachusetts law, defense lawyers are permitted in the jury room, but they cannot ask questions or make statements.

Shockingly, Pina did not ask Ryley any questions about Jeanne's story.

Pina showed Ryley some of the pictures of the victims; Ryley said two, Robin Rhodes and Rochelle Clifford, looked slightly familiar, but he did not know them by name. During most of 1988, he said, he had been living in Brownsville, Texas, and wasn't anywhere near New Bedford. With that, Ryley was excused.

There was another witness called by Pina that day. A woman named Gayle told the jurors that she had known Rochelle Clifford in the winter and spring of 1988. In fact, Gayle said, Rochelle had once called her to ask her to come pick her up. Rochelle, Gayle said, told her that she'd been riding on I-195 with Kenny Ponte, that she and Kenny had been in a fight, that Kenny had tried to choke her, that she'd taken his gun, and had escaped from Kenny's car.

This, indeed, was useful testimony, although far short of definitive proof because of its hearsay nature. If it was true, however, it seemed to indicate that Kenny had once attacked Rochelle Clifford.

The big problem with Gayle's testimony was its lack of precision in timing. Indeed, Gayle's memory, if anything, seemed far worse than Jeanne's, Pina's compliment to Jeanne notwithstanding. Gayle seemed to recall being with Rochelle at Christmas 1988, which couldn't be right, because Rochelle's skeleton had been found on December 9, 1988.

She probably meant Christmas 1987, but that seemed to contradict Jeanne's story, in which Jeanne had said she and Rochelle were pregnant together in December 1987, and Gayle mentioned nothing about Rochelle looking like she was about to give birth.

In any event, Gayle's husband began running around doing drugs with Rochelle, according to Gayle, perhaps beginning in January or February of 1988. On one occasion, she said, Rochelle and Gayle's husband stole Gayle's wallet and tried to use her Sears charge card. The store knew Rochelle wasn't Gayle, and called Gayle to ask her if she wanted Rochelle arrested. Gayle said she did. The police were called, but the officers let Rochelle and Gayle's husband go.

It was some time after that, in the spring, when she'd received a call from Rochelle, Gayle said.

"And she was calling you from where?" Pina asked.

"From Wareham exit off 195."

"She was using the phone off the road?"

"Yeah. When you take that exit, there's a phone booth."

"And what did she tell you?"

"That Kenny Ponte was trying to kill her, so she jumped out of his car. She took his gun. He had a gun. She jumped out of his car."

"Did she say how he was trying to kill her?"

"No. She just said please come pick me up. She's all shook up. And I didn't go and get her."

"You didn't go and get her?"

"No."

Pina then asked Gayle whether she'd told the police that Kenny had tried to choke Rochelle.

"She was in the car. She's—yeah. She was strangling

him, gets out of his car. She got the gun from him. That's
what she told me."

"She was strangling him? Or he was strangling her?"

"I think she was—he was trying to strangle her. I
wouldn't think she'd try to strangle him. She got the gun.
She got out of his car. That's what she said."

Gayle said she told Rochelle to stay away from Kenny.
But later she heard that Rochelle was still hanging around
with the lawyer—"a few months later than that."

What could anyone make out of this story? Taken literally, and together with previously established facts about
Rochelle, it would seem to indicate that at some unknown
point, Kenny had tried to choke Rochelle on I-195, that
Rochelle had taken away Kenny's gun, that she was afraid
of him and called Gayle for help; but then later, had rec-
onciled with Kenny, then apparently stole his gun again
in the burglary of April 13, 1988, then stayed with Frankie
Pina and Nancy Paiva, then returned to Kenny's house "a
few months later than that," by which time, if the forensic
people were correct, Kenny would have been living with
a walking skeleton.

In a courtroom under cross-examination, Gayle's testimony would have been torn to shreds. But Pina wasn't
planning to put Gayle on any witness stand; he was operating his perjury-powered fact-sifter in the hope of un-
covering some new leads.

Pina now tried harder to get a more specific time frame
for these events.

"Did you tell the detectives that after this incident with
Rochelle calling you on the highway—I'm just trying to
refresh your memory, see if this brings your memory
back—you told them you had a phone conversation with
her; and she, Rochelle, said she'd been arrested, and she
was shoplifting?"

"Oh, yeah," Gayle recalled. "She called me from the
police station."

"Okay."

"She called me up from the downtown police station.
And she had got arrested for shoplifting. She told me a
name to use. She didn't use her (real) name. I can't remember her name. Helen, maybe. I can't remember. And

that she was downtown, if I'd go get her out of jail. And I never called back the jail. I never went down there or anything . . ."

"But she was under arrest?" Pina wanted to find out if there might be any police paperwork that would help pinpoint the date of the highway call more accurately. He wanted to show that Kenny Ponte *could* have been with Rochelle after April 27, 1988. If Pina could prove that, he could get around the problem of Dextradeur having last seen Rochelle with Frankie Pina on that inconvenient date. The problem was that Gayle had told the detectives the shoplifting incident had happened *after* the phone call about Kenny's supposed attack. That meant Rochelle was still alive afterward—not good for Pina's theory, at all.

"Yeah," said Gayle. "She was in jail downtown."

"Okay," said Pina. "But the call—so—I'm just trying to get my time right. Okay. The call from the highway was before that or after that?"

"Before I think," said Gayle. "No. After. After she got arrested." One has to wonder at this point about Pina's body language with his witness, along with other questions relating to any possible charges against Gayle's drug-using husband. There is certainly no legal rule against leading witnesses behind closed doors.

"After she got arrested, when she called you to help come and get her away from him on the highway?"

"Yeah. I think so."

"So she got arrested first before that?"

"Yeah. I think so. I don't know. I can't really remember times. You know. Dates."

Eventually, Gayle agreed that the call from Rochelle might have come around two months after the incident in which Rochelle had tried to use her Sears credit card. If only Pina could find a date for that—then what? It was no real help, not with such elastic time estimates from a woman who thought she'd first met Rochelle Clifford two weeks after she'd already been found dead.

—— 46 ——
Return of the Boston Strangler

The following day Pina took more testimony from Ryley; the *Standard-Times*'s Boyle calculated that altogether, Ryley spent approximately four hours in front of the jury. None of this new testimony ever leaked, but it seems unlikely that Ryley ever confirmed Jeanne's story that he and Ponte were in the snuff-film business together; otherwise, Ryley would have been indicted, or at least immunized.

And after Ryley's additional testimony, a man who operated the New Bedford area video production business that was, in Boudreau's opinion, involved in the manufacture of pornography, likewise appeared. Nothing of this testimony leaked either, but Boudreau himself was under the impression that the owner of the video company told the jurors that he'd never heard of either Ponte or Ryley. The man brought his business records with him.

Afterward, Pina termed the testimony "very productive," and told the *Globe*'s Tom Coakley, "We're moving along well. It's exhausting. There is a focus to it. There is a lot of work that has gone into this. At this point we want to see where it leads."

One direction the investigation was leading toward in early 1990 was Diane Doherty, although no one realized this at the time.

By late 1989, Diane and her daughter had moved into an apartment in Lynn, Massachusetts, next door to a private investigator. After a dispute with their landlord, Diane and her daughter were evicted. Diane claimed the landlord was guilty of a long list of building code violations. For about a month, Diane and her daughter stayed with the private eye, who, in turn, happened to be friendly with a retired state trooper who had once assisted in the Boston Strangler murders.

One thing led to another, and Diane began recounting to the private eye some of the stories she had heard about the Highway Murders while she was at MCI Framingham. Over the spring and summer, Diane had composed notes of her musings about the murders on yellow paper. The private eye showed a great deal of interest in these stories, and wanted to see the notes. Diane refused to give them to him, she said later. Later the notes disappeared from her car, Diane said; she suspected the private eye had somehow gotten them.

At this point some of the reality of the Highway Murders begins to merge with the history of the Boston Strangler case.

The Strangler was said to have been responsible for the murders of 11 women in the Boston area from 1962 to early 1964. Eventually, a convicted rapist named Albert DeSalvo confessed to the murders. But DeSalvo was never tried for the crimes, and many police officers who investigated the murders remained unconvinced that DeSalvo was the killer. They thought DeSalvo might have heard the details of the crimes from another man, and then confessed to ensure that his wife and children could get money from the sale of the Strangler story to the movies.

Having obtained a confession, the next stage was to get the authorities to accept the self-proclaimed Strangler's admissions as valid. While the police weren't so sure, several political figures in Massachusetts, notably Attorney General Edward Brooke—then about to be a candidate for the U.S. Senate—gratefully seized on the confession as the answer to a murder series which had terrorized the state. Clearing the cases, whatever else it might be, was good politics.

Ultimately, DeSalvo's confession was accepted; still, numerous people continued to insist for years afterward that DeSalvo had never killed anyone, and that the crimes were "solved" for reasons of political expediency.

Now, in early 1990, another lurid murder series was unsolved; and the person who "solved" them might have every expectation for reaping the rewards for finding the solution.

Whether it was revealed in Diane's notes, or whether Diane simply told the private eye—or instead, as Diane later insisted, the private eye simply made it up—the story soon circulated that while Diane was in MCI Framingham, she had been told that Kenny Ponte had confessed to the murders!

As it evolved, the story was that a prison dorm mate of Diane's, a woman named Leslie Mello, had supposedly told her that one night in New Bedford, Kenny Ponte had broken down, weeping at Leslie's kitchen table, and had confessed to killing six women in New Bedford. Somehow, it evolved that Diane and her daughter had also been present when Kenny made the confession.

However this information came into his possession, the private eye apparently relayed the substance of Diane's story to the retired trooper, who in turn passed it on to others in the state police. Thus, in January 1990, Diane Doherty was issued a subpoena to appear before the Bristol County special grand jury.

Even on the surface, the story was hardly credible. For one thing, Diane and her daughter had never been in New Bedford, although the private eye had no way of knowing that. For another, the "fact" that Kenny confessed to killing six women seemed clearly reflective of the influence of the news stories *at the time Diane had been in prison*, not real information. A casual reader or viewer at the time Diane was in jail in the first part of 1989 would have known only of six victims, not the 11 who now seemed to be dead or missing.

Since the crimes were all linked, why would a confessing Kenny admit to only six? Why not *all* of the murders? The use of the number six was a red flag that the confession story was baloney.

The state troopers heard of Diane's story and quickly dismissed it as more wild prison talk. They located Leslie Mello—one of those who had also been said to have been raped by Flat Nose—and she denied the story about the weeping Kenny from top to bottom. Moreover, she barely remembered Diane Doherty; Diane and Diane's daughter certainly had never been in her kitchen.

After getting her subpoena, Diane told Troopers Gonsalves and Dill that she'd never met Kenny Ponte in her life, and the subpoena was rescinded.

Still, the incident had its lasting effect on the Highway Murder investigation. Eventually, Diane was to contend that the private eye began pestering her to sign an affidavit about Kenny's supposed confession. Diane said she refused to sign. The private eye eventually testified before the jury himself, and offered a written statement about the confession that was said to have been signed by Diane, although Diane later repudiated it. But the main effect of these events was that Diane's interest in Ponte continued unabated, and in the end, Diane was able to insert herself into Kenny's life very deeply, indeed.

By the time the grand jury resumed in January, Tony DeGrazia was finally out of jail. Eddie Harrington had been able to have Tony's bail reduced to $37,500, and Lorraine Scanlon's uncle, one of Tony's former employers, put up the money.

Still, Pina wasn't happy about Tony's prospective release. Just before the doors clanged open, Pina brought another charge against Tony: making threats on Pina's life.

As Tony was preparing for his freedom, a psychiatrist told him that he should be happy, that now he could get his life back together. Tony, embittered, rejected that idea. "I'm not getting my life back together," Tony shot back at the shrink. "Why should I? Pina's made my life miserable. Now I'm going to make *his* life miserable. Then I'm going to end it." The psychiatrist interpreted Tony's remark to mean that Tony intended to kill the district attorney.

It took almost a week, but when Tony showed up at the district court to appear on the long-ago drunk driving charge, he was arrested again, jailed, and charged with attempting to commit a crime. Eddie Harrington was disgusted with Pina. To him, the new charge seemed like nothing more than a transparent attempt to keep Tony locked up, despite the reduction in bail. A judge agreed with Harrington, and shortly before Christmas, Tony was released again.

Then in January, while Pina and the grand jury were hearing from Jeanne, Gayle, Boudreau, Ryley, and the alleged pornographer, Father Harrison took Tony with him on a pilgrimage to Yugoslavia.

In Harrison's view, Tony desperately needed a new perspective, after having been in solitary confinement for almost eight months, and after having been accused of being a serial murderer. His spirits were low, and the bitterness remained. Tony told everyone that the cases against him had been fabricated by Pina and the investigators in an effort to find someone, anyone, to take the rap for the murders and the rapes.

Fulfilling a pledge he'd made to Tony while he was in jail, the priest and his parishioner traveled to the mountainous Balkan country, and made their way to a place where enormous crowds were gathering, after word had spread of a visitation by the Blessed Virgin Mary. Tony had always been deeply religious, and Harrison hoped that some of the faith of the multitudes might help restore Tony's spirits. And when the pair climbed the mountain, an amazing thing happened: a woman Tony had never met before, a Yugoslavian who was said to have seen the apparition, parted the crowds and touched Tony lightly on the shoulder . . . whether in unconscious sympathy, or as a prophecy, no one could say.

Meanwhile, back in New Bedford, Pina was feeling a shoulder touch himself. Looking at the newspaper on February 10, Pina read that a very well-connected New Bedford lawyer, Paul Walsh, was thinking about running for district attorney.

This was real trouble. For one thing, Walsh was the lawyer who represented the *Standard-Times* newspaper. For another, Walsh's father was a former member of the city's school committee, and a politically powerful person who happened to be very close to the one remaining political bloc Pina thought he could count on: the suburban Irish and Italian forces aligned with State Senator Biff McLean. If McLean bailed out on Pina, the incumbent district attorney's political career would be in severe jeopardy.

47

Presumptions

Late in February 1990, one of the most important under-pinnings of the case Pina hoped to develop against Ponte and Ryley was severely damaged.

Paul Boudreau, the detective who had pieced together the complicated theory Pina was pursuing, was accused of improper conduct involving a second drug case involving Whispers Pub. That establishment, of course, was the place police had alleged was the headquarters of a ring that sold nearly $5.2 million a year in cocaine. It was also the place where many of the victims had been known to congregate, and the next-to-last place Nancy Paiva had been seen.

The allegations involving Boudreau were murky, but it appeared that an informant recruited by Boudreau in September 1989—after the first arrest earlier in the same year—may have lied about finding drugs in the Whispers' proprietor's house; instead, the informant may have planted the drugs there. Even worse, it appeared that the informant had stolen a substantial amount of money, nearly $40,000, from the man's house, just before Boudreau had conducted his raid that had been based on the informant's story. The police had seized an additional amount of money that went a long way toward replenishing the drug task force's cash larder for additional investigations. This was a major stinker.

Boudreau claimed that he'd had a second informant as

well, but no one seemed to be listening. It seemed certain
that both Whispers' cases—including 41 indictments returned in the first part of 1989—would have to be dismissed. There was no way to prove that the informant who
had taken the money hadn't also planted the drugs Boudreau found—either the first or the second time.

Other questions swirled about the case as well: had
Boudreau known about the theft? The alleged planting?
What assistance had Boudreau and others rendered to the
informant to get him out of town after the raid? The
bottom line was, Boudreau's credibility in the Highway
Murders was now at risk, and any defense lawyer in the
murder case would be foolish not to zero in on the allegations that the detective's information was not to be trusted,
just as the Whispers' defense lawyers were doing.

Boudreau was furious over the fiasco. His integrity had
been questioned and his usefulness as a police detective
had been shattered. He was sure the proprietor of Whispers had been dealing drugs. The bad informant, he
claimed, had been foisted on him by the state troopers.
Later, Boudreau was to speculate that the troopers were
getting even with him for his work on the Highway Murder case.

And in one other development, Kenny Ponte decided
to replace Joe Harrington as his lawyer with another attorney, Kevin Reddington of Brockton, Massachusetts.

It wasn't that Kenny was unhappy with Harrington's
work, but it was clear that he and Harrington had a difference of opinion on the best way to proceed.

For months, Ponte had been the target of leaks, swipes,
and innuendo from Pina and various other investigators,
most of which wound up on the air, or in print. He resolutely kept quiet throughout, on Joe Harrington's advice.
But Kenny couldn't stand it anymore. He wanted to hit
back, badly.

Joe Harrington was a lawyer of the old school. Making
statements out of court was, in Harrington's view, bad
form, even if other lawyers—read Pina—did it. When
Kenny told Harrington he wanted to go public with his
side of the story, Harrington strongly advised him not to

do it. In the end, Harrington withdrew from the case, and Reddington stepped in.

Reddington was a lawyer from a different era. Thirty-nine years old and the father of four children, Reddington had never been a prosecutor. In fact, he had been an anti-war radical. He believed that everyone was innocent, and he hated it when it looked like someone was being bullied.

"You know we have a presumption of innocence," Reddington said later, "but yet, all you have to do is level the finger at somebody, and even if they're acquitted, their reputation is pretty well damaged." Kenny Ponte, Reddington believed, was "a specific case in point.

"Here's a guy, who, in my opinion, is stone-cold inno-cent . . . he was an attorney prior to these accusations . . . and I really question whether somebody would want him to represent them on anything right now."

Reddington was also experienced in defending murder cases. By his own count, he'd handled nearly 40 of them. And he was aggressive. He was not at all adverse to Ponte's desire to counterattack Pina in the news media, but only after an effort was first made to get a court to order Pina to keep quiet about the case. Failing that, Reddington was willing to publicly throw rocks at Pina all day long, or at least until Pina retreated. .

Ponte called Reddington and asked if he would take the case. Reddington told Ponte to come in and talk to him first.

"After 16 years in a very active criminal trial practice," Reddington recalled, "you tend to get a little cynical and, of course, everybody's 'innocent' anyway.

"So the first thing I said was, 'So you're being accused of this serial killing,' and he gets somewhat histrionic and says, 'I didn't do it, I didn't do it.' And I said, 'I understand you didn't do it, I just want to understand where you stand and what your exposure is right now.'"

Reddington proceeded to tell Ponte how he saw the situation.

"Okay, you've got a D.A. who says you did it," Redd-ington said. "And you've got a D.A. who's leaking things to the press. And you've got this other conspiracy of drug cases kicking around there. You got a criminal charge on an assault with a gun, and one of the missing victims was the person who was supposedly your witness on this case."

That was the situation, Kenny agreed.

"Okay," Reddington said. "The first thing is, I want you to take a polygraph test."

Ponte agreed to take the test. "And he did," Reddington recalled later. "I'm a firm believer in polygraphs, so I had that scheduled." Had Kenny killed the women? The test came back completely negative for deception; according to the lie detector, Kenny hadn't killed the women.

That convinced Reddington that Ponte was innocent.

Now, Reddington decided, he needed to get Pina to shut up. If that didn't work, then Pina would have to take the consequences.

Early in March, Reddington asked for a court order forbidding Pina to discuss the case with anyone from the news media. The order was denied. Immediately thereafter, Ponte issued his first public statement about the case. He denied he was the murderer, and threatened to sue Pina if he didn't apologize.

"No evidence exists connecting me to this crime," Kenny told everyone, "because I have nothing at *all* to do with this crime."

From that point forward, as the spring and summer now unfolded, Ponte and Pina were on a collision course, charted through the increasingly turbulent waters of Bristol County's politics.

SPRING 1990

"His bone leg steadied in that hole; one arm elevated,
and holding by a shroud; Captain Ahab stood erect . . ."
> —HERMAN MELVILLE, *Moby Dick*

48

No Smoking Gun

On March 29, 1990, Ponte and three others—Jeanne Kaloshis, Adele Leeks, and the taxi driver, Arthur "Goldie" Goldblatt—were indicted by a regular grand jury on charges they had conspired to possess cocaine.

"Goldie" Goldblatt's indictment was intriguing for the simple reason that Paul Walsh—the same man who had announced his intention to run against Pina for the district attorney's job—was Goldblatt's attorney. Walsh had made his official announcement in mid-March by going to Weld Square and holding a press conference to lambaste Pina for his failure to suppress crime and drugs in the area.

Using Weld Square as a photo backdrop, after all the publicity over the preceding months, was a stroke of political imagery that couldn't be missed.

And after "Goldie" the taxi driver was charged in the alleged conspiracy, Walsh weighed in again: "I wonder if there are any motivations, other than solid investigative work here," he said.

"I think, maybe, the D.A. feels he has to bring some type of indictment involving this situation," Walsh continued. "Maybe it will make some more headlines in the serial murder case, and this is a left-handed way of doing this."

Walsh had just made it clear: Pina's conduct of the investigation of the Highway Murders—and the attendant publicity he was reaping—was about to become a big-time issue in the election for the Bristol County district attorney.

For his part, Ponte contended Pina had only indicted him because Kenny had criticized Pina publicly when he had denied being the murderer. In fact, Kenny had sent a letter to the *Standard-Times*, accusing Pina of having a great deal in common with the Emperor who had no clothes.

Four days later, Reddington fired off a new barrage: he asked Pina to recuse himself—declare himself too personally involved—and therefore withdraw from the murder case; Reddington instead asked that a special prosecutor be appointed in Pina's stead.

"Mr. Ponte is finished with being harassed," Reddington told assembled reporters at a news conference. "He is done being pushed around by Mr. Pina." And Ponte gave plaintive support to his lawyer's claim:

"I feel completely victimized by the system," Ponte said after being arraigned on the drug conspiracy charges, to which he said he was not guilty. Reddington supported his client: "After all the passage of time, the investigation is really breaking down," Reddington said. "I think it's time for Mr. Pina to step aside, and an independent prosecutor to take over." At his arraignment on the drug charges Ponte was given a new grand jury subpoena—this one for the special panel investigating the murders.

Walsh, Goldblatt's lawyer, and now Pina's erstwhile opponent as district attorney, piped up as well.

"This is a waste of court's resources," Walsh told everyone. The case, he said, was so thin—after all, a *conspiracy* to possess drugs?—that it would probably be dismissed without further ado in the district court. There just wasn't enough specificity as to the date, time, place, and other particulars necessary to effectively prosecute and defend a charge.

"There must be something else to it," Walsh added. "What it is, *I* don't know. I don't let politics affect *my* representation of clients, and I hope the opposite isn't true on the opposition side."

*   *   *

But lashing out at the authorities can bring penalties, as Ponte was to discover later that same afternoon.

After Reddington had left New Bedford to return to his Brockton office, Ponte set out for the airport to return to Florida. He was riding in a car being driven by his friend Daniel Branco when state troopers pulled Branco over. They arrested Branco for driving with a suspended license. They put Branco into the back of a police car and impounded his car. That left Kenny with no way to get to the airport, so Kenny set off on foot, carrying his suitcases in each hand.

As Kenny walked down the road, the police followed him in their unmarked cruisers at a walking pace.

"Having a nice day, counselor?" one trooper asked with a smirk. "Are those bags heavy, counselor? Is there a problem?"

Ponte came to a pay telephone and dialed Reddington.

"Kevin, this is Ken," Ponte told Reddington. "I'm at a pay phone. I'm being followed by the police."

"Whaddaya mean, followed by the police?" Reddington didn't get it.

"I don't know, they followed me. I'm with a guy, they arrested the guy for operating on a suspended license."

"Are they there now?" Reddington asked.

"Yeah," Ponte said, "they're standing up the street, one on the sidewalk, two across the street, two in the car, and they're looking at me . . . do you want to talk to them?"

"Yeah," Reddington said, "I want to talk to them."

"Hold on for a minute." Ponte called to one of the officers. "Excuse me, Officer, would you speak to my attorney? I'd like you to speak to my lawyer."

Reddington heard some mumbling in the background. Ponte came back on the line. "He basically told you to go fuck yourself," Ponte told Reddington. Reddington now gave some equally specific instructions to Ponte.

Ponte next called his older brother Joe, and asked him to come pick him up. Joe Ponte arrived, Kenny got in Joe's car, and the two brothers drove off, the troopers following. Meanwhile, Reddington was working the phones.

Forty minutes later, Reddington's phone rang again. It was Kenny.

"Where are they now?" Reddington asked.

Right behind me, Ponte told him. "Beautiful," Reddington said.

A few minutes after that, Joe Ponte drove his car into the parking lot at Reddington's office building, trailed by one car, with one or two other police shadowers still on the street. Reddington's secretary Jean jumped into her own car, and drove to block the parking lot exit. The lead car trailing Ponte was trapped.

Reddington advanced on the captured police vehicle.

"Good afternoon," he said, "I'm Kevin Reddington, Mr. Ponte's attorney . . . can I ask who you are?" Reddington was surrounded by people with notepads and cameras. In the intervening minutes after first hearing from Ponte, he'd called the news media to come witness the entire event in his parking lot. Now the newspeople were taking pictures and writing down everything that was being said. This was using the news in the same way Pina used it, Reddington thought.

The woman trooper trapped in the parking lot was very embarrassed. She admitted that she was a state police officer.

"What are you doing?" Reddington asked.

"I don't believe this has happened," the trooper said, flushing. "I'm just doing my job."

"That's what got a lot of people in Germany in trouble," Reddington retorted. He told the police to back off and gave a signal to Jean, his secretary. The police left, but they never did that again.

Late in April, Ponte won yet another round, when a judge ordered his special grand jury subpoena quashed. Reddington contended the summons was nothing more than harassment. Pina, however, was undeterred.

"The goal of the Commonwealth and the grand jury has not been affected by the quashing of this subpoena," Pina said. "I think we can do what we want to do in a different way."

So, near the end of April, the special grand jury began

again. This time Pina brought Ryley back, together with two women investigators said were associated with Ponte and his friend, the preppie former jail guard—including Elsa Johnson, who Boudreau was convinced had once lived with Ryley, and not far from the place where the alleged pornography (or even snuff films) was being produced. Pina also called Ponte's friend Daniel Branco. Elsa told the jurors an earful.

Afterward, Pina spoke to the reporters once more. Two new witnesses, he said, had provided some very specific information, and the hour of an indictment was growing closer.

"We don't have a smoking gun," he said, "that one piece of glue that takes us over the top." But Pina confirmed earlier reports that the investigators and the grand jury were now concentrating on *one* suspect—obviously Ponte—and *one* victim, about whom the investigators had the greatest amount of evidence. The victim, of course, was Rochelle Clifford, who was more closely tied by time and location to Kenny than any other victim.

Finding "the one victim's" murderer, Pina added, would help solve *all* of the other cases. "I think she has enough in common with them—how she died," Pina told everyone. "She would be a key. The disappearances and deaths are similar."

But if Pina was talking, so was Kenny's friend, Danny Branco, the same man who'd once been accused of trying to tape the special grand jury as the "clicking witness." Branco told the assembled reporters that the district attorney had asked him whether *he'd* ever brought drugs to Kenny; about the attorney's sex life; about Kenny's relationships with various women; and about the layout of Kenny's old house on Chestnut Street, which turned out to be only a few blocks away from the house of—guess who—Neil Anderson!

Branco, to reporters, now denied that he had told investigators, earlier, that Ponte *couldn't* be the killer, because he, Branco, *knew* who the real killer was!

Thus, Branco denied a statement that no one had yet *officially* had said he'd ever made! That's what came of investigative leaks. Things were getting crazy, all right, which was therefore probably the perfect time for Diane Doherty to make her latest reappearance.

━━━━━━ **49** ━━━━━━
Diane

Ever since the trouble over Kenny Ponte's supposed confession at Leslie Mello's kitchen table, Diane Doherty said later, the private eye who had lived next door to her had been harassing her, to put pressure on her to reiterate the information.

She'd gone to the FBI, the state attorney general, had called the Bristol County CPAC, complaining that the private eye would give her no rest. Along the way, Diane denied she'd ever said *anything* about Kenny Ponte. Finally, in April, Diane found her way to Kevin Reddington.

There she poured out the whole tale: how this mean, unscrupulous private eye was trying to force her to commit perjury. The man was so devious, Diane told Reddington, that he'd even arranged to have her arrested for drunken driving. And worse than that, he'd—get this—arranged for her cat to be hung by the neck until dead!

Reddington nodded sympathetically. Behind his pleasant mask of listening he was thinking: *whoa!*

Diane wanted Reddington to tell her how to get in touch with Kenny. It was important, she said, because she felt sorry for him.

But Reddington, sensing that Diane was trouble for Kenny, refused to tell her where Kenny was.

That didn't deter Diane, however. She knew how to find out. She later said she called John Ellement at *The Boston Globe*, who provided Diane with Kenny's address in

Port Richey. Ellement later denied he'd ever given Diane Kenny's address or phone number, and it seems highly unlikely. Just how Diane actually got Kenny's address remains a mystery. In any event, the next-to-last act of the Highway Murders was about to unfold.

Sorting through all the threads of the Diane Doherty connection, despite the passage of years, continues to be an exercise in convolution. One of the major problems with Diane is that it was extraordinarily difficult to figure out which side she was on. It's likely that Diane herself did not know.

Later, Pina's spokesman Jim Martin was to emphatically reject the notion that Diane had anything to do with Kenny's later indictment. "I can tell you that in my estimation, the indictment against Ponte was based on evidence and on testimony that had absolutely nothing to do with Diane Doherty," Martin said later. "She had nothing to do with it whatsoever."

Yet a grand juror, just hours before Kenny was indicted for murder, called Diane a witness with more "crucial testimony than any other witness we've had in this courtroom in the past 20 months."

Reddington, Ponte's new lawyer, said of Diane just after Ponte was indicted, "I wouldn't walk across the street to present anything Diane Doherty said. If that's the Commonwealth's case, the Commonwealth is in trouble."

And Ponte himself came to believe that Diane was an *agent provacateuress*, a sort of guided Ms. hurled in his direction by a scheming Ron Pina.

But Diane was a cipher; she was the kind of person who collected information the way a ball of felt collects lint. There were all sorts of interesting things attached to Diane's memory; the problem was figuring out where they had come from, and when. Careful extraction and analysis of those bits and pieces might prove instructive, some people later thought; at least it might be a mirror into what Kenny himself knew—*and whether he should have known those things, if indeed he was innocent.* Conversely, however, the way Pina handled Diane shows much about the case Pina wanted to bring against Kenny, and its shortcomings.

* * *

According to her later testimony, Diane's reappearance in the Highway Murders investigation began some time in April or perhaps May of 1990, when she decided to call the private eye with whom she'd been feuding, to patch things up. The private eye warned Diane that he intended to tape-record their conversation, and he apparently did just that.

After telling the private investigator that she wished their relationship hadn't gotten so stinky, Diane began asking him questions about asphyxiation, and an old Massachusetts murder case involving *corpus delicti:* could murder charges be brought against someone even if the authorities had never found the body?

Subsequently—or perhaps before, depending on which interpretation one favors—Diane talked to Reddington, as noted earlier. Diane said that Reddington had told her that the Rochelle Clifford case—and maybe one other—were the only cases the prosecutors had a prayer of tying to Kenny Ponte.

This claim doesn't seem very credible; it's unlikely that a lawyer would tell someone he'd never met before such damaging information about his own client.

The issue here is one of motivation. If Diane talked first to the private investigator, there is reason to wonder whether Diane's subsequent personal involvement with Kenny Ponte was *arranged* to develop evidence against him. On the other side of the same coin, Pina and the grand jurors suspected that it had been Ponte who first told Diane about asphyxiation and the old murder case. That dovetailed with their notion that Kenny was hinting to Diane that he was guilty.

There is no doubt that Kenny later cajoled Diane into making inquiries for him about evidence in the case, as we will see.

But after talking with Reddington, Diane set her cap for Kenny; on April 28, a few days after she talked to Reddington, Diane sent an eight-page letter to Kenny in Florida via Federal Express. In the letter Diane expressed sympathy for Ponte, and told him that if he ever needed financial or moral support, he could count on her.

Kenny then called Reddington, according to the lawyer, and Reddington advised him in the strongest possible terms to stay away from Diane. But Kenny apparently couldn't resist.

On May 5, 1990, Kenny called Diane collect. It was the first of many telephone calls between the two during the month. Kenny always called collect, and later Diane said the month's telephone bill was nearly $500. Almost from the beginning, according to Diane, Kenny wanted her to come to see him in Florida. Diane later claimed she'd sent him nearly a thousand dollars in cash over the month, which raises the question of where Diane got this money.

As the talks between the two would-be lovers continued throughout the month, Kenny occasionally veered into angry denunciations of Pina, contending that Pina was bent on framing him for political purposes. Sometimes the murders were discussed, but Diane later said that she didn't like talking about the subject with Kenny because the topic made him so mad.

But sometime during the month of May, Diane learned two things: that Rochelle Clifford's mother had supposedly said her daughter had once lived with Kenny Ponte, which Kenny had denied; and that Rochelle had allegedly been involved in a burglary at Kenny's house, in which a gun had been taken.

At this point, unfortunately, things become extremely murky.

It appears that Pina and the grand jury were intensely interested in just how Kenny had known that Rochelle had taken the gun. In Pina's theory of the case, this was information Kenny *should not have known unless he'd been with Rochelle* after *April 3, 1988*—and Kenny, of course, claimed he had not seen Rochelle since that date.

In any event, during the last week in May, Diane called Rochelle Clifford's mother for a chat.

The accounts of Mrs. Clifford and Diane diverge, naturally; little with Diane was ever straightforward. Diane's story was that she wanted to find out from Mrs. Clifford just how dangerous Kenny was, before going down to visit him; from a different perspective, however—one adopted by the grand jury—Diane's call seemed a bit like she was fishing at Ponte's instigation to see whether Mrs. Clifford knew anything crucial about Ponte that might foreshadow his indictment.

Mrs. Clifford's version was significantly different. She said Diane called her to offer information about Rochelle. Diane didn't want to discuss it over the telephone, Mrs. Clifford said, so Mrs. Clifford drove to Lynn to meet with Diane. Mrs. Clifford brought a tape recorder with her.

But Diane didn't want to be taped. Instead, according to Mrs. Clifford, Diane wanted her to sign a statement claiming that she'd never said that Rochelle had ever lived with Kenny Ponte. Such a statement would have been very helpful to Kenny, because Pina had already told the court that Mrs. Clifford *had* said that very thing. That might show misconduct on Pina's part, possibly useful in case Kenny was indicted. Mrs. Clifford refused to sign anything. Diane later said that Mrs. Clifford agreed that she'd never told Pina that Rochelle had lived with Kenny, however.

The more critical issue was the gun. Although this was hardly the "smoking pistol" Pina had yearned for, Diane's knowledge about the gun seemed to indicate to Pina that Kenny was, for some reason, concealing the date, place, and time he'd last seen Rochelle. That was inculpatory—an inference that might help lead a jury toward a finding that Kenny was guilty of Rochelle's murder. Why else would Kenny lie about such a thing?

Diane later said Mrs. Clifford told her about the gun. She said Mrs. Clifford told her that Rochelle had admitted to her that she'd taken the gun during the burglary.

Mrs. Clifford later told Pina that Diane was wrong; she'd never said a word about the gun, Mrs. Clifford insisted. The question was, therefore: where had Diane Doherty first heard about the pistol—from Kenny, who supposedly shouldn't have known about it, or from Mrs. Clifford?

"Diane," Pina later said, when Diane was testifying before the grand jury, "Mrs. Clifford came here, and I'm going to tell you that she said she never told you anything about a gun, that Rochelle had taken a gun from Ken Ponte."

"She most certainly did," Diane said.

"She said she didn't tell you that," Pina continued. "I mean, she *knew* about it; but she says she didn't tell you about that, because that was something that was important for her and not to just tell you about that, is what she said."

"How else would I have known if she didn't tell me?"

"I'm asking you," said Pina. "How else would you know?"

The clear implication was that Pina believed that *Kenny* had told Diane about Rochelle's theft of the gun, which in turn showed Kenny was lying about the last time he'd seen Rochelle.

The conversation between Diane and Mrs. Clifford lasted until the early morning hours, according to Diane. And according to Diane's daughter, Kenny called twice during the conversation, each time to ask whether Diane was talking to Mrs. Clifford. This seems to indicate that Kenny knew what Diane was up to when she called Rochelle's mother.

On June 3, 1990, Diane flew to Florida to meet Kenny Ponte for the first time. The plane was diverted from Tampa to Orlando because of bad weather, so Kenny drove to Orlando to pick up Diane, a trip of about two hours.

Later, much of what transpired between Diane and Kenny in Florida received a great amount of publicity. How much of what Diane said happened *really* happened can only be guessed at, however, because by the time it all came out, Diane had provided three different versions, all of them fundamentally contradictory. By then, Kenny was in jail, charged with trying to strangle Diane.

SUMMER 1990

"More than all, his treacherous retreats struck more of dismay than perhaps aught else. For, when swimming before his exulting pursuers, with every apparent symptom of alarm, he had several times been known to turn round suddenly, and bearing down upon them, either stave their boats to splinters, or . . ."

—HERMAN MELVILLE, *Moby Dick*

50

Diane's Florida Vacation

On Monday, June 11, 1990, Kenny got into an argument with the woman who rented the other side of his duplex in Port Richey. The way Kenny portrayed it, the woman had failed to pay him rent that was due; the woman said Kenny refused to return her $50 deposit. The argument unfolded in the driveway, and when Kenny, with Diane, got into his car and drove away, the renter claimed Kenny had tried to run her down. She called the police.

By this time, the Port Richey Police Department was quite well informed about Kenny Ponte. They had already arrested Paul Ryley on the fraud charges, as requested by the Massachusetts authorities, and as noted, Boudreau had established a relationship with the Florida officers and had filled them in on the suspicions about Kenny.

Within a few hours of the renter's complaint, Kenny and Diane were in police custody. Kenny was booked for leaving the scene of an accident; Diane was arrested for violating her probation by traveling to Florida without notifying her probation officer.

When Boudreau's Florida contact, Sergeant William Sager of the Port Richey Police, talked to Diane the following day, he noticed bruises on Diane's neck.

It took some hours to get a story from Diane, but by that night, Sager felt he had enough evidence to charge Kenny with four felonies: aggravated battery, aggravated assault, false imprisonment, and use of a firearm in the commission of a felony.

According to Sager, Diane told him she'd gotten the bruises when Kenny had choked her almost to unconsciousness during an argument over whether Diane could return to Massachusetts. After releasing her, Diane told Sager, Kenny had produced a gun and pointed it at Diane's head while threatening to kill her if she returned to Massachusetts without him. Kenny then refused to let her leave the duplex, Diane said, and said if she went back to Massachusetts by herself, Kenny would have her daughter killed. Diane signed a statement for Sager which also contended that Kenny had raped her with a metal object that caused her to bleed. The language of the statement indicates that Sager wrote the words, not Diane:

"On the night of June 4, 1990," the statement read, "I slept with Mr. Ponte. During the act of intercourse, I was violated by means of an object thrust repeatedly three times into my organs. After bleeding profusely, Mr. Ponte released me from his grip."

The statement continued: "On Saturday afternoon, June 9, 1990, after a long conversation with Mr. Ponte about girls in New Bedford, he appeared to be caressing my neck and then just stopped, but his hand stayed on my neck. His fingers and thumbs began pressing so deep in my neck that I felt like I was going to suffocate, I couldn't breathe or swallow. I thought I would never see my poor daughter again."

Around 11 P.M. on June 12, Sager rearrested the already-jailed Kenny on the new felony charges. The next day, after a search of Kenny's house yielded two bedsheets with blood on them and Kenny's .38 caliber pistol, he notified the authorities in Massachusetts that he had Kenny in the cooler under arrest for choking and assaulting a woman.

That was exactly what Pina wanted to hear. It was the second piece of good news for Pina. Earlier the same day, a Massachusetts judge ordered the hair and saliva samples taken from Ponte in early 1989 to be turned over to the district attorney's office. Pina's enthusiasm was contagious.

"I feel we are very, very, very close," he told the

Standard-Times's Boyle. "I think I have a good feeling in my heart that I know who did it." The context made it very clear that Pina believed Ponte was guilty of the murders.

Over the next two days, lawyers in Pina's office put together two affidavits for the Florida courts. One affidavit recounted the allegations made against Kenny in the grand jury—the assertions that seemingly tied him to the murders. Pina wanted the judge in Florida to authorize a search of Kenny's house in the hope that evidence (such as a snuff film) could be found. The other document was an affidavit supporting a motion to raise Kenny's bail from $5,000 to $205,000. Pina also arranged for State Trooper Ken Martin, the forensic expert, to go to Florida for the new search.

Meanwhile, Diane was being questioned by a Florida prosecutor about the statements she'd made to Sager. Under oath, Diane reiterated her claims, and expanded on them—even going so far as to say that Kenny had confessed to her that he and others had killed the Massachusetts victims in some sort of satanic ritual! By now, Pina was ecstatic.

But on the following day, June 14, 1990, Kenny appeared in a Florida courtroom, and at that point Diane also appeared, saying Kenny hadn't choked her at all, or anything else that she'd told Sager he'd done; she'd only told Sager those things because Sager had been withholding her medicine, she said, and because Sager had promised her she could go back to Massachusetts immediately if she cooperated with the police.

Here was a monkey wrench of the first order: the victim/witness was recanting the whole story. The judge ordered an investigation into Diane's claims, but he refused to release Kenny. The whole situation seemed to be spiraling out of control; all of these people from Massachusetts, all these allegations and recantations. Nobody wanted to make any mistakes, however, and it was decided that the best strategy was to hold everything in place until it could get sorted out.

The next day, June 15, Kenny was brought back to

court again. He was expecting to be released because of Diane's recantation. Instead, he was served with the motion raising his bail to $205,000. Pina's affidavit linking him to the Massachusetts murders had arrived. Kenny was dumbfounded.

"Your Honor," Kenny said, "I find this incredible. The young lady (Diane), the victim stood before you and the state attorney and told the state attorney that the police coerced her for six hours to sign that statement.

"For the life of me, I can't understand why there should be *any* bond when that occurred." Under the circumstances, Kenny said, he should be released without any bail at all.

But the judge wouldn't allow it. Based on the statements in the affidavit, he said—but Kenny interrupted him.

"Your Honor, there have been five people besides me who have been dragged through the mud concerning this matter. Your Honor, the facts of this case are, three of my former clients were unfortunately the victims, and the police questioned me on that and I fully cooperated with them."

The judge shrugged. Obviously, the Massachusetts authorities wanted *more* cooperation, or they wouldn't have supported the motion to raise Kenny's bail.

Kenny went back to jail and called an experienced Florida defense attorney, J. Larry Hart. He also telephoned reporters in Massachusetts and accused Pina of twisting the arms of the Florida police in order to look good for the voters back home.

That afternoon, Diane was grilled anew by the Florida prosecutors about her recantation. In the new questioning, the first thing Diane wanted to know about was perjury.

After a prosecutor explained what perjury was, Diane said she'd kept telling Sager she wanted a lawyer.

"And they kept telling me," she said, "(that) I don't need a lawyer.

"I didn't do anything wrong, I have not committed perjury. I'm a narcoleptic, I drift in and drift out. I can be conscious and then not be conscious for a little while if I get high anxiety.

"I spent that whole day at that police station when I got arrested," she added. "I spent the whole day crying, I throw up blood in the afternoon. It was like an hour, I don't remember what happened. I can remember drifting back in and being in the police car . . .

"So if I did any kind of swearing or anything like that I don't think I should get in trouble for it." In effect, Diane was admitting she was an unreliable witness because of her medical condition, liable to say just about anything, and that she shouldn't be blamed for it.

The prosecutors then showed Diane the two-page statement she'd signed. Diane admitted that she'd signed the statement, but said she didn't remember telling Sager any of the things in the statement. Not only that, Diane added, but the statement simply wasn't true—that none of the things had really happened. Kenny had *never* raped her with a metal object, Diane said.

They'd only had sex once, she said, and then her menstrual period came, which was how blood got on the sheets. Kenny had never choked her, she said, never threatened her with a gun, never held her against her will. He'd never said a word about her daughter, Diane said.

"The guy was nothing but a gentleman when I was at his house," she said. "He didn't do anything violent to me."

Well, where did the bruises on Diane's neck come from?

"I know where these bruises came from on my throat: the first night I made love with Mr. Ponte. I bruise real, real easy." The bruises came during a bout of passion, she indicated. "If you look at them real close, you can see," Diane added.

That same afternoon, June 15, 1990, Kenny's lawyer J. Larry Hart attempted to have Kenny's bail reduced, but failed. Hart then went to see Diane in jail. He interviewed her on a bench in a corridor, and Diane for the third time said she'd never said any of the things Sager claimed she'd said. She again accused Sager of coercing her.

After Hart left the jail, he learned that the court had nevertheless granted a new warrant to search Kenny's house, as Pina had asked. He drove over to the house that evening with his two young daughters, thinking he'd see what was going on, and also pick up a copy of the search warrant and its supporting affidavit, the paperwork provided by Pina's office. When Hart arrived at Kenny's house he was astounded to see it ringed with yellow crime-scene tape; all the television stations for miles around had set up cameras in Kenny's backyard!

Hart stepped over the yellow tape and started toward the house, only to be confronted by Sergeant Sager. This is a crime scene, Sager warned, threatening to arrest Hart (a former prosecutor) for interfering with the search. Hart was taken aback, and then started laughing. Everyone seemed so uptight and self-important, he thought. Did they think he was going to go into the house and find the key piece of evidence with everyone looking at him, and then spirit it away? He stepped back over the tape and told Sager he only wanted to pick up the search warrant. Couldn't he go into the house and pick it up?

No, Sager said. Sager went back inside the house. Hart waited outside as the evening wore on. Finally, after about two hours, Sager came back with the warrant. But the supporting affidavit—the document that contained all the real meat of the allegations against Kenny—wasn't provided. Sager told Hart he couldn't have that—it was being put under court seal at Pina's request.

Although Ponte and his lawyer had an absolute legal right to see the paperwork that authorized the search, this maneuvering prevented it. That meant Hart couldn't begin to figure out a way of getting Kenny out of jail, which was exactly what Pina wanted. But sealing the affidavit also prevented anyone from challenging the factuality of its contents. In effect, Pina was manipulating the Florida authorities to avoid any outside scrutiny of the viability of his theories about Kenny Ponte.

Later that night, officers from the Port Richey Police Department and Massachusetts trooper Ken Martin listed everything they had seized from Kenny Ponte's house.

The big item was videotapes—66 of them, in fact. Almost all of them appeared to be home recordings. Someone would have to sit down and watch them all to see if any one of them contained evidence of the murders. Other items taken included numerous articles of women's attire, some snapshots of women in lingerie, two short lengths of rope, some jewelry, and two identification cards belonging to women—neither of them victims of the Highway Murderer. The house, according to Hart, was a complete mess.

Kenny meanwhile called all the newspapers in Massachusetts and fired off a new barrage at Pina.

"I wish to publicly inform Mr. Pina that there is no way he is ever going to frame me for the highway killings so he can win his upcoming reelection campaign," Ponte told the *Standard-Times*. "It is clear to me that Mr. Pina will stop at nothing to try to win his upcoming reelection. It is my belief that the reason they coerced Ms. Doherty to sign false statements against me was to satisfy the overwhelming desires of the incompetent Bristol County District Attorney Ronald Pina to have the police search my Florida home, which they did."

By Sunday, Diane was still in jail, and yearning to go home. She talked to her brother in Massachusetts. Then she called Sager and told him that when she'd recanted her allegations against Kenny, she'd lied. She did it to protect her daughter from Kenny's powerful friends in Massachusetts, Diane told the Port Richey sergeant. But now her daughter was safe, having been spirited out of the country by her family, so she felt free to tell the truth, and the truth was, Kenny really *had* choked her.

The next day, Diane again testified under oath, reiterating that she'd lied about her recantation—and to Hart, Ponte's lawyer—because she feared for her daughter's safety. The effect of this was to make Hart into a witness for Ponte, which prevented him from being Ponte's lawyer. Hart was exasperated with the flip-flopping Diane. Diane wanted to know if anyone was going to find out about her latest version of the events.

"Let me say this," Hart told her. "I cannot assure you

that others won't learn of this statement. I can't offer that assurance to you."

"Mr. Hart," Diane said, "he told me about all those dead girls. I think I have good reason to be nervous about my daughter." Here was sworn testimony from Diane suggesting that Kenny Ponte had confessed to her—just exactly as had supposedly happened the year before at Leslie Mello's kitchen table!

51

Neighbors

On Tuesday, June 26, 1990, Diane Doherty finally got her wish and was allowed to return to Massachusetts. Troopers Gonsalves and Dill went to Florida to pick her up. On the way back on the plane, Diane told them what happened to her in Florida. Apparently, Diane forgot all about the satanic ritual killings that Kenny supposedly had confessed to. Soon Diane was back in Framingham because of her parole violation.

Kenny remained in jail in Florida, but he was hardly keeping quiet. On the day Diane went back to the slammer, Ponte gave a political endorsement of Paul Walsh for district attorney. It was probably the first time in history that a jailed serial murder suspect had ever made a political endorsement.

Walsh laughed, but knew he had to be careful. The last thing he wanted to do was be seen as believing Kenny Ponte. Who knew what might happen? What if Kenny *was* the killer? "I don't think this is out of any love for Paul Walsh," he said. "I think it's probably his distaste for the treatment he's received from Ron Pina."

Then, at the end of the week, Diane's sworn statement in Florida that Ponte had "told me about all those dead girls" was leaked to *The Boston Globe*. That made Ponte look guilty, especially when Diane's earlier sworn statement—that Ponte had treated her like a gentleman throughout—*wasn't* leaked.

*   *   *

But if Pina and the press in Massachusetts were growing more excited about the prospect of a solution to the
Highway Murders, the authorities in Florida were beginning to believe that they'd been had by their Yankee
counterparts.

The problem was Diane. All of her waffling around on
the facts had destroyed her credibility as a witness. And a
hard look at the affidavits linking Kenny to the Massachusetts murders showed that the most damaging information
was hearsay, and most of that from police officers like
Boudreau—who might have every interest in doing Pina's
bidding. And wasn't Pina running for reelection? The
whole situation was beginning to smell, the authorities in
Florida told each other.

On July 13, Kenny was finally released from jail. "Justice has prevailed, gentlemen," Kenny said, as he was released without bail. "For two years, I've been dragged
through the mud and called everything from a murderer
to a sex pervert, with no charges." Now, said Kenny, he
intended to write a book about the whole nightmare. He
intended to call it *Presumed Guilty*, he said, taking off from
Scott Turow's *Presumed Innocent*.

But on that same day, Pina's spokesman Jim Martin
announced that police protection for Pina would be beefed
up. The reason: one of the earlier witnesses before the
grand jury, Elsa Johnson—Ponte and Ryley's former
housemate—had told the jury that while in Florida Ponte
had threatened to come back to New Bedford and shoot
Pina, his wife Sheila, and Pina's teenaged daughter. Now
that Ponte was out, Martin said, the talk seemed a lot
more threatening.

This was serious, Martin added; and it was particularly
serious because Pina had just learned, for the first time,
that Ponte's sister and mother were living in a house right
next door to the district attorney.

In retrospect it seems almost unbelievable that Ron
Pina could have lived next door to Kenny Ponte's family
for as long as he did without being aware of it. Pina later
thought that Kenny's sister and mother had moved into

the neighborhood after he did, but before the murders or the investigation began. Reddington, however, said he found evidence that the Ponte family had been living in the house for six years, before Pina had moved in. Actually, Ponte's sister and her husband bought the house in May 1989, not realizing that their next-door neighbor was the man investigating her brother.

In any event, in the years prior to the shocking discovery that he was the neighbor of his prime suspect's family, Pina once visited them without realizing who they were. Ponte's mother and sister gave him the cold shoulder, Jim Martin related, but Pina had simply shrugged it off without realizing that his neighbors were in fact the closest relatives of the man he'd been pursuing as a possible serial murderer for nearly 18 months.

Nevertheless, the day after Kenny's release in Florida, Pina's office went to court and obtained an added condition to Ponte's release on the assault and drug charges that had been filed earlier. The new condition barred Ponte from coming within 1,000 feet of Pina's house, and it had the practical effect of preventing Ponte from visiting his mother.

In Port Richey, Ponte erupted once more. "I will never, ever be kept away from my family because of this crazy person who masquerades as a responsible public official," he told reporters. Then he issued a challenge to the district attorney. "Mr. Pina, if you believe that I threatened your life, indict me and I'll go to court anytime I am summoned. Otherwise, why don't you just shut your mouth and leave me alone once and for all?"

Pina's resort to the courts to keep Ponte away predictably brought the criticism of Walsh, who called Pina's action an abuse of his office, and said that it looked like Pina was grandstanding again. "It makes me wonder about the legitimacy of the threat complaints," Walsh said, noting that the alleged threats had been made months earlier, if at all.

"Mr. Ponte was fifteen hundred miles away," Walsh told Boyle from the *Standard-Times*. "The alleged threat was made back in April (actually before that). It was not communicated to Mr. Pina but said to some young lady

(Elsa) who later told him about it. It was made back in April and Pina becomes afraid now? That strikes me as odd."

Jim Martin immediately counterattacked on Pina's behalf. "Shame on him if he thinks a death threat on a 16-year-old is political," Martin said. Pina was *really* worried, Martin added. "They basically became prisoners in their own home." Ironically, Walsh had represented Elsa on bad check and drug charges in 1988 and 1989. The challenger certainly knew something about Elsa's reputation for veracity.

The whole life-threatening circumstance was a Pina reliable, Walsh added. "If you look at his track record, he's done this before." Once, said Walsh, Pina had claimed a Colombian hit squad and the mob were both after him at the same time. "I don't know of any other district attorney who has done this," Walsh said. "I really do believe it is a stunt that he uses from time to time."

"This is far from a political issue," Martin shot back. "And anyone trying to make a political name for themselves because of this, shame on them."

The next day Pina went to court to make the stay-away order permanent, but this time Ponte had Reddington there to represent him. This initial first confrontation between Pina and Reddington had all the atmospherics of two pit bulls meeting each other for the first time.

"We're going to court," Reddington later recalled, "and Pina's there with his wife, Sheila, the former newsperson, and his daughter. They were sitting there, and of course the press interviewed them. Pina was the picture of stoicism. And of course, my guy (Ponte) is down in Florida.

"He had never come up to Massachusetts, had no intention of coming up to Massachusetts," Reddington said. "And this whole thing was blown way out of proportion. I was getting calls from New York news reporters about the D.A., the 'crime-fighting D.A.' with the serial killer moving in next door to him."

With camera lights and strobes flashing, Reddington, Pina, and Veary went into a side room to work out a permanent order. Pina wouldn't look at him, Reddington remembered, or even shake his hand. That made Reddington mad, and Veary finally intervened to calm everyone down.

Eventually, both sides worked out an accommodation. Pina withdrew his request for the court order, and in return Ponte agreed to give the district attorney a day's notice before coming back to New Bedford. The irony of Pina's now wanting to keep Ponte away from town after all of the maneuvering the year before to bring him back wasn't lost on anyone.

Afterward, Reddington told reporters that he'd offered Pina a deal: if Pina would give Kenny immunity on charges other than murder, Kenny would testify before the special grand jury. Even though he'd advised Kenny to say nothing, Reddington said, Kenny was eager to appear before the investigating panel.

"He feels he has nothing to lose and everything to gain," Reddington told *The Globe*. "The man hasn't done anything that would lead the grand jury to think that he is guilty, and he wants them to hear his side of the story."

But Pina was adamant. "There will be no immunity offered by this office," Jim Martin said. "We will not make deals to get to the truth." Pina expanded on this.

"What I would like to know from Ken is ... does he know any of the dead women? How many does he know? When did he last see them alive? And under what circumstances?" he told Boyle.

That was easy, Ponte said from Florida. He had known four of the victims, not seven as Pina kept suggesting: he'd known Nancy Paiva, Sandy Botelho, Mary Rose Santos, and he'd tried to help Rochelle Clifford. And although he might once have called police to have them remove Dawn Mendes from his porch, he wasn't absolutely sure.

Later the same day, Pina announced that the special grand jury would resume taking testimony once more. Walsh accused Pina of using the jury to make political mileage. But Pina denied it. He was neither obsessed with the murders, nor was he grandstanding, he said. He intended to follow the leads wherever they headed.

——— 52 ———

Whispers Wildies

It was during all this uproar over Ponte's intentions toward Pina that Diane Doherty, now safely back at Framingham, began "remembering" things.

When questioned about this later, Diane responded that the whole Florida trip had so badly freaked her out that she had mercifully blotted much of it from her memory. A psychiatrist and priest at the prison were helping her, she said, but it was hard. Still, flashes from the recent past kept creeping back into her mind unbidden. Soon she called a lawyer in Lynn and asked him to contact Troopers Gonsalves and Dill to let them know she had some things to tell them. Thus it was, on July 24, 1990, that Diane Doherty finally made her first appearance before Ron Pina's special grand jury investigating the Highway Murders.

She'd never met Kenny until June, Diane said, no matter what the creepy private investigator had told the jury She'd only gotten involved with Kenny *because* of the private eye—after all, the investigator had been pressing her to sign the affidavit about the confession at Leslie Mello's kitchen table, and Diane knew that had never happened. So she felt sorry for Kenny, and she'd made contact with him at his house in Florida.

She flew down to see Kenny on June 3, Diane said. Kenny had picked her up at the airport, and on the way

280

back to his house in Port Richey, Kenny had made her
give him oral sex the whole way—about two hours.

When she'd objected to this, Diane said, Kenny had
told her, "It's my way or the highway." She didn't get
that at first, Diane said, but later realized that Kenny was
saying that if she didn't do whatever he wanted, he'd kill
her and throw her body out along the highway, just like
the other victims.

The whole week with Kenny was weird, Diane said.
Kenny tied her up and had sex with her, Kenny had in-
serted a foreign object in her vagina, Kenny made one of
his cats have sex with her—it went on and on. Kenny
had ten cats, she said—named Rochelle, Robin, Christine,
Debbie . . .

What about the murders?

Oh yes. The whole thing had to do with a movie, Diane
said. A movie and drugs.

"He said they were, all these girls here, there were nine
girls in this movie," Diane said. Rochelle Clifford was not
in the movie, Diane said. Kenny had told her she was
"different" than the other victims. Kenny wanted Rochelle
dead for his own reasons, she said, not someone else's.
Rochelle was going to testify against him in the gun case,
and that's why *she* was killed.

"Did he tell you why the others died?"

"Oh yeah."

"Okay."

"About the movies."

"What did he tell you?"

"These girls were in the movie," Diane said. "And all
of them die at the end of sexual—you know, like after you
have a movie and you splice it, and you had another part
in. But I guess they owed money for cocaine and heroin,
a lot of money. And they knew he was bringing it into
New Bedford. And so Kenny had to kill most of them
because he owed a lot of money for heroin. That's part
of it."

"Who did he owe money to?" Pina asked. "Did he tell
you? Did he tell you?"

"That's when the name of Mr. (here Diane named the
proprietor of Whispers Pub, the man who'd been accused

by Boudreau of running the $5.2 million a year cocaine ring) came up."

"And who's he? Did he ever tell you anything about (him)?"

"No," said Diane. "He told me he was dead, but I found out he wasn't."

"What did he tell you about that?"

"Mr. (The proprietor) put up the money mostly for the movie itself. And the movie was supposed to go to Canada and Mexico, but it never made it out of the country. And so, these girls that were in the movie were supposed to get a cut ... from the profit from selling the movie.

"And so they started—they were getting lengthy into the time that they wanted their money. And so that's part of the reason, another reason for it. I don't think he had any intention of paying them that."

The name of the movie, according to Diane, was *Whispers Wildies*.

"I Have Nothing to Fear"

In fairness, despite critics such as Walsh and Reddington, Ron Pina truly wanted to solve the Highway Murders. It wasn't only for political reasons, although it was probably difficult for Pina to undertake anything without automatically calculating its political dimensions.

But whatever else he was, Pina was not an unfeeling man. He genuinely grieved for the families of the victims, and wanted to do what he could to ease their pain. He took his responsibility for investigating the murders quite seriously. It was his misfortune to be handicapped by weak technical support, at least initially, in the pathology and forensic labs, so crucial to determining how and when someone was killed; by organizational obstacles that made it difficult for him to exert control over the investigation; by what he, at least, saw as inadequate training for the investigators; by jurisdictional frictions and petty jealousies; and most of all by witnesses whose reliability was the worst that can be imagined.

Yet Pina plunged ahead, just as he had done with the Big Dan's case, because at least he was getting something to work with. With Jeanne Kaloshis, Elsa Johnson, Diane Doherty, and all the other assorted scrapings from the state's jails and prisons, he was at least getting directions to follow; unfortunately, it appears that he was following the line of least resistance, which is not always the right thing to do.

So it was, that by early August, Pina told the grand jury that he and his investigators were done presenting testimony. It would be up to the 23 members of the jury to decide what to do by themselves.

While Pina was telling the jury that the next move was up to them, Kenny Ponte was returning to Massachusetts. A local television show had arranged to interview him live. By now, Kenny had learned to manipulate the media as well as Pina. He called the newspapers to tell them he'd be on the air.

"I intend to discuss the illegal and unethical and nightmarish occurrence of being tried in all forms of the media for a heinous crime I have nothing to do with," Kenny told the *Standard-Times*.

"My only response from the beginning, and now, is that I be treated like a citizen of the United States and be afforded due process of law. It is very unfortunate for myself and the people of Bristol County that Ron Pina does not have the political courage to stand up and tell the truth—the truth being, he has absolutely no idea who committed this terrible crime."

Kenny flew into Boston's Logan Airport and was mobbed by newspeople. Reddington met him and was appalled to see his client wearing dark glasses that made him look like a hood.

Amid the television lights, ordinary people around Kenny were agog. Kenny couldn't resist. One passerby approached Kenny and asked him who he was, since he obviously had to be somebody important. Kenny said he was the ambassador from Iraq, and had just arrived to negotiate a peace agreement for the Gulf crisis. "Stop it, Kenny," Reddington whispered.

Another person, however, recognized him. "Say," the person began, "aren't you—?"

Kenny admitted it. "Yes, hi, I'm Ken Ponte, the famous serial killer," laughing in such a way so that the person *knew* Ponte couldn't possibly be the killer. Reddington was horrified. "Kenny, don't say things like that," Reddington told him, but Kenny persisted in shaking hands with people and making it clear that he wasn't about to hide out.

*   *   *

That night on television Ponte told the show's host that he'd never harmed anybody in his life.

"I have nothing to fear from Ron Pina," Kenny said. "If he has something on me, why am I not indicted now? Ron Pina lacks the political courage to get up and tell the truth. The first rule of politics is to get elected. What does it matter if six months later I'm found innocent? He'll blame it on the liberal judges. I'm sick of it. I want to get him off my back." The television host, Jerry Williams, asked Kenny about the bloody sheets taken by the police in Florida. Matter-of-factly, Kenny said the bloodstains had occurred because Diane had been menstruating.

It was clear to him, Kenny continued, that the police were out to get him. He blamed the Saint, particularly. "At one point he said to me in a very soft voice, 'Ken, why don't you just tell me you killed those girls?' I found the question so insulting and so incredulous. I just said, 'No.' Then he said, 'Until and unless you come down and talk to us, you're going to be screwed by the media.' "

When Williams asked whether he had any sexual hang-ups, Kenny said his only hang-up he had right then was a fear of dating *anyone*.

On the following day, Kenny drove to New Bedford, accompanied by a camera crew from a national television show. Kenny went to visit his mother in the house next door to the Pinas. Each house had a political lawn sign: one for Pina, one for Walsh. Pina and his wife weren't home. The crew from the television show checked to be sure.

The next day Pina learned that the grand jury wasn't happy. He'd left them alone to decide what to do. The room was piled high with testimonial transcripts. Veary recalled later that the jury asked whether they had to read all that material.

"And the grand jury says, 'Let's review this testimony,' and we started saying, all right, here's so-and-so's testimony," Veary recalled, indicating that as the jury asked for each portion, someone would point to the appropriate transcript. "And the response we got from some people in the room was, 'Do you want us to *read* it?' 'Well, of course we want you to read it. We're not gonna stand here and read it. We're not gonna summarize it, because summarizing is unfair.' "

But Pina, Veary, and others in the district attorney's office realized that they had dumped a huge load of information on the jurors, who after all, had full-time jobs, and who didn't have the luxury (or curse) of thinking about the Highway Murders every minute of the day. So Pina and Veary asked Carol Starkey, an assistant district attorney, to put together the components of the case against Ponte on a chart.

"We developed these diagrams of who essentially said what about what and what time period, tracing the victims and tracing the witness statements, and trying to tie this all in together," Veary said later. "I can remember her stopping in the office, it was like a Sunday morning or Sunday evening, there's poor Carol on the floor, cutting and pasting this thing. We've reviewed it before, and decided how best to do it, but she's doing the real work on the thing.

"The idea was, 'Folks, if you want to know how so-and-so says that these two people were together two days after the second of these two people apparently disappeared, if you want to know about that, see line 12, page 18. Now you read here, we're not gonna tell you about it, *you* read it.' " The diagrams essentially provided a road map to the testimony the jurors had been hearing for the previous 18 months, a visual index. So the jury dug into the transcripts and started to talk about the case.

Pretty soon, they had questions.

54

Speechless

On August 17, 1990, Pina's political future and the murder investigation were prominently linked together in *The Boston Globe* in a story written by reporters Tom Coakley and John Ellement.

In "Bristol D.A. Race Seen Linked to Murders Probe," the two reporters suggested that an indictment would clearly help Pina retain his job in the forthcoming election against Walsh. Several politicians and political experts guessed that an indictment would restore Pina's credibility among some voters. And they noted that Walsh wasn't at all adverse to suggesting that Pina had manipulated the whole thing for his own aggrandizement.

Walsh even gave an impromptu press conference on the courthouse steps as the grand jury was meeting.

"I'm very concerned about the timing of all this," Walsh told the reporters. "The reviewing of all the evidence and pushing the grand jury for an indictment 30 days before a tough election ... It has to (raise) one question: Why now?"

Hearing of Walsh's remark infuriated Pina.

"There is nothing political about this case," Pina said. "Why is he trying to make it political? The grand jury proceeds on its own. A political agenda is not going to set its timetable."

The truth was, Pina felt he was in an impossible position. If an indictment *were* voted, he'd be accused of push-

ing for the charge to help him in the election; if the jury
failed to return an indictment, he ran the risk of voters
concluding that he was a failure. One political adviser,
Pina later said, urged him to head off the grand jury so
that no decision would be made before the voting. But
Pina rejected that; he'd already said the jurors had the
power to decide what to do, and if he took that power
away at the eleventh hour, it *would* be political.

A second thread ran through the political speculation,
however. Pina's election campaign had conducted an opinion poll, and rumors were spreading that one question in
the poll was whether an indictment in the Highway Murders would make a voter more likely to vote for Pina.

Pina later said the rumor was untrue: no question was
asked about any indictment. The poll did indicate, however, that the murder case was a high priority issue among
the voters.

The day *The Globe* story appeared, Pina was cornered
by reporters as he left the courthouse. He again rejected
claims that he was using the investigation and the jury for
political purposes. A reporter asked Pina how an indictment would affect his chances of reelection. Furious, Pina
walked away without saying another word—probably a first
for him.

55

Very Crucial Testimony

On the same afternoon, Diane Doherty returned to testify before the grand jury by popular demand—at least, by a demand popular among the grand jurors themselves. The truth was, the jurors weren't sure exactly what to make of Diane, either personally, or of her testimony.

"I wasn't prepared for this at all," Diane said. "Truthfully."

"That's it," said the jury's foreman, putting his finger exactly on the trouble with Diane.

The jurors wanted to test Diane's credibility. By this time, the jurors were telling Pina what *they* wanted to know, not just what Pina thought they should know.

"They're not little people who sit there," Pina said of the jurors, later. "In fact, what you're getting in an investigative grand jury are people who suddenly become detectives ... because once the district attorney or assistant district attorney does what they are supposed to do, a grand juror now can raise their hand and inquire.

"And, these people had heard tons of information, a great deal of things about a lot of people, and they took notes and were very studious, they pretty much were ready to inquire. They cross-examined. I mean, they literally cross-examined the witnesses."

Pina took Diane back over her story, probing for discrepancies. There were, in fact, a number of discrepancies. But Diane resolutely hung on to her assertion that Kenny had confessed to killing Rochelle Clifford, and that Kenny had told her the other victims had all been killed in connection with their roles in some sort of video.

"So," said Pina, "when did this so-called conversation between you and Mr. Ponte take place? How can you remember that?"

"Which conversation?"

"Well, you just said about all these murders. When did you hear that from Mr. Ponte?"

"The night before I left when he showed me, I told you, the movie I talked about." Diane was saying Kenny had actually shown her the fabled video. Previously she had only said that Kenny claimed it existed.

After more questions about the gun Rochelle had supposedly taken from Kenny, Pina returned to the subject of Rochelle herself.

"Did he say why Rochelle died? Did he tell you why?"

"Something to do with testifying against him, first of all."

"That she was going to testify against him?"

Diane agreed.

"Did he say anything else? Was there any other reason?"

"By this time, she was starting to try and blackmail him about these—this movie. All those girls, I guess, were talking too much before when they shouldn't have been. And they all owed money for drugs, too. Like he did."

"What about Rochelle? Let's stay with Rochelle."

"I don't think—I'm not real, real sure about if Rochelle was in the movie or not. But he offed her, as he said."

"He what? Offed her? Is that what you said?"

"Yeah. I think it means murder. Kill. Whatever. And so, because she was starting to blackmail him about that movie. And to who—I don't know who she was blackmailing him to or whatever. But once, you know, he gave into her once, like that, he would have continued blackmailing her, I guess. Plus, I think he loved her, too, of what love is to him. You know."

No, the jury didn't know, Pina persisted. Finally, one juror became exasperated. He or she wanted to know about the video, no more fooling around.

"Would you describe for us again, please, in details the film you had earlier told us Kenny—Mr. Ponte required you to view when you were with him in Florida, in which the murder of these women or some of them was depicted. Would you describe that again from the very beginning and tell us as much about it as you recall?"

That was putting it in plain terms.

But Diane balked.

"Mr. Pina," she said, "I don't want to do that. I don't want to do that. I don't want to go through that again." She'd been sick, Diane said. Couldn't the jurors just look through their notes? "I'm sorry."

Diane said she'd been harassed at Framingham; half the women there thought she'd refused to testify against Kenny in Florida and hated her for that, whereas the other half thought she *had* testified against Kenny, and considered her a snitch.

"Ms. Doherty," said Pina, "let me tell you something."

"What?"

"I think most people are having a tough time believing you."

"Yeah."

"Do you have a problem with that?"

No, said Diane. Even her own family was having a hard time believing her.

But the jurors weren't going to let go of the videotape issue.

"Ms. Doherty," said a juror, "let me ask you this."

"What?"

"If this case goes to trial, you're going to be asked to testify about that movie. Are you still going to (refuse) to testify about it?"

Diane said she thought she'd get better with the passage of time. "I spend a good deal like every day, like I cry for hours and hours. Not like I miss Kenny or anything. Just because of how bizarre this thing happening in my life (is) and happening in my daughter's life."

"Well," said the jury foreman, "you made it happen."

"I didn't make it happen."

"You certainly did," the foreman shot back. "*You* went down to Florida."

"I didn't make him have anything to do with those girls."

"But before you even went down to Florida, that's where we find a huge credibility gap. Okay?"

"Yeah."

"Honestly," the foreman continued, "I think you're a fruitloop. Your daughter told you not to go to Florida. Okay. There's numerous articles pointing toward this man, Kenneth Ponte. Whether or not he is guilty remains to be seen. And why would you even jeopardize yourself and your daughter's safety to do such a thing? Okay? Not because you felt sorry for him."

"Well, I tell you what," said Diane. "I don't like being called names either. So I think you should refrain from calling me a fruitloop or anything else."

"That's my personal opinion."

"Well, it's very unprofessional, too."

"I'm not a professional type person," the foreman said.

Name-calling was something Pina wanted to avoid. He tried to steer the discussion back to more productive channels. "Why *did* you go down there?" he asked. "What did you *really* think?"

"I had to know for myself," Diane said.

"Why?"

"Because I loved him."

A juror was incredulous. "How did you love him? You had never met him."

After another sharp exchange between Diane and the foreman, who as much as accused her of lying, another juror tried to edge back toward the videotape.

"I'd like to ask you, and I sympathize with what you're going through, but it's very important to this grand jury that we know what went on in that videotape. It's very important because we are the ones who have to sit down in the end and make a decision. And we don't want to make a wrong decision, and then have this certain person get acquitted. This is a serious charge. We do have to know what's going on in that video. And I would appreciate it if you tell me what went on in that video and if you recognize any of those persons (the victims) in the video."

"When I was here the last time," Diane said, "Mr. Pina put the pictures on the table. And some of the girls looked like some of the girls that were in that movie. And I'm not going to go through the whole thing again today. If you want to do whatever you have to do to legally make me come back here ... at least I'll have enough time to get more control of myself inside."

But some jurors were insistent.

"We have to know what went on in that video. I think it's very important," said one juror.

"Well," Diane said, "you can reread the notes if you want."

"We've heard it before," a juror continued, "and we want to hear it again. We went through your past testimony already."

"Excuse me?"

"We went through the past testimony about what you said about the video. Now we have more questions about it."

"Does the video exist?" a second juror asked.

Diane nodded.

"Where is it?"

"It's in Florida," said Diane.

Now several jurors started talking at once. "It's in Florida? Where? At his house? Outside?"

"Did he destroy it?"

"What did he do with it?"

"I don't know what he did with it after I left," said Diane.

"What'd he do with it while you were there at the house?" Pina asked.

"We watched it," said Diane. "And then he went back outside, and I went in the bathroom."

"Don't you care about these families, all these little children that they've left behind?"

Diane nodded.

"Why don't you stop thinking about yourself for a minute?" a juror asked.

"Look," said another, "instead of wasting everyone's time, why don't you tell us exactly what happened in that video one more time?"

"Because I'm not going to do it," said Diane. "I can't, I can't handle it."

"Because, just like you weren't going to come home and leave Kenny Ponte," a juror said, turning nasty.

"Just like I wasn't—"

"You left your daughter home that you loved so much to go see this jerk in Florida who may be a murderer. Why didn't he come to New Bedford to see *you?*"

She didn't want Kenny in her house, Diane admitted. She thought he might get in trouble with the police.

"Diane," said another juror, "you've got to realize that there are 11 women missing. Okay, and we've found 9 of them."

"Yeah," said Diane.

"All right," the juror continued. "And there are nine parents out there suffering and wondering who killed these women. Why did their daughter have to die the way she did? And you have given us testimony, very crucial testimony, than any other witness that we've had in this courtroom in the past 20 months. Okay?"

"Uh-huh."

"Now, you gotta stop thinking about yourself. And you've got to think about the rest of the people. And we've got to know what the hell's going on. And you know more than anybody else. And we want to know it. We want to know it because we gotta make a conviction here. And we don't want to pick a wrong guy, and then send him to trial and then have him acquitted because we don't have enough evidence. So you've got to stop thinking about yourself—"

"No," said Diane. "I don't. I *don't* have to stop thinking about myself. I just arrived too. I need to be able to carry on in my life, too. Everything that's going to be my future blew up in my face. It's been a lot of pain and grief for me, too."

"That's your fault."

"Maybe it is."

"Because you're the one who went down to Florida."

"You're the one who went down to Florida," said another juror. "You're the one who spent the time with the man. You're the one who knows all the bullshit. All right.

And we want to know it. And we don't want to hear no more bullshit."

The jury was getting hostile.

"Well, I'm sorry," Diane said, "but I'm not going to go over the whole thing again."

She would, she said, be willing to come back another time.

But the jury wasn't receptive to that. Because, a little more than an hour later, the jury voted to indict Kenny Ponte on one count of first-degree murder.

56
Indicted

Just why the jury voted its indictment remains uncertain, known only to the jurors who were in the room. Certainly Pina hadn't asked for the indictment. As he later recalled, he was as surprised as anyone when the jury voted its true bill.

That there was no definitive evidence to connect Kenny Ponte with any of the crimes seems clear. Even Pina later admitted the case had its problems.

"I'm not going to tell you it was the greatest case in the world," he said later. "No one is gonna have the greatest case in the world when you're dealing with people who are druggies, have bad memories, have been in jail, prostitutes ... You've got to go through this stuff with a rake, and try to figure out what's true and what's not true. I think that we were doing that. And I think the grand jury ... I've got to give those people a lot of credit, I really do.

"They weren't cops, they weren't lawyers, they were normal human beings, who heard all this stuff and they asked questions. They didn't sit there. Nobody spoon fed them. And they didn't come back with, let's indict everybody in the world.

"So, was there a smoking gun? No. Was there a lot of information that, when finally viewed in perspective, let's really analyze it and take it apart, I think that they reasonably, based on testimony that they heard and cross-examined, led to the conclusion that they felt would be sufficient information to bring someone to trial ... that's all an indictment is, not that he's guilty, but bring him to trial for murdering one individual."

But there may have been some other factors involved.

Fatigue, for one. For nearly 18 months, the jury had been hearing testimony from a long string of witnesses, many of them from the lower depths. And much of the testimony was unpleasant—stories about drugs, beatings, rapings, skeletal remains, pornography, snuff films, in short, about the rottenest sort of human behavior. One has to wonder whether the normal human being's mind involuntarily recoils and wishes to put an end to the strain.

And it was obvious that Pina and the others *expected* something. They'd brought in all of the testimony, gone to all the trouble to make a road map, and then had sat back, waiting. It was almost as if the district attorney were saying, See, it's there, all *you* have to do is look for it. Why else would the district attorney have announced there would be no more testimony? Wasn't that like saying the jury now had everything it needed?

And there might have been another factor: the Stockholm syndrome. Just like the hostages in the bank in a lengthy standoff, or the prisoners at Framingham, the jurors may have been captured psychologically by the district attorney's sense of mission. That was evident in the intensity that greeted Diane Doherty, and was even articulated. "We want to know it," one juror said, "because we gotta make a conviction here."

Making a conviction, of course, was *not* the grand jury's job. The grand jury was charged with getting the facts.

While the jury was deliberating, Kenny was on the air again, lashing out at Pina. He was a guest of WBSM's Henry Carreiro.

"In the last two years, my life has been a living hell," Kenny said. "To be called a murderer, or portrayed as a murderer by a district attorney is very powerful. It has bankrupted me; it has caused me the most severe emotional distress that any one human being could ever undergo. I've challenged anyone on the face of this planet to

come forward and prove that Ken Ponte has ever committed a violent act in his entire life. And yet, no one can
come forward with any proof of that."

Kenny reminded the audience that he'd volunteered to
testify before the jury, if only Pina would grant him limited immunity.

"Why don't the families let me go to court and let the
evidence come out, and let the chips fall where they may?"
he asked. "I believe it is a totally unfair, selfish, and obscene political move by Ron Pina to use these families
right now. I don't believe the timing of this grand jury
was accidental—30 days before the election. I walk down
the street of my own hometown in Port Richey, Florida,
and neighbors verbally shout, 'There's the Massachusetts
murderer.' Little children follow me with their bicycles,
and ask me who I killed today. It's been an indescribable
affair."

The jury's vote came on a Friday afternoon. As noted,
Pina was surprised. He immediately asked a judge to seal
the indictment so he could notify the families of the victims. His office sent a fax to Reddington to inform him.
Plans were made to arraign Kenny on Monday, when the
indictment would be unsealed.

But keeping the contents of the indictment secret did
little to stop any of the news media. By the following
morning, the *Standard-Times*'s Boyle had the story in the
paper: "Ponte Secretly Indicted in Highway Killings
Case." Boyle said it appeared the charges were connected
with the death of Rochelle Clifford.

But even as the citizens of New Bedford were reading
about the grand jury's decision, Ponte was once more attacking Pina over the airwaves on Henry Carreiro's radio
show.

"I am truly innocent of these crazy allegations," Ponte
told Carreiro. "I have watched in horror while the newspapers have reported that I am the one in the sealed indictment. No one has told me officially that I have been
indicted other than the media, or other than the fact that
Ron Pina's spokesperson has allegedly leaked this to the
media.

"I greatly sympathize with the families (of the victims). I feel sorry for them. But I want to tell the families that I have nothing to do with the deaths of their loved ones. I miss my father every day, Henry. My father passed away. I don't blame the families for his death. Why are they blaming me for the deaths of their loved ones, unfairly?

"I believe it's a totally unfair, selfish, and obscene political move by Ron Pina to use these families right now. I don't believe that the timing of this grand jury was accidental—30 days before the election. Ron Pina needed to explain why he spent three million on this investigation . . . he needed a scapegoat, and he needed it fast.

"If that indictment has my name, which everyone in the state except me seems to be sure of, I will be found innocent," Kenny said. "There is no question about it. I am not going to hide from anybody or anything."

Now Carreiro played the tape of the conversation that Trooper Jose Gonsalves had with Ponte's friend Norman McCarthy back in February of 1989—the discussion over whether Pina would give Ponte limited immunity to get his testimony about the murder victims. That was the tape in which Trooper Gonsalves acknowledged that Pina *had* discussed the immunity question. The effect of playing the tape was to make it seem as though Pina was a liar.

"Ron Pina will not cooperate in that regard," Ponte said after the tape was played. "I, publicly, once again offer to cooperate. Ron Pina, I will cooperate with any tests that you want. I am in Massachusetts to clear my name, to end this nightmare once and for all. Ron Pina, I ask your cooperation. Allow me to go before that grand jury with the necessary immunity all but for the homicides. Allow the grand jury to hear me. What are you afraid of, Ron Pina? Are you afraid that, once the truth be known, that Ken Ponte has nothing to do with this, that the taxpayers will know, 30 days before the election, that you have *wasted* three million of their money; at least one million chasing an innocent man? That is my opinion.

"The final statement I have to make is, I would like Ron Pina to explain why he wouldn't allow me to cooperate back in February, when Jose Gonsalves informed Norman McCarthy that I would be allowed to testify and tell everything I knew. Basically, which is nothing. I don't know who this killer is. I would like to see this killer caught. I would pull the switch myself if this killer was caught. Certainly I wouldn't protect the nutcase if I knew who did this. Certainly. However, I must also inform you that, if I did, which I don't, I would give this information to the U.S. Attorney, because I don't believe Ron Pina is competent to handle the information. I would provide it to the U.S. Attorney, if I knew, which I don't."

57

Over the Line

On the following Monday, Ponte appeared in court with Reddington as the indictment was unsealed. Just as Boyle had predicted, the charge was for the murder of Rochelle Clifford, "on or about April 27, 1988"—the same day Rochelle had been seen by Detective Dextradeur and Frankie Pina. As hard as he'd tried over the past year, Pina had been unable to authoritatively put Rochelle Clifford in Ponte's company at any time after Dextradeur had last seen her.

The courtroom was packed with relatives of the victims, including Judy DeSantos. Pina had arrived at the courtroom with the relatives, after the entire group walked about five blocks from Pina's office to the courthouse—a trek that did not go unrecorded by the television cameras.

Kenny, Pina now told the court, was an intravenous drug user who had stalked street women in New Bedford in order to use them to buy drugs for him.

Pina said Kenny "crossed the line from the legal community and became a member of the drug community. He used these women because he was an attorney and afraid to go buy the drugs himself. He recruited different women at different times. He brought them to his home," Pina continued. "He did not want it to be discovered by the police that he was buying drugs."

That was why he'd killed Rochelle, Pina said: because

Rochelle was a threat to tell the police that Kenny had been using drugs. That danger became real the day the police discovered that Kenny had pulled a gun on Roger Swire, the district attorney added, and then wanted to interview Rochelle Clifford.

"She made comments to police officers that she was going to come forward and be a witness against attorney Ponte," Pina said. "The case will show a long pursuit by Mr. Ponte, trying to get this witness not to testify and to find her and threaten to kill her."

Boyle reported that Ponte's eyes bulged out in apparent disbelief when Pina said he was an intravenous drug user.

Pina sat down, and the judge asked Kenny how he would plead.

"Absolutely not guilty, Your Honor," he said. Gasps of disbelief rose from several of the victims' relatives.

The judge set Kenny's bail at $50,000 in cash, and Kenny was led away to be booked.

But Judy DeSantos was troubled. Months earlier, State Troopers Gonsalves and Dill, with whom she had now grown quite close, had promised her they would be in court when an indictment was returned if they truly thought the person charged was guilty. Now here was Kenny Ponte, after all these months, pleading innocent, and Jose and Maryann were nowhere to be seen.

After Kenny was taken away and the prosecutors and family members spilled out of the courthouse, there was another news media melee. The family members were the prime target.

Many said they believed that Ponte was guilty of not only Rochelle's murder, but the others as well. Most told reporters that Ponte had known or otherwise been involved with the victim each was related to, far beyond the three or four Kenny claimed. And when it was learned that Ponte would make the $50,000 bail by pledging his mother's house, some family members reacted with bitterness.

"They're going to let him out," said Chandra Greenlaw, the 17-year-old daughter of Deborah DeMello.

"But what about us? That (expletive) can still visit his mother. But what about us? I want him hung."

Later that night Ponte was profiled on the TV show, *Inside Edition*. "It's just amazing to me that this could have happened to someone in America," he said.

No Punctures

In the aftermath of the indictment, the focus of the case turned to the campaign between Pina and Walsh. After all, Walsh had criticized Pina for manipulating the grand jury process, and Pina utterly rejected that. It seemed to some that the vote for district attorney was tantamount to a community-wide decision on whom to believe.

As Walsh and Pina shadowboxed over their respective legal qualifications, experience, administrative skills amid the usual sounds and furies of electoral combat, Ponte was taking another step to show up Pina. He went to a drug-testing doctor in Fall River and subjected himself to an examination. Ponte wanted the doctor to clear him of Pina's allegation that he had been an intravenous drug user.

"Mr. Kenneth Ponte was seen by me on 8/22/90 at 11:20 A.M.," the doctor wrote in his report. "He had requested to be examined for needle marks and to have a urine drug screen for detection of heroin/opiate metabolics and cocaine.

"Mr. Ponte was fully stripped and examined. There was no evidence of any puncture wounds anywhere on his body."

The drug screen was completely negative.

Abandoned

On Tuesday, September 18, Ron Pina was defeated in his attempt to win reelection as Bristol County District Attorney. He lost by 24 percent of the vote—in politics, a huge, crushing margin.

The reason: the Highway Murder investigation. Or so said scores of voters as they left the polling places. Many voters criticized Pina severely for politicizing the grand jury, for indicting Ponte on what some had already concluded was flimsy evidence, for playing to the news media. The trek through the streets with the families of the victims was particularly distasteful to many. Still others were offended by Pina's campaign theme: the cartoon-character Crime Fighter D.A. that Pina's campaign advertising had widely circulated; many thought that sort of approach to the voters was an insult.

All of those perceptions hurt; what hurt Pina even more was the defection of two of his longtime allies in the Democratic party. State Senator Biff McLean had promised to remain neutral, but that hadn't stopped most of McLean's supporters from flocking over to Walsh's camp. Walsh's father, after all, was the very good friend of the powerful state senator. And one of Pina's closest friends—indeed, the best man at his wedding to Sheila Martines, Fall River Mayor Carlton Viveiros had been named a judge by the outgoing Governor Dukakis, and therefore withdrew from partisan politics; that was a double blow, made even more painful when State Senator McLean publicly speculated just before the election that none of Viveiros's supporters would turn out for Pina.

Pina had been abandoned.

Later, he looked back and considered it all. He would have done the same things, he said. The murder case wasn't the only reason he lost, Pina said, but it was painful. Still, he believed that he had done the right thing, and that's what mattered.

Sometimes, when he sailed his boat, *Cyrano*, he considered what might have been. What would have happened had he won, and he had been able to bring Kenny Ponte to trial? What would have happened had he continued to use the special jury to "rake" through the debris of New Bedford's underside? No one could tell, but there was nothing for it but to hold his course.

"I sail," he said later. "One of the things you learn in sailing is that winds come and hurricanes go and you gotta move the boat. The worst thing you can do is let the wheel go, 'cause then you're out of control and so, I take that in life. I held. Feeling the wind will stop. You know, even a hurricane stops eventually. I'm holding, I haven't hit a reef, I'm holding . . ."

Across town, Ponte and Reddington held a news conference celebrating the defeat of Pina.

"Unusual as it may be for a defendant in a Superior Court matter to extend congratulations to a district attorney, nonetheless we obviously look forward to dealing with Mr. Walsh," Reddington said.

SUMMER 1991

"In what census of living creatures, the dead of mankind are included; why is it that a universal proverb says of them, that they shall tell no tales . . . why are all the living so strive to hush all the dead; wherefore but the rumor of a knocking in a tomb will terrify a whole city. All these things are not without their meanings.

"But faith, like a jackal, feeds among the tombs, and even from these dead doubts she gathers her most vital hope."

—HERMAN MELVILLE, *Moby Dick*

60

No Evidence

While Paul Walsh had pledged himself to vigorously pursue the Highway Murder case, once the votes were in, he began to have some second thoughts.

One of the biggest problems was Ponte. After all, Ponte had *endorsed* Walsh. How would it look for the new district attorney to prosecute—or worse, *not* prosecute—a man who had told everyone to vote for him?

Obviously, he would have to find someone else to make the decisions in the case, whatever they would be. But Walsh also had a gnawing feeling that it was too late to solve the Highway Murders. Too much time had passed, too many wild stories had circulated. The trail, other than the one that had led to Ponte, was completely cold. The last thing Walsh wanted to do was wind up like Pina— obsessed, some said, or at the very least the victim of enormous expectations, mostly of his own making, because of promises and pledges. It was far better in the absence of hot new information, to let the whole thing slide back to the level of a normal crime problem, if it could be done.

But how?

By now, everyone would be watching to see what he did with Kenny Ponte. Not only that, all of the victims' families were organized—and vocal. The most persistent was Judy DeSantos. She kept calling Walsh's office to prod him. Finally Walsh stopped returning her telephone calls. Judy sent him letters instead.

Judy kept pressing Walsh to meet with the families.

"I wanted to touch base with him," she recalled, "because it's important that the district attorney, no matter who it is, realize that they are elected by the people, and that victims are a big, important part of their work. And I wanted to say, hey, my sister can't stand up for her rights. When they drew that chalk outline, she could not stand up for her rights anymore, so I'm going to have to do it. And he would never return my calls, we played telephone tag for a long time and finally he did, and he agreed to meet with the families after the election. Which he did and he made some promises, but he never kept them.

"I went in with a list of questions," Judy said. "How come the FBI (Behavioral Sciences Laboratory) in Quantico, Virginia, was never called in? Or, if an FBI profile was done, what happened to it? And whatever happened to the blood samples that were taken from Ponte? And the hair samples? He told me he'd have them answered in a month and he never did. He never answered me and then he said, and a favorite line—this must be a standard district attorney's line number three—'Judy DeSantos must have misunderstood me.'

"And I was so—you know, Pina used us, (and) he (Walsh) was using us, too. The families always 'misunderstand.' Blame it on the victim. Re-victimize the victim. What a nice thing to do."

The next time Judy met with Walsh she brought a tape recorder "because I wasn't going to misunderstand him anymore."

In early March of 1991, Walsh announced that he had appointed a special prosecutor to review the evidence in the Ponte case. Paul Buckley, a Boston-area lawyer, had worked as a deputy district attorney with Walsh years before. Walsh trusted his judgment.

In announcing the appointment, Walsh suggested that the murder case might never be solved. That indeed sounded as if Walsh, in his own judgment, had decided the case against Ponte was meritless. "It is a difficult case and we do not make the promise or a guarantee that we will come up with a conviction in this matter," Walsh told *The Globe*'s Coakley and Ellement. "To do so, would raise false hopes and I just won't do that."

For months, Buckley closeted himself with all the paperwork from the investigation. The more he read, the more perturbed he became. It seemed to Buckley, at least, that there just wasn't any coherent thread to Pina's investigation of the murders. The leads, if one could call them that, went all over the place, and most went nowhere. There was ample indication that many witnesses had committed perjury.

Worse—far worse—there was very little usable information in all the testimony because of the rules of evidence. The rules generally forbade hearsay—what one person says another told him—and certainly frowned upon double hearsay, or what one person says that a second person was told. Hearsay is *not* evidence. But almost everything the grand jury had considered was hearsay if not double hearsay. It would be child's play for almost any competent defense lawyer to keep this unverifiable material off the witness stand.

Finally, in late July 1991, almost a year to the day after Diane Doherty told the jury about *Whispers Wildies*, Buckley announced the obvious: the murder indictment against Kenny Ponte would not be prosecuted.

"It would get to the judge," Buckley told *The Globe*, "and he would rule as a matter of law that there is no evidence."

For Tony DeGrazia, out on bail still awaiting his trial on the rape and assault charges, the news of the decision not to prosecute Ponte was disturbing. Tony thought the dismissal against Ponte probably meant the police would start in on him again. He dreaded it, and it made him mad.

The day of Buckley's decision had been a bad day for Tony, anyway. Ever since January 1991—after he'd been arrested once more and accused of trying to rape still *another* prostitute, which he denied—Tony had been taking Antabuse to help control his drinking. A doctor had prescribed a special prescription medicine to help him with his bouts of depression.

Father Harrison and the church had rallied around Tony, helping him get started in a new business, giving him a place to feel connected to. Friends had raised money to help repair his nose with plastic surgery. He was planning to attend college in the fall, and hoped to get an engineering degree. He was still unhappy about Kathy Scanlon, but was trying to get over it.

The night after he heard about Kenny, Tony called Father Harrison to talk, but the priest couldn't come to the phone. He called his sister Jennifer next. To Jennifer he seemed angry and bitter about the dismissal against Ponte, but assured her he intended to keep on fighting until he was found innocent of all charges.

Next he called Kathy Scanlon. To help him get over Kathy, Ray and Lorraine Scanlon had made their East Freetown house temporarily off-limits to Tony, which he accepted.

In talking to Kathy, Tony seemed a little down, but not too bad. Kathy told Tony that while she loved him, it was important for Tony to go on with the rest of his life and find somebody else to love.

"I guess you're very happy," Tony told Kathy. "Well, I'm going to college, and by the time I get back, I guess you'll be married and have the children we wanted."

"Well," Kathy said, "rather than have somebody else tell you, I'll tell you. Yes, we are getting married, and yes, I am pregnant."

Tony's movements the rest of the night were easy to determine later. Shortly after talking to Kathy, he called Father Harrison again, but the priest was still busy. Next he called Kathy's sister, Kelly. He was weeping. He told Kelly that he probably wouldn't be seeing her for a while, and then he talked to Kelly's children, told them he was going away, and to behave themselves.

Tony hung up the phone and walked around the corner, then up the rural street to Ray and Lorraine Scanlon's house. The Scanlons were out for the evening. Tony went around to the rear of the house and sat on a picnic table for a while. He drank some ginger ale, then walked down to the grave of his old dog—the Labrador he had enjoyed so much with Kathy. He walked back to the picnic table and sat down again. It began to rain, just as it had so many years earlier when Lorraine Scanlon had found him asleep in the woods.

Tony got up and went into the trailer he used to live in during the happiest summer of his life. He removed some tissues and cried some more. It was raining harder, followed by thunder, then lightning. The thunder came closer and closer. He left the trailer and sat on a picnic bench outside, oblivious of the rain. Tony removed the bottle of antidepressant medicine he'd been taking for months. He drank some more ginger ale. He opened the bottle and swallowed its contents. He drank some more.

After perhaps half an hour, Tony passed out. He fell directly forward off the picnic bench, his hands pinned directly under his waist. Within a few hours he was dead.

——— 61 ———

The Real Killer

On the following Monday afternoon, July 29, 1991, the single murder charge against Kenny Ponte was formally withdrawn by the Bristol County prosecutor's office. In a short press conference, Ponte expressed his relief. But Buckley now raised a new possibility: perhaps Tony De-Grazia had been the killer all along.

Tony, Buckley said in his own press conference, had to be considered "a strong suspect" in the murders. Tony's suicide, the special prosecutor suggested, may have happened because of the announcement that charges against Ponte were being dropped.

"To me," Buckley said, "the timing is related." Tony's suicide, coming on the heels of the decision about Ponte, was bizarre, Buckley said, and it "should open a lot of minds." The fact that Tony might have encountered some of the victims, and the fact that he had been identified as a serial rapist of prostitutes made him a logical suspect for the serial killings, Buckley insisted. Of course, if Walsh, via Buckley, could successfully convince everyone that Tony had been the real killer, the pressure on Walsh to continue the investigation would subside, and criticism of the Ponte decision would be muted.

But Tony's new lawyer, Robert George of Boston, rejected the notion that Tony might have been the killer. George instead suggested that Tony might have killed

314

himself because he *feared* that the police would turn once more in his direction, but that didn't mean he was the killer.

"If he felt that attention would have been turned to him again in the aftermath of Ponte's dismissal, that would have upset him greatly, since it was something that he had put behind him once before," George told *The Globe*. "It was a tremendous effort for him to try to survive day to day."

No matter what Buckley suggested, George continued, there was just no evidence to link Tony to the murders. Even mentioning Tony's name in the wake of the decision on Ponte was "a cheap political maneuver to attempt an end to the travesty of justice known as the serial killing cases," George said.

"Any suggestion or statement by the special prosecutor or any other person who knows anything about the serial killing case which infers that Mr. DeGrazia was involved in these killings is reckless, callous, and disrespectful of DeGrazia's family, friends, and supporters," George said.

And what of the victims' families? The decision not to prosecute Ponte was a bitter pill. Some thought that Ponte's background as a lawyer had served him unfairly well.

Debroh McConnell's father, for one, believed that somehow Ponte had talked his way out of trouble. "He's a lawyer," James McConnell told *The Globe*. "He knows how to talk his way out of things, he has a lot of friends, and he has money. When money talks, everything walks."

McConnell told reporters he thought the investigation should be stopped. "They aren't going to do anything about it anyway," he said. "Why don't they just close the books on it and let those poor girls rest?"

Some blamed Walsh. Madeline Perry, for one, thought that Walsh wasn't as interested in solving the case as Pina had been. And she remained convinced that Ponte had something to do with the murders.

"Mothers have intuition," she told *The Globe*. "He knows something. He's involved in my daughter's death. I will never give up on that," Perry said. "It's scary," she said. "It's almost like he smirks, like he knows you are not going to be able to do anything to him. He's so self-confident. He doesn't care about us; he doesn't give a damn about us."

But others blamed Pina. "He bungled the investigation at the beginning," Donald Santos, husband of Mary Rose Santos, told *The Globe*. "It was just one big media circus."

Judy DeSantos had her own perspective. "You put your trust and faith in people," she said, "and then you're blown away."

In retrospect, it seems clear that neither Ponte nor De-Grazia could have had anything to do with the murders. Most telling, both men eventually provided samples of hair and saliva that were compared with samples found at the nine known skeletal scenes. There were no matches. That alone was probably enough to clear them, at least as far as the authorities were concerned.

Additionally, the very fact that Ponte had a personal relationship with some of the victims—or at least, knew them—has to count in his favor, even though Pina saw it in the opposite light. As an almost invariable rule, serial murderers *don't* know their victims. Indeed, the pathology that drives them to kill very nearly requires that the victim be someone *not* known to the killer. It is only by being able to see the victim as an object, rather than a person, that virtually all serial killers are able to murder.

That sort of pathology apparently *was* present in Tony DeGrazia's life—if one believes, as the evidence suggests, that he was responsible for the rapes of prostitutes. After all, Tony did not know any of *those* victims—so much so, that he repeatedly attempted to pick up women he'd already assaulted previously. He simply didn't recognize them.

But Tony almost certainly was not capable of committing murder. As he himself had indicated to the police, had he murdered the guilt would have destroyed him. Moreover, most of Tony's alleged crimes occurred at night, when he was drunk. It's highly unlikely that Tony would have driven so far out of New Bedford to get rid of his victims; indeed, Tony's method appeared to include an almost hysterical haste to get away from the victim immediately after his attack. And Freetown Detective Alan

Alves, who had known Tony almost all of Tony's short
and tragic life, simply doesn't believe that Tony would
have been clever enough to have committed so many murders without it being obvious to everyone around him.

So, if Kenny Ponte didn't kill the New Bedford women,
and Tony didn't kill them, who did?

That remains the darkest mystery, a mystery that was
deepened by the well-meaning struggles among those who
tried to resolve it. The unseemly haste of Ron Pina and
others to find a viable target for their investigation side-
tracked the entire process and prevented the sort of painstaking assembly of information and analysis that is the
heart of any complex investigation, particularly one involving serial murder.

One of the major shortcomings of the investigation was
the lack of truly precise information on where and when
the victims were last seen. Time and resources, devoted to
attempting to make known facts fit suspects, might have
been far more productively invested in delving into the
lives of the dead. It is only by carefully reassembling the
last days and hours of the victims that any serial murder
investigation can hope to produce evidence leading to the
killer. Indeed, even the limited amount of information
known about the 11 New Bedford victims suggests a solid
pathway toward the killer's true identity.

The pathway begins with the comparison of Tony's
alleged victims with those of the murderer. The most
striking result of that comparison is the fact that so few
of Tony's alleged victims knew the Highway Murder victims. It was almost as if there were two different groups,
entirely: the Weld Square victims of Tony, and the Highway Murder victims, who were clearly tied together by
experiences in New Bedford's south end.

Any analysis of the police interviews of Tony's victims
shows that few of those 20-odd women from Weld Square
were familiar with the Highway Murder group, and of
those who did know them, most knew only one or two.
Indeed, most of Tony's victims did not even know *each
other*.

The Highway Murder victims, by contrast, were fairly well known to one another. Their boyfriends knew each other; some of them had actually worked together over a period of years; and several had even lived in the same places. That was the singular fact that had so mesmerized Ron Pina.

But what the Highway Murder victims also had in common was an affinity for New Bedford's south end—the neighborhood around Whispers Pub. Most of the Highway Murder victims were addicted to cocaine—not heroin, as was often the case of the Weld Square population preyed upon by Tony. The Highway Murder victims frequented the south end of the city to acquire drugs; only a few of them could ever reliably be placed in Weld Square. That probably means the killer was someone who also frequented the drug circles of the city's south end, and that it was in that area that the killer truly encountered the victims.

It is unlikely, however, that the killer had personal knowledge of the victims—only that they were familiar objects in his environment. The killer probably knew that the victims were drug users, which further suggests that the killer himself was at least familiar with the drug culture, if not the actual substances. How did the killer make contact with the victims? Most probably by offering the victims drugs, either as part of an inducement to prostitution, or simply as a "generous" offer to get high. So prevalent were drugs within the south end, so common in many personal experiences, that it is almost certain the victims never suspected that the friendly man who shared their drug interest was in fact intent on killing them.

Who might this person have been? There are several intriguing facts that may or may not have relevance. First, the fact that so many of the victims—all except Rochelle Clifford—were found a short distance from the sides of major highways could be an indication that the killer was someone not entirely familiar with the back roads of Bristol County. The major highways were familiar, however, and thus provided locations where a victim could be disposed of quickly. That in turn suggests that the killer was *not* a native of New Bedford, and that he was not therefore cognizant of more secluded areas.

As a major center of fishing activity, New Bedford has long attracted a seasonal population. The very term of the killing season—from April to September—coincides with the peak of the fishing industry. With these facts in mind, it is not unlikely that the true killer was someone who was familiar with the south end drug culture, a temporary resident of New Bedford, who was in town for the fishing season.

What about the white pickup truck? Although several witnesses reported seeing a white pickup truck near the locations where skeletons were found, it would be short-sighted to confine all suspicions only to those who drove white pickup trucks. Serial murder cases in other parts of the country suggest that such killers often vary their means of transportation—chiefly by borrowing friends' and relatives' vehicles. That could well have happened in New Bedford.

So, is it too late to solve the crimes? The passage of so many years makes it far more difficult, naturally, because human memories recede. But it is not impossible. The most productive starting point now would be an effort to reassemble the cultural milieu of the 11 victims—developing a coherent picture of who was who in the south end of New Bedford during the summer of 1988. Police records indicating the identities of those arrested for possession or sale of drugs, particularly at Whispers Pub, is an obvious place to begin. The reinterview of those most familiar with the streets near the pub would reconstruct the timing and movements of those most likely to know the truth, whether they know they know it or not.

With such interviews, an exhaustive process to be sure, eventually the shadow of the true killer will emerge—someone no one really knew, someone quietly ever-present, someone familiar enough to be taken at face value, but who was in fact a secret killer, who destroyed nearly everything he touched.

EPILOGUE

"The drama's done. Why then here does any one step forth?—Because one did survive the wreck . . ."

HERMAN MELVILLE, *Moby Dick*

Outcomes

Ron Pina is a lawyer in private practice in New Bedford, along with his former chief deputy, **Ray Veary**. He is still married to the former **Sheila Martines**. He has considered returning to the political arena.

Kenny Ponte is also a lawyer in private practice, also in New Bedford. The FBI's tests of hair, blood, and saliva cleared him of having been the murderer. Recently he agreed to represent **Tony DeGrazia's** mother in a wrongful death action against Pina, alleging that Pina's statements about her son helped drive him to suicide.

Paul Boudreau took an early retirement from the New Bedford Police Department and moved to New Port Richey, Florida.

Louie Pacheco, the Raynham police captain who is a computer buff, continues in police work in Raynham.

Diane Doherty faded from the public eye, but not until she gave an interview to the *Standard-Times's* **Maureen Boyle,** saying that she first became interested in Kenny Ponte because of a vision she'd had while in MCI Framingham.

Elsa Johnson was found dead on the streets of New Bedford in August 1991, just two weeks after the death of Tony DeGrazia and the dismissal of the charge against Kenny Ponte. She had been in poor health due to years of alcohol and drug abuse. Police believe she died of a drug overdose.

Paul Ryley moved back to New Bedford. All charges were dropped against him, and hair, blood, and saliva tests showed that he, too, was not the murderer. In 1993, he was still in litigation over his great aunt's estate. The theft charge brought against him by Pina in December 1989 was dropped.

John Ellement and **Tom Coakley** continue as reporters for *The Boston Globe*, as does Maureen Boyle for the *Standard-Times*.

Bob St. Jean, aka **The Saint,** returned to his roots in Acushnet, Massachusetts, and started his own contracting business.

John Torres, the Marion detective, joined the Customs Service, while **Alan Alves,** the Freetown detective, still works for his city.

Jose Gonsalves and **Mary Ann Dill** are still investigators for the Massachusetts State Police. Gonsalves is now a sergeant and Dill is a corporal. Dill was transferred back to the highway.

The conspiracy-to-possess cocaine charges against Ken Ponte, **Jeanne Kaloshis, Adele Leeks,** and **"Goldie" Goldblatt** were dismissed. So were the cocaine charges brought against **Donald Santos,** the husband of Mary Rose Santos.

The charge that Ponte had assaulted **Roger Swire** by threatening him with a gun was also dismissed; the charge that Swire had assaulted his own girlfriend in January 1989 was similarly dismissed.

Neil Anderson was convicted of one count of sexual assault, and sentenced to serve 3-to-5 years in prison. He was released early in 1993, and is appealing his conviction.

The Highway Killer remains at large—the one who did survive the wreck.